EAST ASIA
HISTORY, POLITICS, SOCIOLOGY, CULTURE

EDITED BY

EDWARD BEAUCHAMP

UNIVERSITY OF HAWAII

A ROUTLEDGE SERIES

EAST ASIA
HISTORY, POLITICS, SOCIOLOGY, CULTURE
EDWARD BEAUCHAMP, *General Editor*

VILLAGE, MARKET AND WELL-BEING IN A RURAL CHINESE TOWNSHIP

TAMARA PERKINS

Routledge
Taylor & Francis Group

LONDON AND NEW YORK

First published 2002 by Routledge

2 Park Square, Milton Park, Abingdon, Oxfordshire OX14 4RN
52 Vanderbilt Avenue, New York, NY 10017

Routledge is an imprint of the Taylor & Francis Group, an informa business

First issued in paperback 2020

Library of Congress Cataloging-in-Publication Data

Perkins, Tamara.
  Village, market, and well-being in a rural Chinese township / Tamara Perkins.
     p. cm. — (East Asia : history, politics, sociology, culture)
  Includes bibliographical references and index.
  ISBN 978-0-4159-3429-9
     1. China—Rural conditions. 2. Villages—China. I. Title. II. East Asia (New York, N.Y.)
HN733.5 .P47 2002
307.76'2'0951—dc21   2002017805

ISBN 978-0-415-93429-9 (hbk)
ISBN 978-0-367-60474-5 (pbk)

CONTENTS

LIST OF FIGURES

LIST OF TABLES

ACKNOWLEDGMENTS

I WISH THERE WERE A PLACE TO DETAIL ALL THE KINDNESSES AND HELP I HAVE RECEIVED in the process of researching and writing this book; unfortunately this brief and incomplete list will have to suffice.

Funding was provided by a U.S. Department of Education Fulbright-Hays Doctoral Dissertation Research Abroad Grant as well as a research grant from the Committee on Scholarly Communication with China (CSCC). Professor Joe Esherick helped arrange for the Tianjin Academy of Social Sciences (TASS) to be my host institution during my stay in both Tianjin and Ganglong Township. Pan Yunkang, Sun Yanfeng, and other colleagues at the Sociology Institute at TASS were responsible for locating a field site—for which I am indeed very grateful—and coordinating details of my stay with local officials. The people at the Jinghai County archives, particularly Ms. Guo, not only attended to my research needs but were kind enough to provide a quiet place to work during lunch. Xia Qing'an and Li Xiujun conscientiously answered my innumerable history questions about Ganglong.

Back at home, Akos Rona-Tas, in particular, must be cited out for his speedy (usually within hours) response to all my (often less than brilliant) email stats questions—and is of course not responsible for any statistical injustices which may have slipped through the cracks. This book might very likely not have been completed without the gentle prods and sharp feedback on chapter drafts from Johanna Bockman, Julie Broadwin, Berit Dencker and Teresa Swartz, whose comradery I sorely miss. Diane Atkinson and Julie Gonnering provided needed editorial expertise and moral support at crucial points in the process.

My heartfelt thanks goes to the people of Ganglong Township, and especially the Cuitai Villagers and their fearless Party Secretary for their wonderful cooperation, hospitality and friendship during my stay. My apologies to Zhoulong for not having managed to learn to speak with a Cuitai accent. Zhang Gugu of Niudian, Lao Shu and Li Daye of Cuitai provided me with many laughs (but perhaps not as many as I unwittingly provided them), as well as great food and conversation. Meina appeared in those early weeks to befriend me when I needed a friend most—and continued to share her heart and home with me throughout the year.

Li Tie, my staunchest supporter and life partner, can not know how much he has contributed to this project. Through these years he has put up with hours of me tearing my hair out at the computer and other unmentionable abuses with only the most minimal of complaints. Aside from his advice, hugs, bad jokes, missions to bring me food while I was in the field, I am especially indebted to him for helping me drink all that *baijiu* at township and village banquets. And Sweet Leilah arrived just in time to put things in perspective.

VILLAGE, MARKET AND WELL-BEING IN A RURAL CHINESE TOWNSHIP

CHAPTER 1.

INTRODUCTION: DIFFERENTIAL DEVELOPMENT AMONG TWENTY-THREE VILLAGES

WITH A FIFTH OF THE WORLD'S POPULATION AND ONE OF THE LARGEST economies in the world, China has been praised by the international community for greatly increasing literacy, reducing infant and maternal mortality, boosting the rate of economic growth, and improving other social and economic welfare indicators. These successes, however, cannot mask the fact that China's rural development remains extremely uneven: coastal areas flourish while some inland regions are little changed from the days before the Communist takeover in 1949. China's domestic stability and role on the world stage will depend, in large part, on its ability to bring the remaining hundreds of millions of mostly rural people out of poverty. The underlying motivation for this book is to understand the complex processes by which some Chinese villages have come to prosper while neighboring villages lag behind. Its methodology, however, is to focus *not* on the well-known macroregional disparities in rural living standards, but on differences among neighboring villages—where the disparities are stark but the factors accounting for them are more appropriate for controlled analysis.

PUZZLING DIFFERENCES BETWEEN CONTIGUOUS VILLAGES

In December 1994, I arrived at a cold restaurant in a little town in Jinghai County at the southern tip of Tianjin Municipality—a large city about 80 miles southeast of China's capital, Beijing. At a welcoming banquet here I first met the officials who would decide to let me stay and conduct research in Ganglong Township, a small unextraordinary township made up of twenty-three contiguous villages.[1] A few days later when I was settled in, I set out by bicycle to visit each of the township's villages. Based on my reading of existing research on rural China, I expected to find twenty-three villages that looked and felt the same and had similar, relatively high levels of socioeconomic well-being particularly since this area is considered "coastal." I could not have been more wrong. The scope of village variations was striking, especially since the entire township covers only about 14 square miles. The contrast between the two neighboring villages of Langwo and Dingxiang was especially vivid. In my daily field notes, I described the small village of Langwo, which in per capita terms was one of the poorest in the township:

> The village was very cosy—bunches of corn dangling from wooden doorways, goats and chickens wandering around, donkeys tethered in front of mud houses and stables. As we were going into the house where I would do the village interview, two roosters engaged in an impromptu cockfight. This raucous display caught the interest of the Party Secretary and a few other people nearby, who all stopped to watch (VSNotes, Feb. 21, 1995).[2]

The spontaneous, spectator-enticing cockfight scene in Langwo contrasted sharply with life in nearby Dingxiang village. In this village, the Party Secretaries, accountants, other village leaders and residents rushed around on official business and errands. The whole leisurely feel of Langwo seemed a world away from bustling Dingxiang, where the local population and visitors from nearby villages lived by their watches.

Also a small village, Dingxiang is located less than a mile away and across the river from Langwo. In contrast to economically poor Langwo, however, Dingxiang, had the highest per capita income in the township. Compared with Langwo, this village—and its Party Secretary—left an equally dramatic, though less engaging first impression:

> The Party Secretary led us up to his office in a brand-new two-story building at the big factory site. . . . In the office were several pieces of expensive new furniture, including a . . . huge manager's desk which clued you in to who was boss. Then, before talking to—or even acknowledging—us, he made several phone calls on his deluxe new golden-handled telephone (turn of the century US-style). Then he stared at us sternly, waiting for us to speak. Very uncomfortable. He is a big guy, and gave the feeling of a 1930s style Chicago gangster (VSNotes, Dec. 14, 1994).

Dingxiang had three of the largest and most successful rural industries in the township, producing tires, auto parts and pickled vegetables. It was only a few months later, after several Ganglong residents began to trust and confide in me, that I found out the Dingxiang Party Secretary and his whole village (95% of whom had the same surname as the Party Secretary) were disliked by just about everyone else in the township. While partly due to his manner, this universal dislike certainly has some roots in envy of Dingxiang's booming factories, as well as the Party Secretary's arrogance about them.

The above first impressions reflect some of the starkest realities of Ganglong Township.[3] Foremost is the fact that many of the villages have strong village industries, a more "modern," time-is-money feel, and power-ful, domineering party leaders. Others have more distinctly "pre-modern" rural characteristics, extensive landholdings, and a primarily agricultural base. Furthermore, the more industrially-oriented villages are generally on the southeast side of the Grand Canal (now a mere trickle), which runs through the township, while the more agriculturally-oriented villages are on the northwest side.

Langwo's Party Secretary went so far to say that Langwo and the rest of the northwest villages are safer and even more moral than those on the southeast side of the Grand Canal:

> There are no "hooligans" in this [northwest] village, and it is extreme-ly stable and safe—unlike villages on the other [southeast] side of the river. . . . People on the other side of the river are entrepreneurial fiends (zuo maimai gui), while people on the [north]west side are simply farmers (VSNotes, Feb. 21, 1995).

Comments by those living in southeast put themselves in a more positive light, claiming that they are industrious and clever, while northwest villagers are hickish and lazy.

The southeast/northwest and industrial/agricultural split have far-reach-ing implications for village and villager well-being.[4] The more industrial Ganglong villages are doing very well in terms of infrastructure, household income and the ability to provide residents with fairly stable year-round jobs in rural industry. These jobs enable villagers to build and renovate their hous-es, send their children to school and college, eat well, and purchase such modern amenities of life as TVs, VCRs, telephones, washing machines, refrig-erators, etc. At the same time, several other Ganglong villages have been unsuccessful in their attempts to set up and manage rural industry. They lack the funds to pave roads and improve other infrastructure which in turn might attract more outside investment.[5] In these villages, residents generally live in shoddier houses, eat less nutritious food, toil harder and longer in agriculture, and are generally at a socioeconomic disadvantage relative to their more prosperous neighbors.

This study is devoted to answering the question of why such dramatic differences in well-being exist between neighboring villages in the same township, particularly when the existing literature on rural Chinese develop-ment gives no clue that this should be the case.

DIFFERENT APPROACHES IN CHINA'S RURAL STRATIFICATION RESEARCH

Regional differences are a striking and extremely important part of the over-all development picture in China. Consequently, much work has been done to assess the extent and analyze the causes of China's regional inequality.[6] These analyses of macro-level regional distinctions, especially urban-rural and coastal-interior, are a crucial first step to understanding the mechanics of growth and stagnation in China.[7] Ke Bingsheng finds that regional differences in "natural resource endowment, infrastructure, education and technical extension, rural industry, state procurement policy for farm products, [and] regional development policy" are the major causes of disparate macro-regional development.[8]

Another strand of the macro-regional research utilizes comparisons and generalizations from a large, usually nationwide, sample of households in a variety of communities. This sample is then treated as a representative cross-section of China.[9] Large statistical studies such as these generally end up grouping households into suburban (wealthy/industrial), plains (middling/agricultural), and mountainous (poor/pastoral/agricultural) categories similar to those used in the macro-economic analyses mentioned above. In addition to geographic location, these studies commonly cite household-level factors such as nonfarm economic activities, a high ratio of workers to dependents, Communist party membership, high educational levels, etc., as reasons for higher levels of well-being and less incidence of poverty.

While still focusing on individuals or households, many social scientists prefer to conduct smaller, more local studies to assess stratification at the micro-level.[10] The benefit of this approach is that researchers are more sensitive to the local context because they live and work at their particular research sites. These rural stratification researchers are interested in knowing the special characteristics of the people and households prospering under the new market economic system.[11] Research on this topic has revealed a variety of different individual and household attributes which influence the ability to get ahead: education and occupation,[12] political or social connections,[13] degree and success in market participation,[14] life cycle effects and labor endowments,[15] or a combination of these.[16]

What is missing in these macro/regional and micro/household studies of stratification is an entire category of inquiry: to what extent does the community—the village—contribute to the welfare of its residents? A few scholars have mentioned some of the processes by which villages embody decisive features that might affect the socioeconomic outcomes of their residents. For example, in a study of village officials' control over village industry, Pei (1998) inadvertently touches upon one important way the village can make a difference for the welfare of individual residents: village-run rural industries.[17]

Freidman, Pickowicz and Selden (1991) provide historically-grounded evidence that the development of a "model village" in Raoyang County, Hebei Province, was intimately linked to social and political connections and policies. Its unique sociopolitical and historical context, however, meant that this village was *necessarily* different from other neighboring villages. None of the Ganglong villages are model villages.[18]

Noting the many important contributions the village makes to individual and household well-being, Knight and Song write:

> In various ways the village is the most important unit in rural China. Often the village comprises very few clans, giving rise to extensive social networks, social cohesion. Informal income redistribution among households of the village is therefore likely to occur. Village land is allocated among village households on an equal per capita basis (Knight and Song 1992:2).

Summarizing these observations, one of the most obvious village-level factors that can influence individual and household well-being is a village's landholdings, which are for the most part fixed. Therefore, land assets distributed to families are based upon how much land the village has. The high levels of social cohesion found in Chinese villages are due mainly to lineage and kin ties, some of which date back several hundred years, often bolstered by a kin-based village political structure. Similarly, villages also have common histories and "collective" memories which tie them together or threaten to tear them apart.[19] For these reasons (and more which will come clear throughout the book), I have chosen to focus upon the village. Village-level factors have something meaningful to say about the people who live in villages, as well as the process of inter- and intra-village stratification.

Therefore, in addition to the macro/regional and the more local individual and household studies, there is an equally important, meso-level analysis, based on the village. Approaching differential development from the perspective of the villages in one township, one can filter out the possible macro-level regional differences (e.g. political and economic policies, culture, and climate) often cited as causal factors in stratification. By eliminating these kinds of factors, the meso-level approach I use in the study of Ganglong Township allows me to focus on a tightly controlled set of potential causes to account for inter-village differentials among the twenty-three Ganglong villages.

My mid-level approach utilizes both geographic (in this case village) and household-level data.[20] I first employ household surveys and ethnographic information to illuminate *household*-level perceptions and to gather quantitative measures of socioeconomic well-being.[21] The next step then is to aggregate this information to the *village* level. The results of this undertaking confirm that the village continues to be an extremely salient factor for the prosperity of households—even after almost two decades of rural market reform and, especially, the return of labor, land and capital allocation decisions to the households.[22] I argue that the village-level characteristics are primarily responsible for the types of differences between the villages of Langwo and Dingxiang described at the beginning of this chapter.

Parallel to the household/community synthesis described above, another objective of my study is to demonstrate that blending qualitative and quantitative methods in a meaningful way enhances scholarly research. Most contemporary social science research manifests a spurious division of labor, and rural development research is no exception: it is *either* ethnographic *or* statistical, but rarely is it both.[23] I demonstrate that a more sophisticated understanding of any social situation is necessarily anchored in the specificities of time, place, and individual, all of which are accessible by in-depth fieldwork and archival work. At the same time, the ability to identify and summarize larger trends—one of the strengths of quantitative work—supports and enriches ethnographic description and analysis. It poses questions that an ethnographer may have missed herself.[24]

It is my experience that combining sources and methods leads to rich and satisfying explanations which otherwise would have been impossible (see Appendix A for an in-depth discussion of sources). For example, the quantitative archival data alone gives no indication that some of the Ganglong villages had very strong involvement with the market prior to 1953 and still have virtually single-lineage social structures today. Only by discussing village and personal histories with township residents did this information come to light. As readers will discover, historical legacies regarding commerce and kinship strength are crucial for explaining the differences in village and villager well-being today.[25] On the other hand, used carefully, the village quantitative data elicit some very interesting conclusions about the historical and social determinants of well-being in mid-1990s Ganglong.

The multi-stranded methodological approach I use accommodates the variety of sources available; using them creatively allows a more explicit recognition of the complex processes of development - and the ability to specify them.

HISTORY, INSTITUTIONS AND VILLAGE DEVELOPMENT IN GANGLONG

The ultimate purpose of this book is to understand the reasons for differential development among the twenty-three Ganglong villages. While a few of the following chapters necessarily delve into the details of contemporary life in Ganglong's villages and households, a substantial part of the explanation for differential development depends upon unique village histories, dating back to before the Communist revolution. These histories, I argue, are where we find the sources of *institutional change* which have led to socioeconomic prosperity—or stagnation—in the villages of Ganglong Township today.

In part, I take my cue to study institutional change at the village level from an article by Oberschall (1996), who notes that theories of stratification in post-socialist societies are ostensibly theories of institutional change. Consequently, large sample surveys of households using multivariate techniques, most often the basis for such research, are of limited use for understanding institutional change because the crucial local variations in institutions simply are not addressed by such large, cross-sectional studies.[26] The main theoretical inspiration for this study, therefore, comes from economic sociology, particularly the "new" institutionalism in sociology which criticizes and builds upon some of the corresponding theories in the new" institutionalism in economics.[27]

Using this theoretical approach has allowed me to identify four interacting processes of institutional change responsible for differential development in Ganglong. These four processes or "mechanisms" are temporal in nature.[28] The first is the commercialization of particular villages in close proximity to market centers. The market orientation of individuals and households in villages nearer to market centers necessarily emerged over a long period of time and certainly long before the starting date of this study.[29] The fact that some of the Ganglong Township villages faced considerable barriers in getting marketable goods and services to market centers accounts for the differential levels of commercialization in the villages in the era prior to the Communist takeover. (Chapter Two gives a brief history of the area, including the many political and social changes affecting Ganglong development).

The next mechanism is the accumulation of social and human capital in socioeconomic change.[30] This explains how those pre-modern market orientations have persisted until today despite the paved roads, bicycles, motorcycles and cars which now make it almost as convenient for people in the farthest villages in Ganglong Township to get to market as those in villages closer by. Although I argue that it was *villages* closer to market which were more commercialized, this really reflects the fact that a majority of the *households* in these villages were more commercialized: individuals and households produced goods and services for market sale or hire. They had the human capital (skills and knowledge) and the social capital (family ties and other social networks through which to reproduce and exchange skills, knowledge, and scarce goods) necessary for their success in the marketplace.

Human and social capital cannot be obtained over night as tools or machinery might be, but must be accumulated over time.[31] These skills, knowledge and social networks, embodied in individuals and households, were built up over time and therefore did not simply die out after collectivization—despite the fact that communist policies often did a good job of stifling them for more than two decades.[32] Thus, when markets were pro-

moted in the (post-1978) reform period, the villages containing large proportions of people with strong experiences and memories of market activities
were the ones to "get rich first." Villages lacking such skills and experience
have had more difficulties developing the human and social capital to get
ahead.[33]

Ivan Szelenyi (1988) has made a similar argument for the importance of
pre-Communist human and social capital in the context of rural Hungary. He
finds a "correlation between a family's pre-socialist entrepreneurial orientation and current entrepreneurship."[34] Szelenyi uses "cultural capital" to
explain the persistence of the "entrepreneurial spirit" over several decades,
but admits he does not have a mechanism for the reproduction of entrepreneurship over time. My answer to this, of course, is human and social capital
skill are reproduced through the institution of family. The similarities between
Szelenyi's study and this one, for the most part, stop here since his focus is
upon individuals rather than villages. He also assumes that there are no lin-
gering effects of communism (such as the land distribution policies that I
found so important for Ganglong). Still, Szelenyi's use of ethnographic and
quantitative data was an early inspiration for my own methodology.

The lag time involved in creating and destroying human and social capital accounts for some of the path dependence effects found in the Ganglong
Township. Path dependence is "the consequence of small events and chance
circumstances"[35] which over time can determine the particular path a society, economy, technology, or organization, embarks upon and continues to
follow.[36] That villages with little or no past market experience continue today
with their primarily agricultural orientation despite the building of roads and
bridges is one path dependence effect identified here.[37] Another is the hand-
ing-down of market-related skills found among village families, which makes
some villages' economic activities more commercial in nature, while other villages without market legacies remain more agriculturally-oriented.

Institutional constraints are the third mechanism influencing differential
development. Some of the institutional mechanisms responsible for differential development in the Ganglong villages involve policies driven by politics.
These include land allocation policies which locked agricultural villages into
subsistence-based agriculture, while the more commercial villages continued
on a path of economic diversification. Secondly, residence policies made
migration difficult, and therefore locked in preexisting social structures—i.e.
human and social capital. In addition, class labels made some human and
social capital (namely, that linked to the former Nationalist government or
other "counter-revolutionary" forces) disappear from some villages through
"class struggle" faster than others.

A less tangible type of institutional constraint that takes time to change
is human cognition, another key type of institutional inertia or change.[38] The
idea of "mental" or "cognitive" constructs is very much related to cultural

values. Not only do the existing skills and knowledge prompt people in certain villages to rediscover and use their market skills in the reform period; there is also a sense (learned from family and community) that commercial activities are in fact legitimate endeavors to pursue. Likewise, a sense that market activities are corrupting holds back the entrepreneurial initiative in the more agricultural, less market-oriented, villages (see Chapter Three).

The fourth process also involves a set of institutional constraints, but encompasses a process with an internal logic and impact profoundly different from those mentioned above. This set of institutions is the post-Mao market reform of the centrally-planned economy, initiated after 1978. There is no evidence that either type of village economic orientation—commercial or agricultural—was more successful in terms of creating well-being for villagers in the precollectivization era. In fact, commercialization may actually have been a liability in pre-Communist times because reliance on the market may have rendered commercialized villages extremely vulnerable in years of market failure caused by war, famine, and premature entry into international trade.

It is clear, however, that in the institutional environment of the post-Mao period, those villages able to take advantage of market skills and social networks, in either private or collective enterprise, are the ones with higher standards of well-being today. This is where the "increasing returns" aspect of lock-in and path development theory becomes important. Under the new institutional conditions in Chinese "market socialism," entrepreneurial activities now enjoy increasing returns to more commercialization. Simply stated, this generally means that the more commercialized an activity, household or village, the more profitable it will be. This helps spin the villages with long histories of marketization into virtuous cycles of economic development, while a lack of market savvy traps the more agricultural northwest villages into vicious cycles economic stagnation.

The empirical evidence presented here documents the significant differences in levels of economic development that exist among the twenty-three Ganglong Township villages. My analysis demonstrates that these village-level differences are reflected in the economic situations of the households. Even with decollectivization and the individual household responsibility system, the village-as-community still *is* a reasonable unit of analysis for the determination of individual and household well-being in the post-Mao period. Today's levels of village development and villager prosperity are directly linked to the socioeconomic status of the villages—and to the social and human capital of their residents—existing in commune era and even pre-Communist era patterns of village development.

The very different development levels of the villages in Ganglong and the paths they have followed challenge scholars to diversify their approach to the problem of differential development in rural China. Attention to pre-

Communist village histories and village (not simply macro-regional or house-hold) socioeconomic variations yields a more sophisticated understanding of the multiple processes behind rural industrialization and stratification.

HOW THE BOOK IS ORGANIZED

Chapter Two puts Jinghai County and Ganglong Township in historical and regional context. This chapter demonstrates that in comparison to other counties in the Tianjin Municipality and other townships in Jinghai County there is nothing extraordinary about Ganglong Township. Chapter Three documents the diversity among the twenty-three villages—size, location, population, surname composition, etc.—and provides a more detailed look at the different "personalities" expressed by the six villages in which I did the most extensive fieldwork.

The task of Chapter Four is to define the criteria for "well-being" among Ganglong residents in the mid-1990s. It is upon these criteria that the notion of "development" is based. I then measure and compare the levels of aggregate prosperity and development in each of the six survey villages. Chapter Five is a bridge chapter: it moves on from the six-village comparisons based on the household surveys to a more general ranking of all twenty-three villages using yearly accountant records from township archives. I also give evidence that the preliminary differences found between the northwest and southeast survey villages elaborated in Chapter Four can in fact be generalized to most of the Ganglong villages. Chapter Six examines the extent to which precollectivization factors continue to have an effect on the prosperity of Ganglong villages in the mid-1990s, and uses statistical methods to explore many of the hypotheses put forward earlier in the chapter. Chapter Seven (Conclusion) looks at the various implications of this study's findings and raises questions for further research.

NOTES

[1] All Ganglong Township area village and market names have been changed, as have the surnames of officials in each village. "Ganglong" is the actual name of the larger commune to which these villages (and many others even in other counties) belonged during the Great Leap Forward (1958–1961). Throughout the book, I refer to the twenty-three villages in the study as "Ganglong Township villages," "Ganglong villages," "Ganglong Commune villages," "Ganglong area villages" or simply "Ganglong."

[2] I kept several different note files, one for each of the villages in which I conducted household surveys (e.g. "Niudian notes"), one for the initial village surveys (VSNotes), and my own field notes which, for the purposes of this book, I will just call "Notes."

[3] This is not a phenomenon isolated to Ganglong. Knight and Song (1992) use the example of two villages within 20 km of the county seat in Handan County,

Hebei Province, to show a similar pattern: the "rich" village had an average per capita income three times that of the "poor" village.
[4] Throughout the book, I use the terms "prosperity," higher and better "living standards," and "socioeconomic status" interchangeably with "well-being." I discuss different levels of "well-being," both at the household level and at the village level. Household well-being generally refers to the quantitative and qualitative elements of physical well-being: food, clothing, shelter and cash for other necessities, rituals and luxuries. It also includes the more subjective preferences for certain types of jobs and investments in the future (see Chapter Four for details). Village-level well-being is the aggregate level of household well-being, a lower degree of inter-village economic stratification, in addition to village-provided public goods such as paved roads, street-lighting, labor-saving agricultural services, etc. "Rich(er)" villages and "poor(er)" villages refer to villages with more and less of village well-being thus defined. Similarly, "more developed" and "less developed" villages have greater and lesser degrees of well-being, respectively. Village "development" exists on a continuum whereby inadequate village and villager well-being ranges from lack of material necessities, poorer diets, little or no public infrastructure, and higher degrees of household stratification to more than adequate levels of the same.
[5] Chapter Four has a more in-depth discussion of the crucial impact that local industries have on a village's socioeconomy.
[6] See Linge (1997); Linge and Forbes (1990), Pan and Ma (1994); Ma Guonan (1994); Ke (1996); Tsui (1991 and 1998); Knight and Song (1992); Cheng and Zhang (1998); Rozelle (1996); Jian, Sachs and Warner (1996); Guo (1999); Wang and Hu (1999); Johnston (1999). Fan (1997) has an interesting overview of the official Chinese theories of regional development.
[7] However, Quarnstrom (1994:10) believes that by stressing regional income gaps, the Chinese government avoids the problem of class or political factors leading to stratification.
[8] Ke (1996:251).
[9] See Zhongyang (1986), Nongyebu (1992), Griffin and Zhao (1993), McKinley (1996), Knight and Song (1992) and Azizur and Riskin (1998 and 2001).
[10] In their introduction Christiansen and Zhang make an exemplary attempt to point out the crucial role of micro-level factors in differential development, many of which are similar to those important in Ganglong's development.
[11] A good overview of these "transition studies" is found in a Szelenyi and Costello (1996) article.
[12] For example, Ma Rong (1994); Knight and Song (1993); Parish, Zhe and Li (1995).
[13] See Oi (1989 and 1992); Knight and Song (1992); Cook (1998).
[14] Nee (1989, 1991 and 1996); Oi (1994). Nee concentrates on the positive returns to people engaging in the market while Oi focuses upon the fact that poorer/rural people may simply choose not to participate at all.
[15] Selden (1993).
[16] Unger (1994).

[17] More recently, Whiting (2001) looks closely at the institutional constraints and opportunities on local officials which have driven the rural industrialization process in areas just west of Shanghai in central-southern China.

[18] In Mao era China (as well as today), official often experiment with new policies in one location and, when and if they are successful, the first location becomes a "model" to be emulated in other locations. As Friedman et al point out, these models often succeed because a large amount of resources, both human and material, are funneled in to them.

[19] Jing's (1996) *Temple of Memories* is a beautiful demonstration of collective memory in a Gansu village.

[20] I am not the first to do this, however. Putterman (1993) uses *both* collective (village and team) *and* household measures for income to analyze income differentials between brigades and teams in Dahe township for the 1979 through 1985, with additional collective information stretching back to 1970.

[21] An explanation of how the research was carried out can be found in Appendix A, "Note on Methods and Sources."

[22] More about the history and policy atmosphere can be found in Chapter Two.

[23] Summarizing the international development literature, one scholar notes that underlying much of the debate [on development] is a familiar conflict: that is, between those advocates with faith in rigorous and parsimonious models of physical and social reality . . . and associated with positivistic thinking, and others who value pluralistic, narrative, qualitative descriptions (Rodwin 1994:3).

[24] Some examples of rural China research combining statistical, archival and ethnographic materials to come up with something more than just a sum of the parts can be found in the *Dangdai Zhongguo de cunzhuang jingji yu cunluo wenhua congshu* (Village Economy and Culture in Contemporary China Series), especially Hu and Hu (1996) and Wang and Zhu (1996). The pathbreaking study of rural Guangdong by Parish and Whyte's (1978) offers a refreshing combination of methods and some exceptional insights.

[25] This is precisely where Putterman (1993) falls short: he does not look far back in history and thus he concludes that all villages were about the same on the eve of collectivization. Moreover, he assumes that there were no land transfers between villages or teams. Neither of these two points was true for the Ganglong villages, and this had very important consequences for differential village development over time in Ganglong Township.

[26] Xie and Hannum (1996) and Linge's (1997) Introduction include additional arguments about why such large cross-sectional studies are not as representative—or instructive—as they might claim to be. Similarly, economists Benjamin and Brandt (1999:295) conclude from their comparison of North China households in the 1930s and 1990s, that "much of the inequality is coming from within rather than across villages . . . [therefore] in trying to explain overall inequality, much of the focus should be on local institutions."

[27] Histories of economic sociology can be found in Granovetter (1990) and Nee (1998). In recent years, scores of new work have been published in economic sociology. For an introduction to the various currents in economic sociology, see Swedberg (1991). For an introduction to "socio-economics," the name calling attention to the importance of the social in economic activities and systems, see

Etzioni and Lawrence, eds. (1991) and Coughlin, ed. (1991). For a discussion of how economic sociology differs from the new institutionalism in economics and/or evolutionary economics, see Swedberg, Himmelstrand and Brulin (1987), DiMaggio and Powell (1991), Granovetter (1992), Nee and Ingram (1998).

[28] While I am uneasy applying the word "mechanism" to social phenomena because it conjures up images from physics, its use by other social scientists is instructional. I am fond of the idea, attributed to Merton, that mechanisms are a "middle ground between social laws and description" (Hedstrom and Swedberg 1998:6). Further defined, a mechanism is "a plausible hypothesis, or set of plausible hypotheses, that could be the explanation of some social phenomenon, the explanation being in terms of interactions between individuals and other individuals, or between individuals and some social aggregate" (Schelling 1998:32–33). For the purposes of this study, this is what is meant by a "mechanism."

[29] The importance that geographic proximity to markets plays in social and economic development in rural China was first theorized by Skinner (1964).

[30] See Koo and Perkins (1995), particularly Abramovitz's chapter; UNDP (1993); Putnam (1993); Rona-Tas (1998).

[31] Rona-Tas (1998:127).

[32] Wilson (1994) argues that some aspects of social networks *within* villages were actually strengthened after Liberation because villages were divided up into production teams based on lineage and neighborhood. Parish and Whyte (1978) also mention this de facto preservation and strengthening of existing social bonds.

[33] While there is certainly no dearth of "negative" social capital in China, my focus and definition of social capital, however, rely primarily upon the entrepreneurial skills, knowledge and market networks which are passed down within the social context of the family and have propelled Ganglong villages forward in socioeconomic terms. Putnam (1993), for example, discusses how a prevalence of "negative" social capital (personal connections for illegal or otherwise corrupt ends, nepotism, etc.) "held back" southern Italy's economic development.

[34] Szelenyi (1988:210).

[35] North (1990: 94).

[36] The seminal works on path dependence in economic history and economics are David (1985) and Arthur (1988 and 1989). Both of these articles later appeared in book form (Arthur, 1994). More recent work by social scientists from a variety of disciplines include Putnam (1993), Brinton and Nee's (1998) and Rona-Tas (1998). See also footnote 20 this chapter.

[37] Luong and Unger (1998) also note the importance of precollectivization market experience and family histories for contemporary farmer success in the market.

[38] The notion that cognition can be important for institutional inertia and change has appeared in both sociological and economic literature. See Rona-Tas (1998: 123 and ft. 43), Fligstein (1991:335), Zucker (1983), North (1991 and 1998) and Rizzello (1997).

CHAPTER 2.

JINGHAI COUNTY AND GANGLONG TOWNSHIP IN HISTORICAL AND REGIONAL PERSPECTIVE

T HE TWENTY-THREE VILLAGES WHICH MAKE UP GANGLONG TOWNSHIP—THE focus of this study—are today located in Tianjin's Jinghai County. The northern tip of Jinghai county is 35 kilometers southwest of Tianjin proper, but Ganglong Township is in the southern tip of Jinghai County, about 80 kilometers southwest of Tianjin (see Figures 1 and 2 on the following page). The purpose of this chapter is to place the Ganglong villages in their larger geographic, economic, historical and administrative context. It also provides ample evidence that there is nothing extraordinary about this township that should prevent generalizing the findings of this study to many other townships in China.

GEOGRAPHY

The Southern Grand Canal, running north to south through Jinghai County, also runs right through Ganglong Township.[1] Twelve of the twenty-three villages are on the northwest side of the Canal, and the other eleven villages are on the southeast side. Until mid-century, the Grand Canal (now only a very narrow and shallow river) was a source of life—and death—for people who lived nearby. Not only did the Grand Canal provide water for irrigation, protein in the form of fish, and jobs in loading and ferry transport, it periodically swelled with summer rains, flooding fields and submerging houses, drowning animals and village people alike. Access to villages and towns on the other side of the river was rather limited before bridges were built across the river in the 1970s.

Ganglong is almost completely flat: the highest point in all of Jinghai County is just seven meters above sea level and the lowest is 2.4 meters below sea level (Wang 1993:6). Ganglong lies near the Bohai Sea on the

Fig. 1: Tianjin Municipality

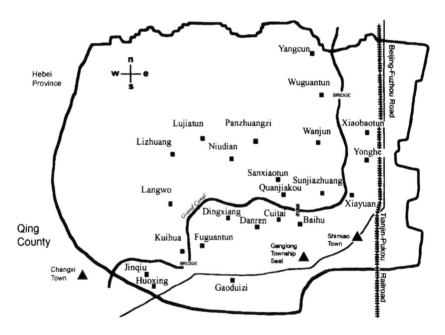

Fig. 2: Ganglong Township

North China Plain, and there are still low-lying depressions throughout the region which are testimony to its millennia under that sea. Along with these depressions are unrelenting summer rains which pound on the large river system found throughout the greater Tianjin and Hebei area. The geography of this region helps to explain the historical battle with floods that Ganglong and Jinghai residents faced on a terrifyingly frequent basis before water conservancy projects in the 1960s tamed the Grand Canal system.[2] Even to this day, the flood-prone nature of the low-lying land and poor drainage discourage high crop yields by promoting a high salt and alkaline content in the soil. In the dry season, passersby on bus or train can actually clearly see the white salt and/or soda on top of the land.

ADMINISTRATIVE HISTORY AND CURRENT ADMINISTRATION

Twelve of the twenty-three Ganglong villages originally belonged to Qingxian (Qing County) in Hebei, while the other eleven belonged to Jinghai County, at least as of the writing of the Jinghai and Qingxian gazetteers of 1929 and 1931.[3] The fortunes of both Jinghai and Qingxian, in turn, have long been linked to the area that encompasses present-day Tianjin.[4] The Tianjin *wei*, a military institution independent of local civil administration (Bian 1986:167), was established in 1404 AD. It included Jinghai and Qingxian, in addition to the area covering most of present-day Tianjin and a large section of Hebei. This was *the* decisive moment for the founding of Tianjin (just a village before then), and a watershed in the development of Jinghai, Qingxian and surrounding counties.

Part of the reason for setting up the *wei* in what is now the Tianjin area—then a meeting point of important grain transport rivers and tributaries—was to protect the grain that passed through the area along the Grand Canal to Beijing.[5] One aspect of the *wei* system was that portions of land, called *tuntian*, were allotted to and tilled by soldiers and, in some cases, their families.[6] A portion of the harvests went for military consumption and into military coffers, while the rest could be consumed or sold by soldiers and their families engaging in *tuntian* cultivation.[7] Many of the villages were part of the original Tianjin *wei tuntian* system in Jinghai, Qingxian and surrounding counties having names which reputedly come from the military official or *"guan"* who first settled the village. (Thus the name Chenguantun would be named after an official surnamed "Cheng"). Eight Ganglong villages have names like this and most of these villages set their founding dates to 1404—the same date as the Tianjin *wei* itself.[8]

Today, Ganglong villages are all administrative villages; that is, they do not contain smaller hamlets as are often found in other regions of China. Each village has its own government, headed up by a Party Secretary (*cunwei shuji*) in charge of the village party organization and overall village affairs, particularly village industrial enterprises, if there are any. Other village officials include a village head or director (*cun zhuren*) in charge of agricultural affairs, and accountants. The accountants are in charge of tallying, collecting and recording household electricity and water bill payments, agricultural taxes, and any other taxes or fees levied on households. It is usually the village accountant(s) who maintain the annual village records, including the demographic, agricultural, financial and social data that I collected and use in later chapters. The village Party Secretary is either appointed directly by township party leaders or elected by villagers from candidates selected by township party leaders.[9] The role of the village Party Secretary is further explored in Chapter Three.

Township officials, appointed by the county, have the task of levying taxes and fees on village industries—this is their main form of revenue.[10] Township leaders also supervise (or at least try to) village leaders over a wide range of affairs: cropping patterns and agricultural procurement quotas, family planning, rural industry, education, public security, village infrastructure, etc. Ganglong Township leaders in turn are supervised by Jinghai County leaders and departments. County officials then answer to Tianjin municipal authorities. As a provincial-level city (*zhixiashi*), Tianjin is under the leadership of national-level Chinese Communist Party and the central government.

COMMERCE, AGRICULTURE AND INDUSTRY IN TODAY'S GANGLONG

One hallmark of rural life in China, both past and present, is the rotating market, analyzed in great detail by G. William Skinner (1964). These markets take place in a fixed location (a market town) every several days. Staple foods, vegetables, fruits, livestock, meats, poultry, clothing and accessories, household goods, as well as the tools, fertilizer and seed for crop agriculture and animal husbandry are the most common items for sale at these markets. The location and time schedule for these market fairs usually makes it possible for local peddlers to sell their wares at one of the nearby rotating markets everyday.

There is no rotating market in Ganglong Township itself, although there is a large market town on both the east and west sides of the township. Today, the closest market is no more than a 40-minute bicycle ride from any Ganglong village on a fair-weathered day, though many older women living closer walk to market because they cannot, or do not want to, ride bikes. One of the two closest markets is actually in nearby Qingxian, Hebei Province. Within a little over an hour's bike ride are the three other Jinghai markets which, along with the two closest, make up the "traditional marketing area" spanning the Tianjin and Hebei border (Skinner 1964). For larger purchases, Ganglong residents might take the half-hour bus-ride to the Jinghai County seat to the north, the hour bus-ride to Cangzhou to the south, or a two-hour trip to downtown Tianjin. Only rarely do they take the four-to-five hour train ride to Beijing, although a train headed there leaves daily from Shimiao town.

Running along the eastern rim of the township is the Tianjin-Nanjing railroad as well as the one-lane Beijing-Fuzhou road, which has done much for local restaurant and vehicle repair business servicing truckers. It remains to be seen what the long term consequences of the two-lane closed highway, which opened in 1995, will be. Because it is closed, those travelling along this new highway must actually exit and detour to the old commercial zone to reach the many local businesses, rather than simply stop on the side of the old "highway" to get a bite to eat or to buy vehicle repair parts. Since much of the traffic is long distance to points along the central and southern coast of China, many Ganglong and Shimiao residents were afraid the highway would adversely affect the local economy.

As in the rest of Jinghai, the main crops in Ganglong Township are still winter wheat, corn and soya beans; sorghum is now only grown on the poorest and/or most distant land. Most families also grow garlic and Chinese cabbage, while people with extra labor will often grow other types of vegetables for home consumption, for market, or for direct sale to the numerous pickled vegetable factories in the area. Villages along the Grand Canal use water from the canal to irrigate fields adjacent to the canal if there is enough water and it is clean enough, and/or rely on well water.[11]

County authorities arrange for water from other rivers to be diverted into the usual trickle that is the Jinghai part of the Grand Canal for winter wheat irrigation in late fall. Normally, there is just enough water to satisfy a few ducks and children's desire to make dams, catch minnows and float paper boats. The canal can be crossed without getting wet with the help of a few stepping stones. In the fall of 1995 the water diverted in was alarmingly black and viscous, but county authorities analyzed it and pronounced it safe for irrigation. Reportedly, the pollutants originated from factories in the Hebei city of Cangzhou to the south of Ganglong.

Due in large part to its proximity to Tianjin's relatively developed industrial sector, Ganglong has a number of very healthy rural industries which generally do subcontracting work for large Tianjin state-run and collective factories. With one exception, there were factories in every Ganglong village in 1995, engaging in a range of endeavors from agricultural processing to clothing, ping-pong tables, and school supplies production, to more heavy industrial car parts and equipment manufacturing. In the mid-nineties, over half of Ganglong's rural industries were classified as "collective," in other words, "owned" and supervised by village leaders or those appointed by them.[12] By county directive, all these "collective" industries are eventually supposed to become "joint-stock companies" with shareholders (including the village-as-corporation), hopefully ensuring that corruption is kept to a minimum and that profits are maximized. Of the remaining enterprises, the majority are contracted out to individuals who generally pay a yearly fee to the village for the use of land and facilities of formerly village-run factories. In this sense, these are de-facto private enterprises. Private factories are still in the minority in most Ganglong villages.[13]

On the other hand, small-scale private commerce is quite common in all Ganglong and surrounding villages. People who sell the vegetables and live-stock they raise, produce handicrafts, process agricultural products on a small-scale (e.g. pressing flour into noodles or making dofu), or who peddle merchandise in the rotating markets are found in large numbers in most vil-lages.

JINGHAI ECONOMY DURING THE REPUBLICAN PERIOD AND PRIOR TO COLLECTIVIZATION (1949–1952)

There is a general lack of demographic, economic or other background information about any the Ganglong villages prior to 1949. Furthermore, there are some important holes in the available data for these villages in the years prior to collectivization and the introduction of the commune system.

Later in the book I will argue that the situation of Ganglong villages on the eve of Communist takeover in 1949 is critical to understanding the levels of village socioeconomic development today. Therefore, it is important to 1) fill in gaps in the Ganglong data with information from Jinghai and Qingxian and, 2) demonstrate that the data I utilize reflects conditions for the Ganglong villages. In comparing the Ganglong data with the (temporally closest) available information for Jinghai and Qingxian (from the 1930s), we find that both sets of data correspond very well.

Today, most families in Jinghai and Ganglong could probably support themselves solely with their jobs in industry, construction or small-scale busi-ness. This certainly was not true before the late 1980s in Ganglong. During Republican times (1911–1937), the majority of Jinghai and Qingxian families relied heavily on what they grew for food, and often supplemented agricul-ture with a variety of sidelines.[14] Crops mentioned in the Republican-era Jinghai and Qingxian gazetteers included glutinous and regular millet, sorghum, oats, sesame, rice and a host of different kinds of beans, most of which are still found in present-day Jinghai.[15] Cotton, a big crop for most of Hebei at the time, was produced in both of the nearby counties of Tianjinxian and Wuqing on a fairly large scale. This was not the case in Jinghai or Qingxian, presumably due to the risk of water-logging which cotton does not weather well (Huang 1985:63). Due to the poor quality of Jinghai land, sorghum was the crop of choice for most farmers.

Table 2.1[16] gives a brief glimpse at the agricultural situation in Jinghai, Qingxian and other nearby counties for 1928–1934, years before both the Japanese occupation (1937–1945) and civil war (1945–1949) disrupted pro-duction. The most striking difference between Jinghai and the other counties shown here is the surprisingly high proportion of tenant farmers (26%), part-tenant/part-owner-cultivators (28.2%), and comparatively low proportion of owner-cultivators (45.8%), especially in relation to Qingxian. In trying to reconcile where to place the Ganglong villages, the best guess is somewhere in the middle. As far as land tenure is concerned, the villages of present-day Ganglong, which are surrounded by Qingxian on the west and south, are more likely to have been closer to Qingxian in the Republican years than to Jinghai. The two Ganglong villages reporting the highest proportion of tenancy in pre-Liberation times are those in the most northeasterly corner of the township.[17]

Grain yields (including wheat, oats, soy beans, corn, sorghum and millet) and income figures show that Jinghai and Qingxian were not only *not* ahead of their neighbors—the other Tianjin area counties and the average for Hebei counties during Republican times—in fact they were *behind* by rather substantial amounts.[18] Both counties have family incomes less than the other counties represented here, and seemingly below other Hebei counties: the range in average gross household income among the thirty-two Hebei counties for which I have information is 113 yuan to 552 yuan, not counting the Tianjinxian anomaly. Tianjinxian numbers are suspicious: only 10 yuan in annual income and 245 yuan expenses for owner-cultivators was reported.

Of the surveyed Jinghai households, 86.1% are reported to have been predominantly agricultural—slightly above the Hebei average of 85.6%. There are two Hebei counties with proportions as high as 99.8% (Tangxian, Xinzhen) and one county with a percentage as low as 52.1% (Cheng'an). Tianjinxian, in the center of today's Tianjin (which, even in the Republican era, was fairly urbanized), matched the Hebei average for percentage of households engaged in agriculture. This indicates that in the earlier part of this century, most of Hebei—even the counties adjacent to large urban areas—was preoccupied with grain crop agriculture.

Although grain-crop agriculture was the main economic activity for Jinghai and Qingxian families during the Republican era, sidelines (handicrafts and small-time peddling) helped households avoid the risks of flood, drought, wind, hail and locusts, as well as provide cash for weddings, funerals, clothes, gifts and other goods which could not be self-provided. Table 2.2 looks at commerce and the various industries in Tianjin area counties organized by central workshop, factory and home handicrafts during the middle-Republican years.

The number of fixed-location commercial shops indicates once again that both Jinghai and Qingxian lag behind the other area counties. Unfortunately, there are no figures for how many people in Jinghai and Qingxian were involved in small-scale peddling, and this may have been as important or more important than home handicrafts. The trend for Jinghai and Qingxian to lag behind other counties economically continues with artisan workshops. Of the seventy-nine Hebei counties surveyed, one county had no workshops at all, but there were two counties with over five hundred

Table 2.1. Basic agricultural indicators for Jinghai, Qingxian and other counties, 1928-1934.

Counties	% Owner-cultivator households* (and income in yuan**)	% Tenant farmer households* (and income in yuan**)	Mean arable land per capita*	% House- holds in agriculture+	Grain yield in jin per mu++	Major crops in order of land occupied in 1928**	Average # of people per household
Jinghai	45.8 (170)	26.0 (210)	6.5	86.1	83.4	Sorghum, corn, beans, wheat	5.2
Qingxian	81.0 (210)	8.8 (120)	4.6	92.0	89.2	Sorghum, corn, beans, millet	6.4
Baodi	83.6 (425)	11.2 (271)	4.9	86.8	116.2	Beans, sorghum, corn, millet	5.7
Wuqing	55.0 (300)	6.9 (300)	6.1	85.0	129.9	Beans, sorghum, corn, wheat	6.1
Ninghe	na	na	2.8	73.7	121.2	na	5.3
Jixian	na (175)	na (252)	3.7	77.3	104.3	Wheat, millet sorghum, beans	6.9
Tianjinxian	6.3 (10)	12.0 (na)	na	85.0	92.8	Sorghum, corn, millet, wheat	na

*Source: Hebeisheng gexian gaikuang yilan, 1934.

**Source: Hebeisheng shengzheng tongji gaiyao, 1928.

+Source: Zhongguo jingji nianjian (Vol. 6, agriculture), 1934-1935:46-47.

++Source: Hebeisheng nongye gaikuang guji baogao, 1933.

Table 2.2. Commerce, handicrafts, sidelines, and industry, 1928-1934.

Counties	Number of commercial shops*	Number of artisan work-shops**	Percentage of surveyed people engaged in sideline industries+	Percentage of family income from sidelines++	Number of factories*
Jinghai	318	42.0	8.2	29.4 (42.9)	0
Wuqing	851	76.0	3.2	0.0 (0)	1
Baodi	488	na	2.0	1.8 (7.7)	1
Jixian	600	na	12.6	30.6 (30.6)	0
Ninghe	450	na	60.7	na	6
Qingxian	262	64.0	3.2	23.8 (16.7)	na
Tianjinxian	na	157.0	21.1	na	na

* Source: Hebeisheng gexian gaikuang yilan, 1934.

**Source: Jicha diaocha tongji congkan, Vol 2(5), 1936-1937, but data for 1933.

+Source: Zhongguo jingji nianjian, Vol. 6 (agriculture), 1934-1935.

++Source: Hebeisheng shengzheng tongji gaiyao, 1929(?). Figures not in parentheses indicate the percentage of income from sidelines for owner-cultivator households with less than 50 mu of land, and those in parentheses are for tenant households working on less than 50 mu of land.

workshops. With 42 and 64 workshops respectively, Jinghai and Qingxian are again toward the bottom of the list. In addition to carpentry workshops, metalsmith and dying workshops, the types of artisan workshops in Jinghai and Qingxian in 1933 included those producing cloth, soya-sauce, alcohol, jewelry, shoes, pastries, dofu, oil (for cooking and lighting), roof tiles, and carts.[19]

Weaving braid for straw hats, mats, baskets and other straw and reed products was a predominant cottage industry from at least the Republican period, and certainly much earlier.[20] This continued to be an important sideline right up through the 1970s in some Jinghai villages, and a few households in the Ganglong area continue to weave baskets and brooms today. Particularly significant during the 1920s was weaving the straw braid for export to Europe where it was sewn together into the latest-style hats. By the 1930s however, the market for straw braid diminished.

One type of industry prevalent in the Ganglong area, paradoxically, did not make it onto this list. The industry that put Jinghai on the map, so to speak, is its preserved cabbage industry. Marketed by the name *Tianjin dongcai*, this product is an extremely salty chopped pickle made from the distinctive long narrow Chinese cabbage grown in the Jinghai area—with a strong dose of garlic added. Production of preserved cabbage began in the Qing Dynasty in nearby Cangzhou, but it was actually Jinghai preserved cabbage that became famous in the Republican period.[21] As early as the 1930s Tianjin preserved cabbage was exported, mostly to Indonesia, Singapore, Malaysia, Vietnam, Thailand, Cambodia and Laos. Today it can be found in Asian food stores in Western countries as well. Jinghai County is currently still the main base of production for Tianjin preserved cabbage, and along with other pickled and freeze-dried vegetables, has become a main export product in the (post-Mao) reform period, accounting for a large portion of Jinghai exports. The preserved vegetable industry is very prominent in our Ganglong villages today; almost every village has at least one such factory.

GANGLONG VILLAGES ON THE EVE OF LAND REFORM (1949–1952)

In the few years after the official establishment of the People's Republic of China (1949), Ganglong witnessed a period of socioeconomic recovery from the ravages of Japanese occupation and civil war. During this time, the new administrative organs of the local Communist government, including village governments, were still being set up and new leaders were being located and trained. Land Reform, in which land and possessions deemed as superfluous were confiscated from landlords, rich peasants and some middle peasants and redistributed to poorer villagers, occurred at this time.[22] The free markets of Shimiao, Changxi and other surrounding markets prospered. But in late 1953, a national policy of unified supply and marketing went into effect in Ganglong, and this greatly curtailed what could be bought and sold on the free market. This one policy had wide-ranging ramifications for the socioe-conomy of all Chinese villages, including those in Ganglong, and makes a logical endpoint to the early recovery period.

Again, since the available information for pre-Land Reform times in Ganglong is limited, the ability to use 1930s data for clues to fill out the pic-ture is key. Given the disruptions due to the Japanese occupation, civil war and a terrible flood in 1939, we can assume that little changed with regard to technology, investment, or other factors which might have led to a sub-stantial increase in agricultural yields or the quality of life for Jinghai-Qingxian people between the 1930s and 1949. If anything, one would expect a decrease due to war. Table 2.3. offers some evidence for the idea that there was not much difference between the 1930s and the early 1950s as far as basic indicators are concerned.

For the most part, figures for Jinghai and Qingxian in 1933–1934 are consistent with Ganglong figures in 1952. This is strong evidence that both sets of numbers, those from the 1930s and those from 1952, are reliable. Because 1952 was a very good year weather-wise, I included the cumulative averages for 1949–1952 in parentheses. These figures are even closer to the Jinghai and Qingxian grain yield and grain output per capita twenty years earlier. Varying definitions for what constituted arable land, population increases, and changes in administrative boundaries account for why per capita arable land in Ganglong in 1952 and the earlier county figures are so different (refer to Table 2.1 above). The situation for sidelines, peddling and other non-agricultural business perhaps provides the largest discrepancy between the 1930s and the pre-Land Reform years (1949–1953). This is especially true in villages where war disrupted planting and harvesting, and other means of survival had to be found.

COLLECTIVIZATION, COMMUNES, AND BEYOND—A BRIEF OVERVIEW OF GANGLONG'S POLITICAL ECONOMY, 1954–1995

The years from 1954 to 1964 were a time of political, economic and envi-ronmental turbulence, both in Ganglong and nationally. Seasonal and year-round mutual aid teams (MATs), in which groups of farmers pooled labor, tools and draft animals, had been promoted in Communist-held areas prior to 1949. But beginning in late 1952, these MATs were pushed a little more aggressively in Ganglong. There was only one Ganglong village with season-al MATs in 1949, but by 1954 there were eleven villages with MATs, some of them year-round (Ganglong Document #1). The promotion of MATs was the first phase in the Chinese Communist Party's collectivization process. The next steps followed closely: first, elementary co-ops, where private land was counted as shares in the cooperative and a unified production plans were fol-lowed; then advanced cooperatives, where an entire village was collectivised;

Table 2.3. Comparison of Ganglong villages' agricultural indicators (1952) with all the Tianjin counties (1952), Jinghai and Qingxian (1933-1934).

	Average # mu arable land per capita	Grain production per capita in jin	Grain yield in jin per mu	Draft animals per 100 people	Major crops ranked by amount of land occupied	Average # of household members
Ganglong Villages 1952*	3.2 (3.3)	251.8 (241.6)	95.2 (90.8)	11 (11)	Sorghum, corn, wheat, millet+	5.1 (5.1)
TJ suburbs & counties 1952**	1.9	256.2	119.0	5.6	Sorghum, corn, wheat, beans	4.6
Jinghai 1933-1934++	6.5	na	83.4	11.5	Sorghum, corn, beans, wheat	5.2
Qingxian 1933-1934++	4.6	na	89.2	na	Sorghum, corn, beans, millet	6.4

*Source: *1949-1960 nian jiben shuzi tongji pian:* Ganglong Document #1. Figures in parentheses are cumulative averages for the years 1949-1953. I use 1952 figures to be consistent with the data from the other present-day Tianjin counties.

**Source: *Tianjin nongye jingji gaikuang,* 1985. Includes six suburban districts of Tianjin as well as the five counties now part of Tianjin municipality.

+ Source: *Xiaguantun cunzhi,* 1995. Unfortunately, the only crop information is from one village.

++Source: *Jicha...*Vol.2(5), 1936-37 (1933 data).

finally, the communes themselves appeared, where entire townships were collectivized.

The Ganglong (Steel Dragon) Commune, of which all present-day Ganglong villages were a part, came into being in August of 1958,[23] ushering in the Great Leap Forward. Along with a push for rapid industrialization based on sheer human motivation, the central government embarked upon some very ambitious water conservancy projects. Village-based cafeterias and childcare centers were set up to make more time for all, especially women, to participate in production. Through a combination of bad weather, labor diversion away from the fields and into industrial and water conservancy projects, and the free-rider problems associated with the lack of incentives to work under the communal production system, the Great Leap Forward ended up falling flat on its face. Mass famine resulted, forcing the central government to scale back the institutions of the Great Leap and reinstate material incentives.[24]

In 1961, the larger communes were broken up into smaller communes, and more liberal policies encouraging agricultural production were put into effect, thereby signalling the end of both the Great Leap and huge communes. In the fall of 1963 there was a terrible flood on the North China Plain, in which people and livestock died and houses were destroyed in large numbers. It affected all the Ganglong villages on the northwest side of the Grand Canal, and several on the southeast side as well. This put a damper on Ganglong's Great Leap recovery. Thus the period from 1954 through 1964, encompassing collectivization, Great Leap and flood famine, is a dark period for Ganglong village and villager prosperity.

In March 1965, the twenty-three villages of present-day Ganglong were split off from the Shimiao market town into their own Ganglong Commune. From this time through 1977, Ganglong brigades (villages) steadily increased grain and handicraft production, and began to set up small factories. Large jumps in villager well-being occurred at this time, and inter-village stratification was, for the most part, kept in check. I refer to this period as "the high years of communism" because of the egalitarian policies, political and economic stability and marked improvement in living standards experienced during this time.[25] Another flood in 1966 devastated that year's harvest, although it thankfully caused little other damage. Other than the 1966 flood, these were years of increasing prosperity. Perhaps surprisingly to some, even during the more radical years of Ganglong's Cultural Revolution (1968–1970), there was almost no decrease or negative effect on physical well-being (income in cash and kind, grain consumption, etc.) for the average resident.

MARKET REFORM AND THE HOUSEHOLD RESPONSIBILITY SYSTEM

A deliberate increase in grain procurement prices (prices the government paid farmers for grain) and large-scale reinstatement of free markets in 1978 marked the beginning of market-oriented reform. The most far-reaching and momentous by-products of the increased prices for agricultural products were the new organizational incentive systems accompanying the new prices. In Ganglong, as in many other rural areas, the new incentives were gradual, often beginning with modest contracting out of agricultural work to small collective production groups *(baogan dao zu)*.[26] The culmination of this process was the Household Responsibility System (HRS) in which production team or brigade (village) lands were divided up, by population and/or labor power, and then contracted out to individual households to till (or even not till) as they saw fit. Although these experiments with different types of responsibility systems took place in most Ganglong villages by 1980,[27] the Ganglong Commune did not dissolve officially until July of 1983.[28] Still, by late 1982, almost all village land had been distributed to individual households. Because the winter wheat crop harvested in spring 1983 was still officially part of the commune system; the first full year of the HRS was therefore in 1984.

Taking advantage of the revived free markets, a few ambitious Ganglong villagers began to set up small shops or engage in small-scale peddling, specialized agricultural production (e.g. large-scale chicken and pig farming), transport, and home-based handicraft industries as early as 1978. These new economic market activities, in addition to the new organizational forms in agriculture, radically influenced household incomes and well-being for the successful.

In the decade beginning with 1984, free market activity increased rapidly for Ganglong township residents. For the most part, grain production continued as it had before the commune dissolved, the major crops being wheat and corn, mainly for subsistence consumption. But now almost all farming families found a multitude of non-grain opportunities in cash crops and animal husbandry. These included growing tubers and other vegetables for pickling at the new pickled vegetable factories or to sell fresh; hot peppers and garlic to be dehydrated at a new township-run factory; sunflower seeds, sesame seeds (mostly for oil and paste); large and small-scale pig, chicken and goat farming, etc. Township-, village- and privately-run factories and cottage industries sprang up (and closed down) in unprecedented numbers, giving township residents an ever-increasing ability to work year-round in non-farm jobs paying cash wages. Cash wages have allowed villagers to eat and dress better, build newer, larger houses furnished with modern appliances like refrigerators, fans, gas stoves, TVs and, in recent years, air conditioners and VCRs, telephones, in-home hot showers, and central heating.

SOCIOECONOMIC DEVELOPMENT IN JINGHAI AND GANGLONG IN THE MID-NINETIES

In the past decade, Jinghai has become well-known for its dynamic rural industrial sector. The infamous story of Daqiuzhuang, a Jinghai village which rocketed from being one of the poorest in the county mid-century to the richest in the whole *country* in the 1980s and 1990s, is Jinghai's claim to fame.[29] It is also the topic that first springs to mind whenever Jinghai is mentioned inside or outside of the Tianjin area. The impression that most people have, and that the official figures give, is that Jinghai's rural industry is highly developed. But growth is uneven, and much of Jinghai industry is concentrated in a few townships, towns and villages. In fact, a Tianjin sociologist reports that the industrial output of Daqiuzhuang accounts for half of all Jinghai industrial output.[30] But even if this report is true and Jinghai's gross value of industrial output (GVIO) was cut in half, Jinghai would still be close to the top of the list of counties in China with regard to gross value of industrial material output.[31]

Table 2.4 shows that, by comparison with its Tianjin neighbors and with Jiangsu, Jinghai does fairly well with respect to the available indicators. Although I will argue in later chapters that per capita income is not a reliable measure of socioeconomic performance at the village level, with no other better data available and for our purposes here, it gives a cursory sense of where the counties, municipalities and provinces are economically. Shanghai and Beijing, unsurprisingly, have the highest per capita incomes, Jinghai and the other Tianjin counties (except for Jixian which has difficult mountainous terrain) are several hundred yuan per person per year above the national average, and quite close to the Jiangsu level.[32]

Table 2.4. Measures of industrialization and per capita income for Jinghai, the other Tianjin counties and Qing County, 1995.*

Counties	Per capita rural net income in yuan**	TVE income per capita (total rural pop) in yuan	TVE income per enterprise per year in yuan	Average # of TVE laborers per all TVE enterprises	TVE income per laborer in yuan	Ratio of agricultural to industrial output
Jinghai	2313	47,324	15,215,447	69.60	205,152	0.07
Wuqing	2,343	27,429	10,628,556	96.89	107,029	0.19
Baodi	2,300	20,648	1,909,926	10.45	108,592	0.20
Jixian	1,856	9,571	968,751	6.15	80,503	0.34
Ninghe	2,544	24,710	6,180,860	2.79	333,649	0.19
Qingxian	1,966	7,462	614,653	Na	na	0.32
Tianjin	2,406	na	na	13.75	na	0.06
Hebei	1,669	na	na	4.75	na	0.22
Beijing	3,224	na	na	15.72	na	0.08
Shanghai	4,246	na	na	85.85	na	0.03
Jiangsu	2,457	na	na	10.01	na	0.13
China	1,578	na	na	5.84	na	0.18

* Sources: *Tianjin tongji nianjian,* 1996; *Hebei jingji nianjian,* 1996; *Zhongguo nongcun tongji nianjian,* 1996. All yuan amounts are in current 1995 prices.

**The column categories from left to right in Chinese are: *nongmin renjun nian chunshouru; xiangzhen qiye zongshouru* divided by *xiangcun zongrenkou; xiangzhen qiye zongshouru* divided by *xiangzhen qiye danweishu; xiangzhen qiye zongshouru* divided by *xiangzhen qiyedanweishu; xiangzhen qiye zongshouru* divided by *xiangzhen qiye renshu; nong lin mu yu ye zongchanzhi* divided by *quanbu gongye zongchanzhi.*

Again, Wuqing, Baodi, Jixian and Ninghe Counties are the other four counties belonging to Tianjin Municipality. Hebei's Qingxian, as mentioned earlier, is the county that borders Ganglong Township to the west and formerly encompassed several of the villages currently belonging to Ganglong Township. Because Tianjin is an autonomous municipality with the same administrative status as Beijing and Shanghai, I have included both Shanghai and Beijing averages for comparison. Jiangsu is the province held up as the model *both* for successful agriculture *and* rural industry. Note that the average for Tianjin also includes thirteen urban *qu* (districts) in addition to the five counties.

Figures for the Tianjin area counties include the size of township and village enterprises (TVEs)—numbers of workers and enterprise income—which can be compared.[33] Jinghai's rural enterprises average almost seventy workers each, lower than Wuqing and Shanghai, but still Jinghai enterprises are quite large. Among the Tianjin counties, Jinghai TVEs are the most productive in terms of income per enterprise. Labor productivity is better than all Tianjin counties - excepting Ninghe, which on average has very small enterprises.

The fact that Jinghai has the smallest ratio of agricultural to industrial output among all the Tianjin counties, demonstrates that at the same time as it has a strong industrial sector, Jinghai has a much more modest agricultural sector, as can be seen more clearly in Table 2.5 below.

Table 2.5. Basic measures of the strength of agriculture in Jinghai, Tianjin counties, Qingxian and other relevant municipal and provincial comparisons, 1995.*

Counties	Percentage rural labor force in agriculture**	Number of mu arable land per capita	Grain output in jin per capita	Grain yield in jin per mu	GVAO in yuan per mu	GVAO in yuan per capita
Jinghai	47%	2.45	1,428	582	1,438	3,529
Wuqing	55%	2.47	1,864	753	2,087	5,159
Baodi	57%	2.07	1,619	782	1,958	4,055
Jixian	59%	1.59	1,416	890	2,030	3,230
Ninghe	58%	2.08	1,563	751	2,305	4,793
Qingxian	na	2.30	975	423	1,042	2,400
Tianjin	48%	1.61	1,047	649	2,085	3,362
Hebei	69%	1.84	1,029	560	1,174	2,156
Beijing	40%	1.61	1,399	867	2,745	4,428
Shanghai	27%	1.11	1,073	967	4,195	4,651
Jiangsu	57%	1.25	1,235	985	2,528	3,170
Nation	73%	1.55	1,018	563	1,428	2,219

*Sources: *Tianjin tongji nianjian,* 1996; *Hebei jingji nianjian,* 1996; *Zhongguo nongcun tongji nianjian,*1996. All yuan figures in 1995 current prices. Per capita figures calculated with rural population (not labor) figures.
**The column categories from left to right in Chinese are: *nong lin mu yu ye laodongzhe renshu* divided by *xiangcun laodongli; zong gengdi mianji* divided by *xiangcun renkou; liangshi zongchanliang* divided by *xiangcun renkou; liangshi zongchanliang* divided by *gengdi zongmianji; nong lin mu yu ye zongchanzhi* divided by *zong gengdi mianji; nong lin mu yu ye zongchanzhi* divided by *xiangcun renkou.*

Compared with the other Tianjin counties, Jinghai has the lowest percentage of its rural labor force in agriculture (47%), though it is much higher than Beijing and Shanghai (40% and 27%, respectively). This is despite the fact that Jinghai actually has a rather high land-to-rural population ratio. With the exception of Qingxian, Jinghai's grain yield is the lowest of all other comparison areas. Again, this is certainly partly a function of poor quality land as well as a rural labor force preoccupied with non-farm employment and therefore unwilling or unable to allow for the intensive field management necessary to induce higher yields. Not surprisingly, Jinghai also shows the lowest Gross Value of Agricultural Output (GVAO) per mu of the Tianjin counties, Beijing and Shanghai, and only squeaks in slightly above the national average. Besides poor land quality and the availability of off-farm employment, another factor accounting for Jinghai's dismal showing is that it has not developed its cash crop, livestock and fisheries industries the way its northern neighbor, Wuqing, has.

All in all, Jinghai is above average with respect to the number and size of its rural industries and strength of its state industrial sector, and below average with respect to its agricultural endeavors. As far as per capita rural income goes, Jinghai is about average in relation to the other Tianjin counties, though much lower than Beijing and Shanghai (which certainly have higher standards of living all around). Jiangsu's per capita income is surprisingly not much more than Jinghai's, perhaps more a function of the poorer areas in northern Jiangsu than of Jinghai being up to the Jiangsu level.

GANGLONG TOWNSHIP'S POSITION WITHIN JINGHAI

According to official figures and discussions with Ganglong Township officials, Ganglong appears to be in the middle range with respect to economic indicators, as far as Jinghai townships go.[34] The numbers are rather misleading, however, for reasons explained below and in further detail in Chapter Four. For example, Hexi Township, just northwest of Ganglong, would seem to be one of the poorest in the county by the indicators in Table 2.6 below. In fact, there is a great deal of private business and the people there are much better off than the numbers allow us to imagine.

The low figures for per capita income do not reflect the very healthy commercial sector which, by conservative estimates, would increase the Hexi per capita income figures by at least 50%. However, the per capita income figure is a very important one in China: despite its inaccuracies, most official programs and policies helping poor areas go by this figure. Because it is seen as the one piece of information which conveys the most about the socioeconomic situation in a given village, township or county, per capita income is not going to be displaced any time soon. As a matter of fact, I found myself using it when trying to gauge Ganglong's place in Jinghai county—mainly because there were only a few indicators available. Chapters Four and Five are devoted to finding a more meaningful way to measure village development levels and well-being.

Table 2.6 contains information about ten townships, each on the basis of per capita income figures in the low, medium and high range in geographically varied locations across Jinghai county. Also shown are figures for the county seat (Jinghai zhen), the market town closest to Ganglong (Shimiao zhen) as well as Ganglong Township itself. Sunguantun and Xiaocaizhuang border Ganglong on the north and east, respectively. Even if there were more data available, we would find that nothing about Ganglong sets it apart from the other townships in Jinghai.[35]

The two categories where Ganglong stands out the most (though in neither case is it the extreme) in Table 2.6[36] are the low fertility rate and large gap between highest and lowest village income. The low total fertility rate is most likely due to a very strong set of family planning policies in Ganglong combined with enthusiastic enforcement.[37] Note that the large gap in highest and lowest income is not a feature unique to Ganglong; this is further evidence that the differences I found in Ganglong—and will begin describing in the next chapter—due not belong solely to Ganglong Township.

CONCLUSION

In this chapter we have seen how Jinghai and Qingxian counties compare with other areas in their corner of the North China Plain (as well as other relevant areas) both historically and contemporarily. From the Republican years to as late as the establishment of the People's Republic, Qingxian and Jinghai residents, including those in the Ganglong villages, were living fairly spartan lives—at least as spartan as people in neighboring areas. Between the 1950s and 1995, Ganglong villages became increasingly industrialized. By the 1990s, Jinghai residents' living standards in general improved dramatically.

Although Jinghai lags behind other area counties with respect to agriculture, Jinghai has still exceeded its provincial neighbors Hebei, and especially Qingxian, in the areas of agriculture, commerce, and industry. Ganglong Township itself does not stand out, and in fact, was considered among the less successful townships in Jinghai until the very late 1980s. Even so, it only ranks in the top third now and, unless something spectacular happens, will probably not make much headway toward the top position in at least the next twenty years.

As far as intra-village comparison is concerned, we will find in later chapters that most of the Ganglong villages previously belonging to Qingxian are today still more like the Qingxian villages they border: they have more land, are more reliant on crop agriculture, and have fewer rural industries than their fellow Ganglong villages on the southeast of the Grand Canal. Before we delve into those issues, howeve, Chapter Three is devoted to giving a more intimate description of Ganglong's villages.

Table 2.6. Socioeconomic indicators for 10 of the 28 townships in Jinghai County, 1992.*

Township	Average per capita income in yuan	Arable land per person (agricultural population)	Grain yield in jin per mu	Population density per sq. kilometer	Birth rate per 1000 people	Spread between highest and lowest village per capita income in yuan
Ganglong**	1,065	2	342	435	2.4	2,005
Dongshuangtang	1,533	3	480	270	2.0	3,870
Gaozhuangzi	1,280	3	300	209	8.2	1,438
Sunguantun	910	2	314	327	4.9	781
Beishaolou	983	3	356	435	9.2	696
Fujunmiao	701	3	394	340	11.5	307
Hexi	666	3	364	396	10.1	310
Xiaocaizhuang	665	3	212	253	3.1	547
Shimiao zhen	1,165	1	484	1,216	22.5	265
Jinghai zhen	1,294	0	186	3,528	9.5	1,250

*Source: Jinghaixian guomin jingji he shehui tongji ziliao, 1993. All yuan are in 1992 current prices.

**Ganglong, Gaozhuangzi, Sunguantun, Hexi, and Xiaocaizhuang are pseudonyms; the others are not.

NOTES

[1] The Grand Canal north of Tianjin is considered the Northern Grand Canal.

[2] In the 175 years 1736 through 1911 alone, there were 88 recorded floods of the southern Grand Canal which affected Jinghai County and, most likely, our Ganglong villages. This is despite the fact that there are no records for 38 of these years (Shuili . . . 1981). Two huge floods occurred in 1939 and 1963: the first killed many people, but both wreaked havoc on animals and crops in the Ganglong area.

[3] *Jinghai xianzhi* (1929); *Qingxian xianzhi* (1931). Gazetteers are overviews of local - in this case county - history, culture, and economy. Some counties and prefectures have gazetteers that date back hundreds of years.

[4] The links between Jinghai and Qingxian go as far back as 1265 AD when they belonged to the same administrative district, and the connection probably extends back even before that. Both were part of Tianjin *zhou* when it was set up in 1725, and continued to be a part of Tianjin *zhou* when it was raised to the status of Tianjin *fu* in 1731 under Zhili Province (today Hebei Province) jurisdiction. They both stayed under Zhili and then Hebei rule until after Communist takeover. During the Great Leap Forward, from 1958–1961 Qingxian and Jinghai (as well as a few villages from Dacheng county) were actually combined into one huge county for a little more than two years, still under Tianjin in Hebei (Li 1987; *Tianjinshi zuzhi shiliao* 1992). Tianjin became a municipality under the direct authority of the central government in 1967, and six years later in 1973 Jinghai was placed within Tianjin's jurisdiction, where it has stayed until the present, while Qingxian continues under Hebei provincial authority.

[5] Guo (1989) argues convincingly that, in pre-modern times, the importance of Tianjin rose when Beijing was capital, and fell when it was not. Interestingly however, contemporary policy makers and scholars alike in the greater Tianjin area see the proximity to Beijing as a liability in the post-Mao reform era. They argue that more liberal social and economic policies are not permitted in Tianjin by the central government in Beijing precisely because Tianjin is so close and there is a fear of instability spreading to Beijing if things got out of control in Tianjin. In fact, one of the reasons often given for why Tianjin is one of the three municipalities under direct central government rule is that it is "the door to Beijing."

[6] The *tuntian* system was tried as early as the Jin Dynasty, but was not long-lived (Guo 1989:56–57).

[7] Yu (1986:19–20).

[8] Historically speaking, Jinghai County is quite young, mainly because the area it occupies was either covered by the Bohai sea or marshes while the rest of China was busy making human history. Jinghai County received its current name (sporting a different Chinese character for "Jing") in the Jin Dynasty, 1115–1234 AD (Yin 1988:9). But even after that the area was sparsely settled. It was not until the beginning of the Ming Dynasty (1368–1644 AD), with the establishment of the Tianjin *wei* (Tianjin military garrison) and the *tuntian* (military settlements) system of land administration, that permanent settlement and cultivation began (Guo 1989). It was also at the beginning of the Ming that Jinghai County received the name Jinghai, as it is now written.

[9] See Epstein (1997) for a discussion of village-level elections.

[10] In boundaries and administrative scope, the "township" government generally corresponds to the former "commune."

[11] Well water, the only potable water source, is so salty to the taste in some Ganglong villages that a reasonable amount of tea leaves cannot mask the flavor. Guests from outside the area are therefore often treated to hot salty water with sugar in it, prefaced by many apologies for the bad taste.

[12] "Ownership" is used loosely in the rural Chinese context. For analyses of rural enterprise ownership, see Byrd and Lin (1990), Ho (1994) and Chen (1996).

[13] Chapters Three and Four contain more detailed descriptions of the different types of rural industries found in Ganglong and their impact on the local social and political economies.

[14] "Republican" refers to the years of Nationalist Party rule under Chiang Kai-Shek, 1928–1937. See Spence (1990) for an engaging history of China from the late 16th century up until 1989, including a few chapters on the Republican period.

[15] Gazetteers are overviews of local - in this case county - history, culture, and economy, and date back hundreds of years in some cases. In recent years, the PRC has reintroduced county gazetters; a Jinghai County gazetteer was published in 1995 by the Tianjin Academy of Social Sciences.

[16] The information in Tables 2.1 and 2.2 are taken from a study of millions of rural households all over China, but there is no further information about how the survey was done. For Table 2.1 and all subsequent data I use, I am assuming that the year in which the data was actually collected is one year earlier than the publication date (given in the "Sources" below the Table) unless otherwise indicated. Readers may find it useful to refer back to Figure One to locate the surrounding counties which are compared to Jinghai and Qing Counties in the subsequent tables. Note also that the sources for these years often disagreed with each other—even when dealing with the same year. Both Table 2.1 and Table 2.2 should only be used as general guides to similarities, differences and trends, rather than a decisive summary of the way things were.

Adding the percentages of owner-cultivator and tenant farmer households together and subtracting from 100 gives the number of households who both own their own land and rent land. The mean *gross* income figures are for owner-cultivator households with less than 50 mu of land, and the average *gross* income figures are for tenant farmers renting less than 50 mu. Both include sidelines industry income and are in current yuan. I use gross income figures because they can be compared with incomes in data sources available in later years. Net income figures tell the same basic story: Jixian, Jinghai and Qingxian are at the bottom with negative net incomes.

[17] Indeed, for a time in the Republican period, these two villages belonged to another township altogether, one bordering Ganglong on the northeast.

[18] There was no average yield for Hebei, but a bar chart showing acreage and production data for Hebei indicates that it was about 117 jin per mu.

[19] *Jicha diaocha tongji congkan* (1936–1937).

[20] *Qingxian xianzhi* (1931: 879); *Jinghaixian xianzhi* (1929, renminbu:7; *Hebeisheng gongshang tongji*, 1931:214–215).

21 Jiang (1987). See also, the wonderfully complete book, *Tianjin gudai chengshi fazhanshi* (Guo 1989:47), which cites evidence that the pickled vegetable industry in the area can be dated back until at least 200 BC.

22 Actually, in some of the Ganglong villages, land reform took place in 1948, while in others it did not occur until 1950.

23 *Tianjinshi Jinghaixian zuzhishi ziliao*: 78.

24 The "Great Leap Forward" (1958–60) whereby China would supposedly, by sheer human will and labor, "overtake Britain in fifteen years," ended up throwing the country into famine and hardship. See Yang (1996) and *The Cambridge History of China*, vol. 14 for a more in-depth look at this period. Lin (1990) gives an assessment of the Great Leap Forward impact on agriculture.

25 I would like to stress that unlike the characterization Yan (1992) gives about non-Chinese researchers mistakenly believing uncritically the egalitarian rhetoric on the part Chinese government, I am well-aware of the fact that a certain degree of household stratification was present among villages during commune years. On the other hand, the empirical evidence that I have shows that inter-village stratification in Ganglong was indeed much less pronounced then than it is today.

26 Kathleen Hartford (1985) gives an excellent account of the rural reform process.

27 See Yang Dali's (1996) account of how and why experiments with the household responsibility system first occurred in areas most devastated by Great Leap Forward policies.

28 *Tianjinshi Jinghaixian zuzhishi ziliao*: 308.

29 Gilley's (2001) book is all about the rise of Daqiuzhuang.

30 Personal communication with Sun Yanfeng of the Tianjin Academy of Social Sciences. For some reason I was not allowed access to county socioeconomic data for other Jinghai townships, though collection of in-depth data for Ganglong Township itself was strangely never questioned.

31 I should point out that not only counties themselves, but actual urban districts of major cities, are considered in the 100 top counties list by the Chinese State Statistical Bureau.

32 The fact that Jinghai outperforms Jiangsu on some of these measures is probably due to two factors. One is that northern Jiangsu is much poorer and brings down the Jiangsu provincial average, and the second is the fact that Jinghai's overall strength is heavily weighted to one or two very prosperous townships/villages (such as Daqiuzhuang, mentioned above).

33 It is unfortunate that the same types of information found in the Tianjin Statistical Yearbook are not found in the other municipal and provincial yearbooks: a comparison of the fiscal performance of rural industry nationally would be instructive.

34 According to the current Party Secretary of Ganglong Township (who may have a special interest with regard to this question), Ganglong used to be close to the bottom of the list as late as the mid-1980s.

35 Sifting through the Tianjin Daily for the 1980s and 1990s turned up only a handful of tiny news flashes about Ganglong, none of any interest whatsoever.

36 Unfortunately I was unable to obtain any industrial or commercial indicators; in fact these 1992 data are the only at all recent comparative data I could get access to for the townships in Jinghai County.

37 The township employs none of the physical methods so decried by international organizations and individuals. Instead it uses incrementally steep fines for each breech of the family planning policy, and has the staff ready and willing to enforce them. This, combined with increasing numbers of women in off-farm labor, women who are more and more inclined to provide as much as possible for their only children, keeps the fertility rate low.

CHAPTER 3.

ONE TOWNSHIP, TWENTY-THREE VILLAGES

ONE OF THE PURPOSES OF CHAPTER TWO WAS TO SHOW THAT, ON AVERAGE, the twenty-three Ganglong villages were also average in another sense: in comparison with nearby villages and counties, they had no particular advantage in agriculture, sidelines or industry; they neither produced much more nor much less than the overall Jinghai, Qingxian or even Hebei averages, nor were they outstanding in any other definable way over the past forty-odd years. While these villages understandably have many points in common, this chapter will begin to differentiate them, using both basic quantitative data and ethnographic information to highlight how much the villages today actually do differ from each other.

By overlooking the distinct village level social, historic, geographic, economic and political realities, we overlook important clues about the process(es) of development. In emphasizing the variety of these villages—different sizes, economic activities, kinship structures, political leadership and orientation—by no means do I want readers to think that this variety is something unique to Ganglong. My point is rather the opposite: the variety within townships and counties is much greater than students of China have really ever noted. In all its diversity, then, I believe that Ganglong is quite average.

VILLAGE DIFFERENCES

These twenty-three villages occupy a very small geographic area, only about 14 square miles. A superficial glance at the different villages finds clusters of similar kinds of houses, arranged in a central location surrounded by village agricultural land. Chickens, pigs, goats and draft animals are a prominent feature in some villages, while others seem to have none at all. Many villages have lighted paved roads leading to them and through them, while others sport only dirt roads which turn into mudded ruts difficult to negotiate during the rainy season. In some villages the houses are lined up very neatly in east-to-west and north-to-south rows; in others houses appear in the middle of alleys, some built up on higher ground than others, and giving a very cluttered and chaotic appearance. Day visitors to a few of the villages would find men and women of all ages chatting as they stand or squat about in groups, but in most villages the days are quiet, as many or most of the adults work in local factories, government offices or schools, etc.

The major differences between villages are summarized in Table 3.1: size (both population and land holdings), lineage structure, degree of industrialization, and amount of consumption goods. In population terms, the largest village is seven times larger than the smallest, while the village with the most land is almost five times larger than the smallest. The size of the households and numbers of dependants per household are very similar in the twenty-three villages.

Because some villages have much more arable land per capita than others, it makes sense that these same villages would have a more agriculturally-based economy, although theoretically speaking this does not necessarily have to be the case. While actual grain yields do not differ that much between all the villages, the output per capita, number of draft animals and proportion of village income from agricultural activity varies quite widely. Generally speaking, it is the more agriculturally-oriented villages which have fewer durable goods and phones. The agricultural villages also have lower per capita incomes which, as mentioned earlier, are based almost exclusively on the strength of the industries within villages. Thus, those villages with the highest GVIOs per capita are inevitably those with the highest per capita incomes.[1] For the most part, these agriculturally-oriented villages are found on the northwest of the Grand Canal and the more industrially-oriented villages are on the southeast side.

The variation in surname structure is quite pronounced: the highest proportion of households sharing a single surname in one village is ten times greater than in the village with the smallest proportion.[2] Although the largest proportion of households sharing one surname in any Ganglong village is 98%, there are two other villages with one single surname accounting for 90% or more. Considering the common perception that single-surname villages are generally not found in northern China, this was a rather surprising finding.[3] Additionally, in at least three more villages, the proportion of families related through the female side of the family would also exceed 90%.[4] The importance of surnames will be tackled later in the book. Suffice it to say here that there seems to be a positive relationship between surname structure and village socioeconomic performance.

Table 3.1. High, low, average and standard deviation figures for various dimensions of socioeconomic development in the twenty-three Ganglong villages, 1994.

Dimension	High	Low	Average	Standard Deviation
Number of households	410.0	59.0	188.9	93.3
Number of people	1525.0	214.0	654.5	328.6
Arable land per capita in mu	4.1	0.9	1.9	0.8
Grain output per capita	1035.2	321.7	662.8	192.4
Grain yield in jin per mu	656.0	390.0	501.8	76.1
Number of draft animals per 100 mu of land	9.2	0.2	4.4	2.4
Ratio of agricultural income to total gross village income	0.7	0.0	0.3	0.2
Per capita annual gross value of industrial output (GVIO) per capita in yuan	275553	79	18373	56784
Per capita village income	1569.6	321.7	788.5	281.6
Proportion of largest surname	98%	10%	50%	3.0%
Number of consumer durables (TVs, fans, washing machines, refrigerators) per household	5.9	1.3	2.6	0.9
Number of phones	78.0	0.0	19.4	20.8

My first impressions of the two villages, Langwo and Dingxiang, which I related in the Introduction, drew attention to the importance of the northwest/southeast split, as well as to the village Party Secretary. The Party Secretary can in many ways make or break the village's chances to harness outside investment and take advantage of government policies and programs on the village's behalf by lobbying for their villages at township and county levels. Within the village, Party Secretaries are usually the defacto managers of village-run "collective" factories but, if they are not, they have the final say on who actually gets those jobs.

The term "collective" enterprise gets murkier and murkier as market reforms in China go forward.[5] For my purposes here, village-run industries are those the township rural industry office classify as "collective" and whose incomes and expenses are considered part of total village income and expenses.[6] These types of factories were often set up by the brigade or team under the commune system, using funds rightly considered by villagers to be fruits of collective labor.[7] These collective factories still have a high degree of participation by village officials: village officials appoint and fire factory managers and other staff, and also have a say in how profits are used.

A "good" Party Secretary is also able to mobilize residents for public works projects (e.g. extending and deepening irrigation ditches) or simply get them to pay their agricultural taxes on time. In the area of extra- and intra-village relations, Ganglong Township has its share of both effective and very ineffective Party Secretaries. Ostensibly chosen by an election of villagers, in almost all Ganglong villages Party Secretaries are chosen by township party committees regardless of villager sentiment, and where elections are actually held, the candidates must be chosen or approved of first by township officials.

Public perception of what it takes to be a Party Secretary in Ganglong inevitably includes being able to milk the system for private use, whether it be outright embezzlement, nepotism or private use of public/collective goods and services.[8] Thus, the Party Secretaries who care about public perception find themselves looking for ways to appease villagers' grumblings by engaging in infrastructure investment and other activities which directly benefit villagers. Examples range from paving roads throughout the village, to giving monetary gifts to all village households from village industry profits at New Year's, to arranging with other villages' officials to send cars for villager marriage convoys (which traditionally fetch the bride from her natal village and deliver her and her entourage to the groom's village). There is an unsurprising circularity about which villages get "good" Party Secretaries and which do not. Villages with good leadership have successful enterprises which in turn attract future good leadership. The opposite holds as well, and corresponding virtuous and vicious cycles are born—a topic to be taken up further in Chapter Six.

A CLOSER LOOK: THE SIX SURVEY VILLAGES

Because one year would not be enough time to study each of these villages in detail, I relied on preliminary village interviews to narrow help my focus. As criteria, I used three basic dimensions to choose six villages for more in-depth study: northwest or southeast of the Grand Canal, large or small in both population and land, and better or worse levels of well-being (based on discussions with local officials and my own preliminary observations). Village "well-being" here is a very loose concept which includes, among other things, thriving rural industry, prosperous households, decent infrastructure and prospects for continued successes. The next chapter is devoted to a more operable definition.

Of the six villages chosen, three are on the northwest side of the Grand Canal (Langwo, Niudian and Wanjun) and three are on the southeast (Baihu, Cuitai, and Yonghe); two are large (Yonghe and Wanjun), two medium-sized (Cuitai and Niudian) and two are small (Langwo and Baihu). Similarly, I chose two on each side of the river that seemed to be doing very well in socio-economic terms (Cuitai and Niudian), two which were not doing so well (Baihu and Langwo), and two others in the middle (Yonghe and Wanjun). I tried to stay away from extremes in the "well-being" category, which means that neither the richest nor poorest of the villages on either side of the Grand Canal are represented here. Three of the villages are close to one another and close to the township seat, while the other three are either to the east, west or north of the township seat. Although one might infer from this small sampling that village size and "well-being" go hand in hand, there are examples of both large and medium villages which fall into the "poor" category, and small villages which are "rich."

I introduce each of these six survey villages in more detail below as six "characters" with specific personalities. Readers hopefully will get a better sense of these six villages through their observable characteristics and the one person, the village Party Secretary, who can most tangibly influence the village's fate - either through strong positive leadership or strong negative leadership—simple inaction or poor decision making. Again, this should help accentuate the variety found in the Ganglong villages.

THE TOWNSHIP SEAT: BAIHU

Normally, when one thinks of a county or township seat in rural China, it is usually larger, a bit more tidy, more modern, more "on show" than the surrounding area. This is certainly not the case with either the Ganglong Township office compound or Baihu Village itself. The township office compound (which is all there is to this "township seat"), houses township

Communist Party and government officials overseeing agriculture, industry, education, family planning, public security, and health. It is located on the southern tip of the residential part of Baihu, right on the main Beijing-Fuzhou road. Unlike the new four-story freeze-dried vegetable factory (a township-run enterprise) next door, the township offices are drab, single-story and almost invisible.

Baihu is similarly invisible. It is one of the smaller villages in both land area and population and, at first glimpse, does not seem to be a village at all. It consists of a bunch of scattered houses, many of them made of mud-bricks, along dirt paths with deep ruts, all located behind the township offices and a few other roadside businesses. About 100 yards from the main road running through the southern part of the township, Baihu sits on the western border of the bustling market town Shimiao. The *"daduibu,"* or village office compound, is a ramshackle L-shaped structure that is deserted most of the time.

Baihu has 146 households and 485 rural residents.[9] There are 50 more people who were born and raised in Baihu but do not have village residency and an additional 60 more who are not from the Ganglong area at all, but have come here to work and live. Those born and raised in Baihu, but without village residence, are people with either non-agricultural residency (i.e. they work permanently for the township or other agency or enterprise allocating such status) or are newly-born children who have not yet been given their residency cards.[10] Most of the immigrants—of which there are more here in Baihu than in other village—are from the bordering provinces of Shandong and Hebei, and virtually all are from areas with much fewer opportunities to work for wages.[11]

There are 660 mu (about 109 acres) of arable land and more than 100 more mu which are occupied by buildings. Agriculturally, most families just grow enough wheat and corn to sustain themselves, and a few families let others till their land or let the land lie fallow because they do not have the interest in, or time and energy for, agricultural labor. Technically, Ganglong area land is not supposed to be turned over to people without village residency, but Baihu officials admitted that about 110 mu of village land have been contracted out (*zhuanbao*) to households from a nearby village in Hebei province for twenty to thirty yuan per mu annually. There are also several fishponds in Baihu which have been contracted out to individual village families since 1987 or 1988. The contracts run for 10 years and the contract fees were 300 yuan each (worth about US$37) in 1995.

There are no village-run industries in Baihu; village leaders explain this as due to a lack of good managers. There are seven larger enterprises, including a paint factory, a gas station, a metal parts factory, an oxidation shop (painting metal goods like bicycles), a welding shop, a pickled vegetable factory, and a meter plant. Nominally, the first four are "village-run," but the Baihu

Party Secretary and accountant conceded that they are, in practice, contracted out to individuals. However, the township cadre in charge of enterprise work said that none of these are officially classified as "village-run." The only point at which the "village" participates at all is in taking the contract fee (which is really best seen as a property rental fee), and the average villager does not actually see any of it. The factories were all set up between 1979 and 1993, and employ between five and thirty people. In the past few years, they have had either to cut staff or even shut down when the business climate was inhospitable for a few months or longer (as is true in many other villages). Although net profits were reportedly only a modest 50,000 yuan, the gas station is the largest money-maker, with a gross annual income in 1994 of one million yuan. The other factories and the three shops in the village are operated entirely by individuals or partnerships.

Baihu's largest surname group only accounts for about 10% of all village surnames, making it the lowest of the six villages, and very close to the bottom of all twenty-three villages.[12] With a hunch that the surname structure in a village would be important, I asked about this in all the villages, and discovered what seemed to be a positive relationship between large proportions of one surname, village cohesiveness and economic performance—a point to be explored more in later chapters. In Baihu, there certainly was little evidence of any village spirit or village cohesiveness.

I met Party Secretary Li of Baihu very early on in my stay. He seemed to know a lot about the history of the area and was quite personable with me. After completing a few household surveys however, I was surprised to find that villagers spoke openly—and with verbal daggers—about their Party Secretary. Party Secretary Wang from the Garden Village (and a good friend of Li's) commented that Li was a good leader who simply had not had the right kind of opportunity to develop his village. But the villagers in Baihu told quite a different story: among other things, they spoke of Li's tyranny, embezzlement and his mismanagement of a brick factory in which the village went almost one million yuan into debt.[13]

Several families made sharp-tongued digs about Li, who had been in office since the early 1980s, but the most detailed accusation came from a man who said that Li would not give approval to this man (or others) to build a new house unless Li was given a large bribe. Other people said that other lower-level village officials were not paid under Li's regime and that he was pocketing money from the new highway project in which the state had purchased village land for highway construction.

Right before I returned to the U.S., a friend from Baihu excitedly related an incident between Li and a fellow Baihu woman. Apparently this woman and her husband wanted to contract one of the village factories, but Li decided to contract it out to someone from a nearby village in Hebei Province instead. The couple was angry that, in a sense, Li betrayed the whole village (not to mention township, county and municipality) by contracting village property to outsiders instead of a Baihu resident. She reportedly slapped Li across the face. He, in turn, was allegedly so humiliated that he ran off to the county hospital where he stayed for several days until the Cuitai party secretary coaxed him back.

Whether any or all of this is true is impossible to know, but the strong negative feelings unleashed at the very mention of Li's name in Baihu are certainly undeniable.[14] If one of the functions of village government is to mobilize people to work together on village infrastructure projects and in other ways for the benefit of the village or larger community, then it is easy to see that this is almost impossible in Baihu.

THE GARDEN VILLAGE: CUITAI

In contrast to the slipshod appearance of Baihu, Cuitai has a neat paved road with street lights leading several hundred yards into the heart of the village from the main road, as well as a brand new road which rings the outer perimeter of the residential part of the village. The houses are neatly lined up along these roads and are, with a very few exceptions, all brick and quite new. The tidy village office compound is paved with interlocking red bricks, swept daily, has a garage housing a Volkswagen Santana (produced in Shanghai, it is the equivalent of a Volkswagen Fox), and sports a newly-painted red and white brick perimeter fence. The village government staff come to work daily at 8 a.m. or earlier and spend the day working at the office compound. This way, villagers know when and where to find them, creating an environment in which villagers feel they have a place to go to air grievances or for help in solving a problem.

On the south side of the compound there is a room with a telephone and staff on hand to answer it around the clock. Village residents without phones may make and receive calls here—if they don't mind a room full of people listening in. This same room contains the microphone government staff uses to alert residents that they have a phone call, summon them to the village offices for other reasons, or inform them of what agricultural tasks need to be performed, or that taxes and fees need to be paid. Local peddlers use the microphone to announce they are selling fresh produce, fish, clothing, etc., while the formidable Cuitai Party Secretary Wang and other village officials use it to lecture the villagers (often at 5 am or earlier). The room just to the left of the telephone room was my home for the year.

Cuitai is a mid-sized village with 255 households, 837 official residents, 40 more people with non-agricultural residence, and about 8 immigrant families mostly from the northeast province of Heilongjiang. While there are a large number of surnames present in Cuitai, 63% of household heads are surnamed Wang, while another 23% are surnamed Fan. There is a fairly amiable and close relationship between the Wangs and the Fans, with much intermarriage between these two main surname groups.

There are 850 mu of land designated as grain land, and another 150 which is "garden land" (*yuantian*). In 1995 (as for the preceding several years) Cuitai was the only village in the township to provide villagers with mechanical plowing and planting of wheat and corn, as well as mechanized harvest of wheat.[15] The quality of village garden land is quite good (as it seems to have been historically), and there are over 30 greenhouses operated by villagers growing vegetables and flowers for sale at market -which is at least twice the number of all the other greenhouses in the township. One gardener reported annual net sales of over 30,000 yuan from his three greenhouses.

The mechanization of almost every aspect of grain cultivation frees up villagers to engage in other activities. As in Baihu, virtually every household has at least one member working in a factory or other non-agricultural job although, unlike Baihu, a large proportion of these jobs are right there in Cuitai village itself. There are at least 10 enterprises of various types in Cuitai, of which 5 are classified as "village-run" by both township and village officials. The largest two of these are a construction materials company and pickled vegetable factory employing over 40 workers each. The smallest (only 5 employees) of these "village-run" factories is a wood materials company joint-venture with another company in the northeast of China. There are 3 partnerships, all fairly small-scale: two are vegetable oil mills and the other a metal parts factory, all run by sets of brothers. Enterprises run by individuals include a fodder mill, a jewelry workshop and a fertilizer factory. There are quite a few peddlers in Cuitai who sell their wares daily at stalls in the five local rotating markets that make up the standard marketing area (Skinner 1964). I also met several people who did a very entrepreneurial business of buying a variety of things (usually strawberries or other highly seasonal produce) at low prices in one market, often quite far away, and selling them for a higher price in another market, usually urban Tianjin. Though very tiring, one could make 100–200 yuan or more daily doing this type of thing. There are three small general-store-like shops in Cuitai and two medical clinics run out of people's homes.

Cuitai has a long history of stressing the importance of education, so it is not surprising that both an elementary school (grades 1–6) and the only township middle school (grades 7–9) are located here. When plans were made to build a new middle school in 1996 because the old one was not big enough, it was again Cuitai (or, more appropriately, Cuitai's Party Secretary) which offered the land for a building site.[16] Elementary schools in the township typically serve a few villages. In addition to schooling the village's own children, the Cuitai elementary school serves Baihu and Daren children. As in other villages' schools, children of migrant workers can attend for a fee—usually several times that of locally-born children with residency. The middle school takes children from all township villages.

Even though the Cuitai Party Secretary is himself a Wang, this does not stop even the other village Wangs from grumbling about his heavy-handed manner, though few complain about his actual leadership performance. Party Secretary Wang is a broad-shouldered man in his late 40s with a very stern demeanor and a voice which absolutely roars when he is agitated. On the rare occasions when he does smile, it is quite disarming because it gives him a shy boyish look that does not at all correspond with his generally intimidating presence.

Wang came to be Party Secretary in the mid-1980s and has been very astute about building village enterprises, expanding close connections with other villages, townships, county-level enterprises and officials and improving village services.[17] In doing the preliminary village informational interviews, I always asked which other villages had particularly close ties with the village I was visiting that day. Almost all village officials in the township said that they were closest to Cuitai and its Party Secretary Wang. He was elected to the Chinese People's Consultative Conference and was invited to attend the national meetings in Beijing in 1995, which is quite an honor for the party secretary of a village. The year I was there he was hailed by people all over the township for his bold steps not only to get Cuitai reimbursed for village land being occupied by the new highway, but to get a nice new bridge built over the closed highway so that villagers could easily access their land on the other side. Additionally, he managed to get the highway construction crew to pave a road running the perimeter of the village.

An uncle of Wang's told me that, because of Party Secretary Wang's good management of Cuitai, he had several job offers to work in the Ganglong Township government. Wang's uncle went on to say that Party Secretary Wang had declined these offers because it would mean he would then have a boss—someone above him—while as village party secretary he *is* the top gun. The people who did not like Wang talked about how he must have made a lot of money on the road construction deal. They pointed at the big new house Wang just completed building for his eldest son, and asserted that this was certainly not built on the meager salary of a Party Secretary. While there was no way to confirm the not-so-covert embezzlement allegations, the symbolism of the high brick fence around Wang's son's new home—reminiscent of the fence around the Qing Emperor's abode in Beijing, the Forbidden City and painted in the same red and white as the village's office compound fence—was not lost on villagers who joked about the "Wang Dynasty" in Cuitai.

Both Cuitai's Party Secretary Wang and Baihu's Party Secretary Li were accused of personally profiting from the road construction project (and other village endeavors).[18] They differ, though, in that Wang made sure the village profited from the new prosperity—through new roads, village agricultural services, etc.

THE "POOR" VILLAGE: LANGWO

On my very first day of work in Ganglong Township, I was told that there was a "poor" village (*pinkuncun*) in the township. The labeling of "poor" is part of the Chinese government's effort to target and eradicate poverty-stricken areas in China: a "poor" village gets subsidies, loans, special consideration as far as electric supply, tax breaks and other goodies which are supposed to help the village get on its feet and prosper. Langwo was given this special status for three years, 1993–1995. Because of my interest in differential development, the prospect of visiting a "poor" village was very exciting to me. I am rather ashamed to admit my disappointment in Langwo for not really exhibiting any of the outward signs of poverty that I was expecting.

Between the time I first visited in early 1995 and November 1995 when I conducted household surveys there, Langwo had already moved up in the ranks of the Ganglong villages, and was no longer the poorest, and certainly not a "poor" village by county standards. The type of poverty I was expecting in Langwo certainly did not even exist in 1992. The "poor" status in reality is more a reflection of *village* assets and profits from economic endeavors which could provide the township government with tax revenue, rather than individual or household manifestations such as dilapidated houses, inadequate clothing and malnutrition. In fact, Langwo Party Secretary Bu himself noted that the households in Langwo were wealthy but the village (*dadui*) was not, and that families all over the township were about as well off as each other (a point unfortunately not quite proven true by household surveys). He said that currently at least one person in each Langwo household worked off-farm, and that this had been the case since the late 1980s. In fact, he claimed there was a shortage of labor so that migrants were hired to work in Langwo factories.[19]

Langwo is located on the opposite (northwest) side of the Grand Canal from Cuitai and Baihu, and its western neighbors are Hebei villages, native home to many Langwo brides. It is one of the township's least populated villages, containing just 59 households and 241 residents. There are another 8 people with non-agricultural residence and about 25 laborers from Heilongjiang, Shandong and Henan living and working at village factories. Langwo has 638 mu of arable land, 38 mu of which are apple, peach, pear and apricot orchards. This works out to about 2.65 mu of land per person, the fifth highest per capita land holdings in the township. At the beginning of 1995, all county land had to be (if it was not already) divided into two types of land: subsistence land *(kouliang tian)* and contract land (*chengbao tian*). Subsistence land is distributed according to the number of people in the household and is meant to produce enough grain for a family for a year.

Those families interested in working more land can contract more, for a yearly fee of 30 yuan per mu. Perhaps because of the amount of land available, people in Langwo seem to take their agricultural work more seriously, as one young woman (originally from Baihu, but who married into Langwo) noted when asked if she had contracted land:

> Everyone in Langwo is eager to contract land, but I already have more than enough to do with our *kouliang tian*, so I didn't contract any land. I feel a little strange about [my decision] knowing that everyone else was lining up for contract land. People in Langwo aren't like Baihu people who don't care about the land: Langwo people are really into working the land. If you till it well, you can actually make a lot of money, but as far as I am concerned, it is just too much work.

Although Langwo officially shed its "poor" status at the end of 1995, it still does fall behind many of the other villages with respect to village services and scale of its few enterprises. Party Secretary Bu said that while Langwo does not provide any plowing, seeding or harvesting for its residents, mechanization of agriculture is a high priority, and is something he hopes to have in place by the year 2000. Langwo has only four households with telephones (as opposed to over 60 in Cuitai homes), though there are more in the factories.

Bu said that this village had historically been an exclusively farming village. Up until a few years ago this was still true. Even today there are no private businesses (as there are in Cuitai and Baihu) besides three little stores and three people who have small transport businesses. There are five enterprises, and the village has a stake in all of them: 20%, 33.33% and the rest 50%. Interestingly, the county waterworks bureau (*xian shuili ju*) has a 1/3 stake in one of the two pickled vegetable factories, while the other 1/3 belongs to an individual. None employ more than 20 people, but this is as close as the village gets to large private enterprise. The three smaller factories (all under 10 employees) include a brass bed factory, a knitting enterprise and one that produces school supplies. All village factories are contracted out to a manager. Even though the village has a stake in the business, the contract fee is required whether or not an enterprise makes a profit, so there really isn't much in the way of risk involved for the village; it is more like a rental fee. Animal husbandry entrepreneurs are few: one family owns more than 30 goats and two more households raise more than 10 pigs.

Socially, Langwo seems, at least on the surface, to be a fairly harmonious village. The largest surname, Liu, only accounts for 25% of the households. The year I arrived, Langwo had just created a *yang ger* troupe (they do a traditional dance while beating drums and clanking cymbals) to perform at festivals and the whole village is involved. As mentioned in the Introduction,

Party Secretary Bu claims that there are no "hooligans" in Langwo, and that it is extremely safe. The *pailou* (a traditional entrance gate) and large "screen" recently built at the entrance to Langwo are lucky symbols villagers are hoping will bring prosperity to the village.

I never heard anything negative about Party Secretary Bu, probably because the village does not have much money which village officials could be accused of misusing. In fact, Bu's mother told me that if it were not for the fact that Bu's wife had a good job, his family would not be able to survive on the 200 yuan Party Secretary wages. Furthermore, she claimed his wages often went unpaid because there was no money in the village accounts.

NIUDIAN: THE VILLAGE WITH ROYAL ORIGINS?

Niudian is a mid-sized village of 635 people, 98% of household heads surnamed Hao.[20] There is a great history behind this village, even if some of it is borderline fiction. The village chief (*cun zhuren*) told a colorful tale of how originally Daren, the neighboring village to the south on the other side of the river, used to be located where Niudian is. The equivalent of the Qing Dynasty (Qianlong) Minister of Defence (*bingbu shangshu*), Hao Songnian, had an audience with Emperor Qianlong. After kowtowing to him, Hao stood up and brushed himself off. The Emperor offered Hao the Emperor's chair— the throne—and Hao sat down. The Niudian village chief chuckled at his ancestor's big mistake: one should never be so bold or arrogant as to sit in the emperor's chair, even if it is offered. The Emperor got angry, fired him, and exiled him to the original site of Daren (which the Qianlong might have seen on a trip down the Grand Canal). In any case, a flag indicating the former residence of a high Qing Dynasty official flew in Niudian right up until the Cultural Revolution.

I searched for Hao Songnian and his other name, Hao Mengtao, in the book of Qing officials but did not find either of them.[21] In a subsequent visit to Niudian, I met another man who said he had seen the four Hao family trees (one for each son) before they were burned in the Cultural Revolution, and Hao Songnian was not as high up as the village chief had said. While the village chief had said the founding Hao was a *bingbu shangshu*, the man who had seen the geneology said that the founding Hao was a lesser official in the Qing defence (*bingbu silang*). There was no Hao Songnian in the book of Qing officials under this title either. At least this much seems to be true: Hao Songnian won a battle and the emperor gave him the land where Niudian now sits. This basic story, as well as the fact that the Qing flag flew over Niudian until before the Cultural Revolution, was corroborated by many non-Niudian people.

The second informant said that he had memorized the introduction to the Hao family tree which told Hao Songnian's story. The founding Hao reportedly did not have to farm or do any other work because he could collect tributes from grain boats on their way to Beijing from the south along the Grand Canal. Hao Songnian was originally from Zhejiang's Guiji County, and apparently cut his ties with that place to start a new line with him at the top in the North.

Whatever his origins, Hao had four sons who took over each of the four corners of the village. To this day, the graves of the descendants of each son are still at the same four corners. Although the Haos are all related, they do talk about being from different "doors" (*men*), which is a reference to the lineages as traced back to each of the four sons. Most of the oldest son's descendants are in Beijing or elsewhere, though the Party Secretary and woman in charge of "women work" are his descendants. The third son's descendants are mostly in Tianjin. Most of the people still in the village today are descendants of the fourth son.

Niudian is also just across the Grand Canal from Cuitai. During the dry season when the Grand Canal is, at best, a trickle, the river can be crossed on stepping-stones from the northwest corner of Cuitai. Otherwise, it takes about a half an hour by bike to get there from Cuitai over the Shimiao bridge. People in Niudian have a little over 3 mu of arable land per person, the second highest in the township. The farthest plots are 8 li away (more than 2 miles). The village provides mechanized plowing of the big plots of land (a total of 2000 mu). People use draft animals on smaller plots and there are about 70 draft animals in the village (there were none in either Cuitai or Baihu in 1995).

Generally speaking, the land in Niudian is quite good and it has the best garden land on their side of the Grand Canal. Niudian has a few fishponds and just planted about 350 mu of date trees on former *kouliang* land. Although the village did not charge any money for planting the date trees on people's *kouliang* land, people who harm or kill the trees will be fined. A lot of people complained about the trees because they have prickers which jab them while working the land: grain is still planted on the land around the trees.

There is only one village-run enterprise, a clothing factory which, in addition to cutting and sewing clothes, recently started designing them too. It seems to be doing pretty well because the profits have been apportioned 600,000 yuan to build a large new food seasoning factory (most likely processing hot pepper, garlic and possibly making pickled vegetables as well).[22] The buildings for this new factory are already completed, and they are planning to start operations soon. This new factory will need cucumbers, *jiecai* (a large root commonly used for pickles), garlic and other produce. The village leadership decided that instead of searching elsewhere for the produce the factory would need, they would contract out Niudian's own garden land to villagers and get them to grow the needed vegetables. That way people would know they had a sure market for their crops and the village factory would be saved the time and resources of trying to buy enough at reasonable prices from other villages. Apparently there were more people who wanted to contract the land than the number of plots, so they drew straws. Another pickled vegetable factory in the village opened in 1994: it is a joint-household operation among five related households. There are more than 10 migrant workers (from Henan) who live at the factory manager's house and work in this factory. There are three privately-run construction teams in Niudian, two little stores, three households that do business (selling aluminium pots and utensils at the market) and five carpenters. In addition, two households raise more than 40 sheep/goats, two raise more than 10 pigs, and four or five households raise about 1000 chickens.[23] Another five-household joint-household enterprise used to sell popsicles, but it reportedly went out of business because the five parties involved did not see eye to eye on how to run the business.

When I asked about school-age kids who did not go to school, Accountant Hao said that there were a handful, but that these were ones who were "too stupid" (*tui ben*[24]) to go to school. The school here has only kids in the first grade—the rest go to Lujiatun and Panzhuangzi for second and third grades, and to Lujiatun for fifth and sixth grades. I was told that Niudian wives were mostly from the surrounding villages because this village is fairly well off. In previous years, though, there were some brides from the northeast. Because the northeast was reportedly poorer than Niudian even when Niudian was not doing well, women from the northeast were willing to marry in to Niudian while women from surrounding villages were not.[25]

Niudian is very neatly laid out. In fact I would say that it was the neatest in appearance of all the Ganglong villages. All the houses seem to be lined up with exact precision along the one paved road running north and south right through the village, as well as along the many non-paved roads. Plans for the future include a village office building and three more electric pumps for irrigating the garden land to ensure a good vegetable crop for the new factory. The current Party Secretary, not surprisingly a Hao, has been in office since before the breakup of the commune system and is generally held to be a congenial man. Interestingly, he officiates most village marriages and funerals, a role that most pre-Communist village heads performed. To my knowledge, no other Party Secretary in Ganglong conducted these ceremonies.

THE LARGE AND ONCE DYNAMIC VILLAGE: WANJUN

Wanjun is on the northwest of the Grand Canal. The Wanjun village office compound rivals the Baihu one as the most humble of all in the township. It is set back a bit from the northeast edge of the paved ring road surrounding the whole residential part of the village. The compound gate is a rickety wooden one, and if you walked straight ahead, you might miss the three-room village office building to the left and run straight into the only village enterprise to speak of, a pickled vegetable factory.

The office building is a dark, dank place with dirt floors, but is probably decades newer than it looks. The middle room is twice as large as the rooms to either side and is pretty much empty except for a dirt-covered, baby blue wooden bed frame, a huge weigh scale, a bench, and some other nondescript clutter. The one-room main office, which is primarily used by the accountant and person in charge of electric and water bill collection, etc., is the darkest and dankest room in the building. The walls are (literally) mud brown, and the brightest, newest thing in the office is the white family planning chart on the west wall which was supposed to be used to document who is using what form of birth control and who is pregnant (it was blank). A huge wooden desk sits next to the only window (southern exposure, naturally) and a nicely-aged bamboo bench. A wonderful old safe that looks like it could have contained buried treasure now has a less flashy job; it functions as a stool. Apparently it was taken from a landlord during Land Reform days. As in all village offices, there is a PA system which, in the many times I have been in the office, I have only seen used twice: once to advertise a roving household appliance repairman was in the village, and the other time to announce a peddler's sale of fresh spinach—five jin for one yuan (or about five pounds for 12 cents). A coal stove for boiling water and providing heat stands in one corner, opposite a big padlocked cupboard which no doubt contains years of yellowing records and a stash of imported cigarettes for special guests.

The village itself has a slipshod appearance as well, and it is difficult to imagine that, pre-1949, Wanjun was the vibrant seat of a smaller township, complete with its own *yang ger* song and dance troupe and a martial arts team. In the first two decades after Communist takeover, Wanjun continued to be a dynamic village, winning county model status for agricultural and industrial production. It was in the wake of the Cultural Revolution that Wanjun started declining.

Wanjun is a larger village of 946 people and 272 households, and is located almost directly north of the township seat on the north side of the Grand Canal, though its fields extend west to the Hebei border. Eighty percent of all people have either the surname Tang or Tong. By per capita income standards in 1995, it was the third poorest village in the township, ranking even behind "poor" Langwo. As in Langwo, several people have said that the Wanjun village as a collective (*dadui*) is poor, but the households are rich. From many of the households I have seen, it looks like some have "gotten rich first": as in Baihu, there seems to be a large difference between the richest and poorest households.

Most of Wanjun land is in a low-lying depression where there is much salt build-up. But as far as the proportion of people working in agriculture, this village by far has one of the highest in the township—about 25%, of which women make up about 60%. Besides a village-run electric pump used for irrigation and a wheat threshing machine, the village has no agricultural services. Apparently they tried mechanizing wheat sowing last year, but only on some of the village land; the rest of the plots were all too small to do it on a large-scale. Although there used to be wasteland—land too poor on which to grow anything—the village has since contracted it out (it is far away but at least one villager contracted 37 mu of it).

There are also a few families planning to set up greenhouses. Additionally, last year, the village required each household to plant three date trees per household member at a cost of one yuan per tree. The village bought the trees and distributed them to people. They will bear fruit in two to three years. The village construction team takes care of a twenty-plus mu orchard with apple, pear and peach trees. The profits are split this way: 30% to the village, 30% to the village school, and 40% to the construction team itself.

In response to a question about why it was that Wanjun people did not seem to grow much, or in some cases any, wheat when this was their primary food source, the person in charge of daily affairs had this explanation: everyone used to plant wheat on a big stretch of land to the west of the village, but last year the river water they use for irrigation was red from pollution. After using it to irrigate, all the wheat died. Corn, sorghum and other crops do not have to be watered so there is not this same risk from polluted water for these crops.

When I asked about village assets and income, the young Wanjun accountant became a bit despondent and said that Wanjun was poor and had no industry. When I asked what he thought the problem was, he said that there were not the "rencai" (talented people) necessary for starting and managing successful industries. I was later told that there are plenty of talented people but they have all left the village and are doing business outside of Wanjun. Looking at the types of industries the village does have, it seems clear that they do not have a very good idea of what will sell. Villages throughout Jinghai County, including Ganglong, have set up pickled vegetable processing plants and steel polishing factories which have certainly saturated the market, but these are the industries that Wanjun has decided upon.

As far as industry goes, there are only three village-run enterprises: the construction team, the steel polishing factory, and pickled vegetable factory (which was actually contracted out to an individual in 1994). These three enterprises employ only a total of forty full-time workers. A clothing factory and a glass factory were set up in the mid-80s but have since shut down. The reason given was lack of raw material availability. The construction team hires part-time laborers when needed—about 100. Private industry provides about

60 jobs. Interestingly, a joint-household-run metal factory run by 8 house-holds employs 30 people. Other private enterprises include the ping-pong table factory run by the current Party Secretary (partially accounting for his disinterest in village affairs), another metal factory, and a condiments processing plant. In addition, there are eight or so other small private business-es—bicycle repair, oil milling, four small shops, etc., and also quite a few households that raise chickens, pigs and goats on a small scale.

The current party secretary has served only one year. I was told that there have been several changes in leadership in the past several years—perhaps one reason for the poor village performance. The current party secretary seems unconcerned with village affairs and is not around the office much; his own enterprise undoubtedly takes up most of his time.

A VILLAGE OF LARGE FACTORIES: YONGHE

Yonghe is located in the northeast corner of the township and, population wise, is the second largest village in Ganglong with 1119 people and 339 households. When I last visited Yonghe at the end of 1995, the rutted dirt roads through the village were about to be paved. This will do much to tidy up the appearance of the village. Considering the officially-documented wealth of the village, however, it is puzzling that its roads were not paved long ago. Still, the surprising number of older houses conveys an appearance belying the figures and popular opinion which rate Yonghe as one of the more successful villages in Ganglong.

While Yonghe does not have the largest factories in the township (Dingxiang, mentioned in the opening anecdotes of the Introduction, has that honor), what does distinguish Yonghe is that almost all Yonghe adults who work in factories actually work in Yonghe factories. Village officials are proud of both the fact that the village pays high enough wages to satisfy village residents and that the hiring of migrant workers is not necessary in this village (though there are 7 or 8 migrants who live here and work in neighboring Xiaobaotun).

The largest factory is a village-run automobile bearing factory which employees 130 people and, according to village and township officials, is doing quite well. Doing less well is the bottle factory employing 110 people. To try to tighten up management and make the firm more efficient, village officials planned to contract it out to an individual in 1995 at a price of 100,000 yuan per year. They started producing beer bottles, but the quality was not up to par, so they lost the contract. Now they are producing little horseradish bottles, and probably will not be able to pay the contract fees to the village; they cannot even pay their employees.

Another car parts factory employs 70 people and is also reported to be doing well. In addition to these, there are 7 more small village-run enterprises located within the larger factories, including a couple of smaller car parts factories and (the ubiquitous) pickled vegetable factory. People I met all across the township are particularly admiring of the fact that, for the past three years, the Yonghe (and Xiaobaotun) leadership took profits from village industries and distributed these in 100–yuan bonuses to all village households at New Year's. When people say a village is doing well, this is one criterion they give; that when a village-run enterprise does well, it actually does benefit the villagers.

Yonghe has four small private enterprises, the most lucrative making a rare part for railroad cars and earning, by the entrepreneur's own admission, 200,000 yuan in net profits per year. (Surely this figure is conservative). Besides the three shops in the village, the other private enterprises include two clothing workshops, a tool factory, and a restaurant. Altogether these private enterprises have about 60 employees. As in the other villages, small peddling businesses, including buying and selling leather jackets and fruit, exist in Yonghe. There are also five households raising 200–300 chickens each.

Yonghe has 1618 mu of arable land, which works out to about one and a half mu per person. The land here is not suitable for growing vegetables like cucumbers, which can be grown in the western part of the township. The water here is also supposedly not good for the crops. However, the drinking water here is better tasting than the salty water in Cuitai: Yonghe has a shallow well especially for drinking water that serves the village. This year (as it has every year since the collapse of the commune) the village did a unified plowing for the wheat crop on all land that could be accessed with the large machinery. On the same land, a mechanized sower planted the fall 1995 winter wheat crop for the first time. As in Cuitai, a small fee is collected per mu for these services and for the hybrid wheat seed. About 80 mu of land has been occupied by the new highway, but as of the end of 1995, Yonghe had not been paid for it.

The most distinctive feature of this village was its young, rather wild, Party Secretary. In 1993 at the age of twenty-nine, Party Secretary Tan was the youngest in all of Jinghai County. He himself admits that few people like him because he has a rough personality and manner. He said he took on the party secretary job because no one else would do it but, according to him, his appointment was still controversial—both in his village and at the township level where such decisions are made. Another reason he gives for not being liked is that there are fewer than 20 people with his surname in the village. Thus, he claims that, unlike Cutai's Party Secretary Wang, he does not enjoy the support and protection that a lineage majority typically provides.

Tan has long hair past his shoulders—almost unheard of for a Ganglong villager and certainly unheard of for a village (or any other level) party secretary. A few years ago he began going up to Heilongjiang (in the northeast, bordering Russia) to do business: he buys a truckload of ramen noodles (*fangbianmian*) or other goods that are in short supply in Russia, and hires fellow former soldiers to help sell it. Taking advantage of the empty trucks on the way back, he often buys goods from the Russians to sell back home in the Tianjin area. He does not speak Russian, nor do the Russians he deals with speak Chinese, so they hire a translator at 500 yuan per meal and make deals over dinner. In doing business with the Russians, he said that they all fight and that if you are going to get their respect, you have to prove you are worthy of it. He showed us scars on his arm from when he either burnt himself or cut himself right in front of them. Though that was several months ago, his scars are all still quite big. At least some of the money he makes from trade with the Russians this goes to the village. He said he feels like the burden of the whole village is upon his shoulders: if he does well (i.e. brings money in) people complain about his methods, and if he does poorly, they complain all the louder about his risk-taking and mismanagement.

I got another side of the story from a former Yonghe official whom I happened to meet one day on a bus to the county seat. He was a factory manager from 1985–1987 in one of the three bearings factories then in operation. This former official was disgusted with Party Secretary Tan, saying that all Tan does is eat, drink and womanize, with the village footing the bill. Indeed Tan told me himself that he has already consumed over one metric ton of *baijiu* (strong Chinese liquor) in his four years as Party Secretary— though his point was to demonstrate the "sacrifices" he has had to make in the position. He also gets chauffeured around in a sleek black Audi.

The same obviously disgruntled former official said that the Yonghe collective factories have not had one new customer since they opened in the mid-1960s; so they really have not made any new advances or connections, but instead are relying on the old structure and connections for current success. He also said that these factories are often unable to give workers their salaries. I was unable to corroborate this allegation, except at the now contracted-out bottle factory.

CONCLUSION

Because the villages exist in a very similar geographic, political, economic and cultural environment, the close proximity of the Ganglong villages would seem to indicate that differences between the villages should be minimal. Superficially, this is true: within the township the dialect is the same, fashions and lifestyles are similar, houses built around the same year look very much the same across villages, and almost all the villages have pickled vegetable factories and other similar social and economic activities.

A closer look, however, finds that there are also sizable and, in many cases, quantifiable differences over many demographic, geographic and social dimensions, as well as economic activities and effectiveness of local leaders. Ethnographic evidence corroborated and clarified the quality of these differences. These differences suggest that more micro-level processes and factors are at work causing this socioeconomic differentiation.

This chapter has touched on a few of the important factors that will resurface again in later chapters: the initial village endowments of population, land holdings, social (lineage) structure, economic activities, village leadership, and geographic characteristics such as location in respect to the Grand Canal. The next chapter will focus on formulating a working concept for socioeconomic status or well-being. Only then can we go on to explore the reasons behind the various differences introduced in this chapter.

NOTES

[1] In fact, the correlation coefficient for village distributed income (a form of net income) and village GVIO is .8438, p=.000.

[2] The proportion of a given surname in a village is based on the surname of the head-of-household, usually male. Often, if a man has died or has non-agricultural residence (e.g. works at the township government offices), his wife would be considered head-of-household. Therefore, a simple count of household-head names may not reflect the actual number of people of a certain surname.

[3] Freedman (1958); Huang (1985:65), citing Hsiao (1960:326–327).[4] For example, a woman surnamed Xia from Xiayuan who marries a man surnamed Chen from Xiayuan and therefore continues to live in her natal village, would not be counted as part of the majority Xia lineage when it came to surnames because her husband would be the head-of-household. This is true even though, lineage-wise, she is just as much a Xia as her brother who is considered a full-fledged Xia.

[5] See Rozelle et al (1997) for a categorization of the types of collective enterprise regimes—who is responsible for what and to what degree.

[6] While I was in Ganglong, there was a Tianjin-wide effort to convert all township- and village-run collective enterprises into "joint-share" systems (*gufenzhi*) in order to make factory ownership rights (and therefore rights to profits and responsibility for losses) more explicit with the aim of minimizing embezzlement and other abuses. Very few village leaders, however, were enthusiastically following orders to do this.

[7] Jang (1998:124–125) and Yang (1994:160–170) also found in the villages they studied that villagers felt the factories in their villages were still, in part, theirs. This is a bit more surprising in the village Yang researched because the factory there was actually a private shareholding firm rather than one originally set up as a brigade or team factory during the commune years.

[8] See Rozelle and Boisvert (1994) for an analysis which shows that rural industrialization is the primary way local leaders can and do milk the system. Whiting (2001) gives a more detailed description of the institutional factors shaping local leaders' behavior in their management of rural industry.

[9] I will continue to use the present tense to discuss the villages, although the numbers of people and other details certainly will have changed since I did my fieldwork in 1995.

[10] People without village residence do not get land allocated to them, but may sometimes get grain or other food subsidies or grants from their employer. Residency is linked to mother's residence status: if the mother has village residency, so will her children, but if she has non-agricultural residence, her children will be allocated jobs in government or industry when they come of age. This is assuming the system for job allocation in the countryside does not change in the future.

[11] It is very unfortunate that I was unable to formally interview any of these immigrants, though I did get to know many on a casual basis, and will comment on them when appropriate throughout the book.

[12] I was unable to look at the household-by-household residence information for all twenty-three villages. Therefore, the proportions I have for the remaining seventeen (non-survey) villages come from the party secretaries, accountants, and other village official estimates.

[13] I knew of the problems with the brick factory from Li himself, who explained that it was a cooperative venture between his village and one in another township. He said the problems were due to conflicts between managers from the two villages, in addition to market saturation.

[14] I asked a few of these disgruntled Baihu villagers why they had not complained to the authorities and they replied they had indeed talked to township officials about it, but that nothing had been done. Their explanation is that Li "kissed up" to (*pai mapi*) the township officials.

[15] A few other Ganglong villages had plans to mechanize in the coming years.

[16] The Party Secretary undoubtedly scored points with township officials for volunteering his village land for the new building. Cuitai residents were not happy about the decision, though a village election by hand was held after fielding comments and criticisms. The main objections were that a cemetery would have to be moved (to which many cultural taboos are attached) and that good growing land would be sacrificed.

[17] Perhaps Wang learned his leadership skills from his father, who was the first Party Secretary in Cuitai and served from the early 1950s until he was ousted in the Cultural Revolution.

[18] Incidentally, Baihu's Li was also targeted as corrupt by his fellow villagers for building a five-room house for just him and his wife at a time when most other families could only afford a three-room house.

[19] Probably, the reason for "needing" migrant labor is that the Langwo factories do not pay enough to entice enough of Langwo's own residents to work there.

[20] Even those who are not surnamed Hao are very often related. Of the families I met NOT surnamed Hao, more than half were families in which a non-Hao man had married a Hao woman and moved into Niudian (instead of the usual patrilocal practice whereby brides move to the husband's village). Since the surname of the household is based upon the husband's surname, officially these are not Hao families.

[21] Since these are aliases, readers will not find them either!

[22] Apparently this money was not enough because, according to one of the households in the village I interviewed, Niudian village officials went around to

villagers asking for loans to get it started . The informant also said that not many people were willing to loan money to them.

[23] By the end of 1995, however, all these large chicken farms went out of business because the price of grain fodder went up so much that it was no longer a profitable business.

[24] "*Tui*" is the local dialect pronunciation of Mandarin "*tai*" (meaning "too").

[25] See Lavely (1991) for more about the idea of a "marriage market."

CHAPTER 4.

OUTLINING WELL-BEING IN GANGLONG, 1994–1995

COMMUNE-ERA POLICIES TIED THE SOCIOECONOMIC STATUS OF VILLAGES TO the well-being of families in those villages. A large part of this study is directed at finding out whether, over a decade after the commune system was dismantled, the village still plays an important role in individual and household well-being. This chapter documents how households in the six villages do indeed embody characteristics specific to each village, and that the larger village community is still a determinant of villager well-being. Here I will identify the local standards of well-being and show where households in the six survey villages stand in relation to these standards. To this end I use ethnographic materials to give a sense of what prosperity means for the 554 Ganglong residents whom the survey covered, as well as present quantitative data from household surveys conducted in these six villages for comparison.

Measuring how well villages are doing—their relative socioeconomic performance—is not quite as easy as it may sound. What does "socioeconomic performance" or "well-being" mean and whose criteria are to be used? Perhaps the most common single measure of socioeconomic status used both globally and in China is per capita income. The most commonly used method in China to calculate per capita village income does not tell us much about actual household or individual living standards for those living in the villages. Before laying out the different aspects of well-being which I found relevant in Ganglong, let me first elaborate some of the problems with the per capita income figures so often used in discussions and analyses of development in China.

Theoretically, village per capita income figures are calculated from net village income—the income from all crop agriculture, animal husbandry, fisheries and forestry, industrial enterprises, and commerce—ostensibly from both collective and private activities in each village. Expenses from these productive endeavors are subtracted along with village taxes, fees to the township, and monies put into village public welfare. The result is net village income: per capita income simply divides net village income by the number of people officially registered in the village.[1]

There are two tangible problems with village per capita income as a useful measure of household and individual living standards: 1) the inability to collect all the component information, and 2) the fact that definition of village (and consequently per capita) income currently does not take into account important extra-village factors. Private agricultural endeavors such as animal husbandry, fishing and non-staple food crop farming change from year to year and household to household and cannot be accurately calculated by a village accountant who has neither access to—nor authority to access—individual income information. Similarly, income from private commerce is almost impossible to acquire but can be very sizable in some villages. Therefore, per capita village income in the Ganglong villages is primarily an indication of the amount of collective (village-run) rural industry in each village. This is the most important type of income for village economy and administrative purposes; it is taxed by township authorities and therefore provides a major portion of the township revenue base.

The second reason why village per capita income figures are inadequate is due to their faulty calculation: by subtracting expenditures and taxes from all village enterprise and agricultural income, the income generated by village residents employed at enterprises in *other* villages and townships is left out of the equation. Therefore, actual household income in villages labeled as "poor" by official statistics (because the villages lack strong collective enterprises) is generally much higher. On the other hand, actual household income in supposedly wealthier villages may be lower than reported because of a high proportion of non-village laborers, taxes and other siphoning off by village or higher government levels. Villagers and local officials alike recognize this and distinguish between rich villages (having village industries) *without* rich households and poor villages (without village industry) where households are rich.[2]

However, the main reason to find a measure for living standards beyond per capita income is that village per capita income tells us nothing about how life actually is for typical *people* in the village, which is (or should be) the essence of research on development. The Chinese government policy of awarding worthy villages the title "xiaokangcun" (loosely translated as "prosperous villages") is an acknowledgment of the fact that there is more to a given village's state of development than per capita income.[3,4] This idea of *xiaokangcun* follows global trends which include infant mortality, average life expectancies, and the availability of social services such as health care and education in calculating well-being or socioeconomic status.[5]

Household surveys are the most direct way to measure the well-being of individuals because they collect information about actual family income, expenditures, assets and liabilities. While this type of survey has its own drawbacks, such as under- or non-reporting of income and assets, it surely reflects a household's socioeconomic status more accurately than the per capita net village income figures. McKinley (1996) uses a Chinese State Statistical Bureau (CSSB) survey which sampled over 10,000 households throughout China in 1988.[6] He employs the concept of "wealth" to capture the present and future well-being in perhaps the most thorough study to date of relative household socioeconomic status all across China.

Aggregated, household surveys conducted in two or more villages can, in fact, tell us much about the qualities of these villages—whether or not some villages seem to contain higher concentrations of individual income, consumer goods, newer houses, and all the other amenities of prosperity. In trying to assess the village's role in impacting household socioeconomic status, however, the type of data McKinley and others use is very limited. It contains too few households in any one village to make any conclusions (or even wild guesses) about the relative ability of villages to offer social and economic benefits that augment individual wealth. Obviously, conducting enough household surveys in each of several villages to make any definitive statements about the relationship between village and household prosperity on the national scale would be time-consuming and costly. But it can be done on a more local level and this is what I have done for six of the Ganglong villages.

The most tangible measures of individual prosperity in Ganglong revolve around the basic needs of physical well-being: food, shelter, clothing and other necessities. Quality is very important in those physical necessities as well as in other factors like occupation, work conditions and luxury items that contribute to well-being. Other components which are not so immediate but still impact the quality of life are village-level factors such as village location and infrastructure, as well as information which might indicate the leadership's commitment to village residents, etc. The rest of the chapter will outline what Ganglong people believe constitutes individual- and village-level socioeconomic status (well-being): income and expenditures, housing, consumer goods, land assets, and level and quality of industrialization. Unless otherwise specified, all the information provided in tables will be from the 150 household surveys.

DIMENSIONS OF WELL-BEING: HOUSEHOLD-LEVEL FACTORS

MONEY BROUGHT IN AND MONEY SPENT: INCOME AND EXPENDITURES

One of the main points of the household survey (the World Bank's Living Standard Measurement Survey) that I adapted for use in Ganglong is to detail all conceivable household expenditures during one year. Thus this survey gives a better sense of household income than asking households to report income from all sources. Indeed, in each of the six villages, average family expenditures exceeded reported income by 339 yuan (in Wanjun) to over 5,268 yuan (in Cuitai). Although forty families reported lending out money (which might account for this discrepancy), others may have been dipping into savings to buy house building materials, wedding gifts, necessities, etc. But for many families, this gap between income and expenditures indicates an under-reporting of income, particularly in Baihu where two obviously wealthy, private businessmen refused (though graciously) to tell me either their gross or net income.

Table 4.1 gives figures for annual household incomes and expenditures; the official village per capita income figures are shown for comparison. All the tables in this chapter will be arranged in the following way way for reasons which will quickly become apparent: the three southeast villages (Cuitai, Baihu, Yonghe) are on top of the list, while the three northwest villages (Langwo, Niudian, Wanjun) are on the bottom.

A glance at the figures for household income and expenditures shows huge differences.[7] A reasonable conclusion might be that the more income brought in, the more it is under-reported: Cuitai and Baihu have the highest discrepancies between income and expenditures. Between 8 (Cuitai) and 14 (Yonghe) families in each village (a total of 69 households) reported more income than expenditures, an indication that they were either saving their money, borrowing money or over-reporting income (which, except for one case, I think is unlikely). In fact, almost a third (22) of these same families were borrowers. Throughout the year, several people told me (not in the interview setting) that most families have between 5,000 and 10,000 yuan in the bank - or hidden somewhere, as the case may be. A few more of the surveyed households volunteered that they were barely paying the bills and often had to borrow money to make ends meet.[8]

Compared to per capita household income or expenditures, the official accountant record figures for per capita village income are one-third to one-fifth of the results from the household surveys. Moreover, the ranking of the villages is not the same when using household survey or village-level income information. Taking the per capita expenditures as the most accurate reflection of actual per capita income, we find Baihu on top, whereas it is in third place among the survey villages in the official figures. Wealth here is total household expenditures (rather than financial assets) plus the net value of

Table 4.1. Mean household and per capita income, expenditures and wealth from household surveys compared to average village per capita income as calculated and reported by village accountants.*

	Household expenditures from survey in yuan	Household income from survey in yuan	Per capita expenditures from survey in yuan	Per capita income from survey in yuan	Household wealth from survey in yuan	Per capita household wealth from survey in yuan	Official village per capita income in yuan
Baihu	16,166 (13,475)	11,930 (8,440)	4,857 (3,867)	3,630 (2,791)	37,762 (36,303)	12,054 (9,582)	915
Cuitai	17,455 (11,261)	13,887 (9,494)	4,574 (2,712)	3,638 (1,756)	46,481 (33,474)	13,088 (7,930)	1,619
Yonghe	14,025 (8,971)	13,185** (6,843)	3,831 (2,382)	3,842** (2,612)	45,690** (36,490)	12,201** (8,634)	1,119
Langwo	12,572 (6,949)	10,750 (6,134)	3,830 (2,436)	3,145 (1,931)	39,180 (25,931)	12,030 (7,994)	910
Niudian	12,096 (7,939)	12,531 (7,701)	3,320 (1,804)	3,447 (1,763)	32,498 (20,882)	8,888 (5,125)	900
Wanjun	10,329 (7,654)	12,338 (11,222)	2,637 (2,080)	2,980 (2,241)	32,780 (29,794)	7,773 (5,312)	800

*Standard deviations for each village and variable are in parentheses under the bolded means.

**See footnote 7, this chapter, for further explanation of these figures.

housing and large productive assets, including livestock, land and any private business assets.[9] In wealth terms, Cuitai comes out ahead of the other villages; Niudian is still at the bottom of the list with Wanjun.

The three southeast villages (Cuitai, Yonghe, Baihu) lead in every aspect as the northwest villages (Langwo, Niudian, Wanjun) trail in every aspect, with two exceptions: in both household income and household wealth, Baihu trails two northwest villages. One explanation for Baihu's poor showing with regard to household income is that it was under-reported in Baihu. The other explanation is that there is a fairly large income stratification in Baihu. The more expensive houses found in Langwo account for that village's higher rating with respect to wealth, and this will be discussed in a later section on housing. The ranking of the northwest villages is consistent over all variables in Table 4.1: Langwo is first, Niudian next, and Wanjun is at the bottom of the list. The southeast villages, however, take turns for first, second and third place. For instance, Cuitai comes in first for household expenditures, household and per capita income, but Baihu is first for per capita expenditures, while Yonghe ranks first for per capita income.

Thus we find that household income and expenditure figures offer evidence of a substantial difference between the more modest incomes of northwest households and the often outright extravagant ones found in the southeast villages. Note, too, that the standard deviations, which indicate basic stratification, are generally lower in the northwest villages. This northwest-southeast split will be a recurring theme in this chapter, and will be explored in more detail in Chapters Five and Six.

"THE PEOPLE SEE FOOD AS HEAVEN": EDIBLE CONSUMPTION

It does not take long to figure out that food—especially grain—in addition to being the basis for physical existence and well-being, is an extremely important status symbol and an indispensable element of ritual in China, and the Ganglong area is no exception. As many students of China have noted, the most common way of asking how someone is doing in the countryside has been "Have you eaten?" Ganglong residents, like those in many other places, still use this greeting. And eating refers, not simply to food, but specifically to staple foods—grain. A meal without grain is not a meal. Even today if you were to ask someone in Ganglong what is for dinner, the answer inevitably is the main grain-based food (e.g. rice, pan-bread, buns, noodles) rather than any of the accompanying vegetable and meat dishes. When villagers asked me what Americans eat, an answer of vegetables, meat, fruit was not enough. They wanted to know what grain foods Americans eat.

For rural Chinese even today the importance of grain as the basis of their diet cannot be overstated. Until just a few years ago, neighbors would talk enviously, suspiciously, or even maliciously about a family able to afford white flour—a high status food—more than a few times a year. Noodles at wedding engagements and one-month old baby celebrations; boiled or steamed meat and vegetable-filled dumplings (*jiaozi*) prepared by the bride's family to accompany a bride to her new patrilocal home so she will not be homesick; *jiaozi* for Spring Festival; and steamed white-flour buns (*mantou*) at funerals; these are just a few of the examples of the ritualistic uses of grain-based food.

Most Ganglong villagers now eat staple foods prepared with white flour - noodles, *jiaozi, baozi, mantou,* as well as leavened and unleavened white bread. Corn porridge (*nianzhou*) and other corn-meal foods—steamed corn meal buns (*wotou*), thick corn meal griddle cakes (*tie bingzi*), steamed corn meal buns filled with vegetables (*cai tuanzi*)—are also very common. Non-grain foods consist of vegetables, meat, fish, eggs and oil for cooking. The most commonly eaten vegetable in the Ganglong area, as in most other areas of China, is Chinese cabbage (*dabaicai*) of one type or another. With the use of fertilizers and irrigation, 2000 jin (about 2000 lbs) of cabbage can typically be grown on one-tenth of a mu. This cabbage will be the main vegetable for most of the winter. Household pigs will dine on the cold-damaged outer leaves.

After the fall harvest of cabbage (and carrots, potatoes, turnips, radishes, etc.), families in the Ganglong area dig huge pits in the ground to keep these vegetables fresh all winter. These pits are covered with huge, woven mats made of straw. Prior to the arrival of greenhouses in the early 1980s, these cold cellar vegetables were often the only "fresh" vegetables people had to eat between December and April. Now all families (at least all 150 that I surveyed) bought fresh vegetables at the local markets at least some time during the year, if not all year round.

In addition to cold cellar vegetables, most families eat pickled turnips, garlic and cucumbers, among a wide variety of other pickled vegetables. While pickling used to be done at home using vegetables families grew themselves, with the advent of the reform period and the subsequent re-emergence of Jinghai as a hotbed of pickled vegetable factories, there are many other alternatives to pickling one's own (or bought) vegetables.[10] These pickles are puckeringly salty, and are used to give a little flavor to whatever grain-based food is being served; it would be hard for a Ganglong area person of any age to imagine eating their staple food without these salty pickles. Hot peppers are similarly grown by Ganglong families and used for flavoring.

Pork is the main meat consumed in Ganglong, although I found that people buy and eat quite a bit of ready-to-go roasted chicken. Pound for pound, however, fish is probably the most widely consumed protein product, followed closely by eggs. The Grand Canal, other nearby waterways, ponds especially for fish-raising, and the Bohai Sea provide plenty of fresh fish. Only a few families eat mutton, rabbit, dog (road-kill only) and donkey, and these are in small quantities.

Table 4.2 compares food consumption in the six villages. With the exception of Wanjun, the overall mean value of food consumed per person in the six villages is almost the same. Wanjun is interesting in that the residents there consume a very high proportion of their diet in grain (32%), and virtually all of it self-provided. Since Wanjun also has, on average, lower total expenditures, the fact that their food expenses are proportionally much lower than the other villages is not surprising. Cuitai has a ratio of food to total cash expenditures of only 29%, but this is still a large proportion of total expenditures and shows the importance of food in the Ganglong household economy.

Soya bean oil and fresh vegetable consumption in jin per person is quite similar in all of the villages. The Cuitai residents I surveyed reported a quarter to one half more fresh fruit consumption than the other villages, which is rather odd considering the fact that the northwest villages all have fruit trees and Cuitai does not. Meat consumption in Wanjun is substantially less than in the other villages, although I had expected a lowered amount in Cuitai and Niudian because quite a few vegetarians live in these two villages. While this vegetarianism is most likely a vestige of Buddhist sects which used to thrive in the area, when asked why they were vegetarians, people would typically answer simply that it was because their mother or grandmother did not eat meat.[11]

All in all, however, the southeast villages fork out more cash for their food, and eat more vegetables and fruit than their northwestern counterparts.

CONSUMER GOODS

During my first visit to China (1982–1983), I remember hearing that a man had good prospects for marriage (*hao tiaojian*) if he was 1.8 meters tall, had a house or apartment, a good job and family background, and was able to provide his future wife with "sixty-four legs" (*liushisi tiao tui*). These legs would at least include those on a bed, a dining room table, chairs, an armoire, sofa, coffee table, etc. The only mechanized consumer durables mentioned at this time were the sewing machine and bicycle. Throughout the 1980s the ante was upped to include three—and then four—"machines" (*sanji, siji*): fans, televisions, washing machines, and then refrigerators to accompany a bride to her new home. In more recent years, all these earlier goods have become so common that they seem not worth mentioning anymore. The latest saying to sum up state-of-the-art wedding prerequisites puts forth the "three golds" (*sanjin*)—gold earrings, necklace and ring—as embodying what a truly good catch in a husband should provide. Although I do not recall actually hearing this new saying about the "three golds" while I was in Ganglong, in practice it was certainly the fashion, along with an even newer status symbol: matching leather jackets and pants.

Table 4.2. Six village comparison of mean household food consumption and expenditures.*

	Value of all food per person in yuan**	Per capita cash food expenditures in yuan	Proportion of total cash food value which is grain	Grain per person in jin	Meat per person in jin	Soya oil per person in jin	Vege-tables per person in jin	Value of fruit per person in jin
Baihu	1,595 [.30] (1,088)	1,220 (1,167)	22% (12%)	277 (112)	68 (40)	25 (8)	206 (149)	315
Cuitai	1,556 [.29] (649)	1,118 (652)	22% (10%)	320 (118)	66 (46)	27 (11)	227 (132)	444
Yonghe	1,502 [.35] (686)	986 (558)	22% (8%)	347 (162)	72 (41)	29 (14)	274 (171)	210
Langwo	1,449 [.43] (845)	815 (628)	25% (9%)	362 (150)	62 (53)	23 (8)	231 (145)	223
Niudian	1,445 [.42] (638)	902 (588)	26% (16)	336 (113)	71 (48)	28 (12)	186 (101)	278
Wanjun	1,183 [.52] (440)	566 (319)	32% (10)	408 (184)	56 (46)	27 (18)	127 (67)	271

* The standard deviations are in parentheses below the means.

**The value of food consumed as a proportion of total cash expenditures is in brackets.

The most visibly wealthy household I visited was that headed by the son of a former landlord in Baihu. They had a karaoke/compact disk stereo system (he said he wanted a Panasonic brand one but it was too expensive). They also have a VCR, Atari video game set, refrigerator, color TV, solar panel heater for showers, motorcycle, tractor-trailer set, and leather jackets; his wife also has two 24–K gold rings with matching necklace and earrings.[12] Almost any urban Chinese household would be envious of all these possessions.

It was only after 1980 that the first televisions (black and white until about 1984), fans, washing machines, refrigerators, motorcycles and telephones were bought (in this basic order) by Ganglong families. When I asked people during my household interviews how old their TVs were, a few were quick—and quite proud—to tell me that their 1982 10–inch black and white television sets were the first, or among the first, in their village. Today, almost every family has one television if not two, and a large proportion have big imported Japanese color television sets, usually costing twice what we would pay here in the US.

As seen from Table 4.3, the sample households from the six Ganglong villages follow Tianjin trends fairly closely, and are much higher than the national average. Again, the top three villages listed (Baihu, Cuitai, Yonghe) are on the southeast of the Grand Canal, while the bottom three (Langwo, Niudian, Wanjun) are on the northwest side. Cuitai leads with the largest number of consumer durables in almost all categories. The only item where a northwest village leads is bicycles, where Wanjun has the most. This is because bicycles are primarily bought and used by individuals rather than households. Looking at per capita bicycle figures, Yonghe (a southeast village) is at the top with 78 bikes per 100 people.[13]

In my analysis, there are three kinds of consumer durable. The first relatively inexpensive and/or by local standards indispensable type of consumer good can be found in almost every household—fans, televisions and bikes. The second type includes items in flux: washing machines and gas stoves for cooking used to be a luxury but are rapidly becoming less expensive and more common, while sewing machines were once indispensable but are now rarely bought by younger people since ready-made clothes are increasingly less expensive and usually more stylish.[14] More expensive items considered a luxury—refrigerators and motorcycles—make up the third type of consumer durable. One indication of a higher degree of socioeconomic stratification is found by looking at the differences in the numbers of the first and third types. Villages with fewer than average goods of the first type and more of those in the third type, for example Baihu and Wanjun (lower in TVs and fans but higher in refrigerators and motorcycles), will be more stratified. The reasoning is that there are some families without the most common and/or practically useful goods at the same time that there are those with enough money to buy luxury goods.

Table 4.3. Mean number of consumer durables per 100 households.*

Table 4.3. Mean number of consumer durables per 100 households.*

	Fans	Televisions [color]**	Refrigerators	Motorcycles	Washing machines	Gas stoves	Bikes	Sewing machines
Baihu	140 (96)	96 [48] (35)	24 (44)	16 (37)	72 (46)	68 (48)	236 (119)	68 (48)
Cuitai	176 (109)	124 [60] (44)	16 (37)	12 (33)	84 (55)	96 (54)	272 (128)	92 (28)
Yonghe	152 (82)	112 [60] (44)	8 (28)	16 (37)	56 (44)	68 (48)	260 (104)	92 (49)
Langwo	132 (69)	104 [40] (35)	8 (28)	12 (33)	40 (50)	72 (46)	248 (112)	60 (50)
Niudian	116 (62)	120 [56] (65)	12 (33)	4 (20)	56 (51)	72 (46)	256 (158)	76 (44)
Wanjun	116 (90)	108 [40] (40)	20 (50)	10 (29)	52 (65)	56 (51)	284 (125)	60 (50)
Tianjin	119	119 [68]	29	5	62	na	234	92
China	89	81 [17]	5	10	17	na	147	66

* Source for Tianjin and national statistics: Zhongguo nongcun tongji nianjian, 1996. Standard deviations for all household survey figures are in parentheses underneath the bolded means.

** The subset of color TVs within the category of all TVs is shown in bold and brackets on top.

The only other items of significant worth falling into the consumer good category are motorized vehicles—cars, trucks and tractors. There was only one truck owned by any of the surveyed households. It was cooperatively-owned by two relatives and a friend who had started a transport business. I know that the young privately-run factory owner in Yonghe was in the process of learning to drive so that he could buy a car and that at least one, if not two, families in Cuitai had their own minivans for private transport businesses. Most of the independent transport businesses use tractors, however, and their main business is hauling bricks for the construction industry. Still, there were only seven tractors among the 150 survey households.

In brief, there was a northwest/southeast difference in the survey households in regards to ownership of consumer durables: overall, northwest village households owned fewer per household than southeast villages. Cuitai had the most in virtually all categories, while Langwo had the least consumer durables per household. The importance of consumer durables as a measure of Ganglong village and villager well-being will be explored further in the next chapter.

HOUSING

Housing has a fascinating twofold character. On the one hand it has a direct bearing on a family's physical well-being as protective shelter. At the same time, the size, newness, cleanliness and quality of a house and its contents has been, and continues to be, a symbol of a family's wealth and/or social resources and cultivation. Wilson (1994) concludes from research in suburban Shanghai that houses actually represent an owner's social networks because house-building necessitates recruiting labor and/or capital, and this can be done only through a family's social networks.[15] For some Ganglong families, the actual condition of their houses can be more important than being considered "rich" in cash terms when it comes to how they are perceived by society.

For example, one wealthy household I interviewed had a very lucrative vegetable- and flower-raising business, though one would not know it by looking at their house. It's big, airy, clean, but by no means extravagant in the same way people with much more modest means tend to build. Only one of a handful of such households in the village, they still have cement rather than tile floors. The head of household said he was planning to redecorate in 1996 (he estimated this will cost more than 10,000 yuan) because his daughter was planning to be engaged: he was afraid that the potential son-in-law's family might think they are too "farmer-like" and call off the engagement.[16]

Marriage in China, rural China particularly, is the time when most of a couple's most expensive possessions and assets will be acquired. In Ganglong, the vast majority of families live in the house the couple lived in when they were first married (almost exclusively built by the groom's parents). They can expect to live in this same house for the rest of their lives. When they do build a new house, it will almost certainly be in preparation for their own son's marriage.

One rather graphic example of the importance of a good house to a marriage is found in Baihu. A few years ago, the Niu family—parents and three grown sons—discussed splitting up their large extended family household into nuclear households. The second son's wife saw that the parents and other brothers all had red brick houses while she and her husband only had a one made of mud-bricks, and this made her wildly angry. She wanted the family to give them money as compensation, and when they did not give in to her demands, she ran away, leaving a toddler son behind. Although Niu's wife went to quite an extreme when she and her husband were not given a red brick house, her strong negative reaction to living in a mud-brick house is understandable given the context. Chances are that she would be living there the rest of her days while her neighbors lived in bright new red brick houses with shiny tile floors. Niu has since decided to build a new brick house. This is both an attempt to spite his wife whom he adamantly declared he would never welcome back, as well as an acknowledgement of the importance of having a brick house for wooing a potential second wife.[17]

Not surprisingly then, families with male children start saving early for the materials for houses to be built before their sons are married: men without their own houses in Ganglong today are very unlikely to find wives. The main reason is that young women do not want to live under the constant watchful eyes of their mothers-in-law, and will not agree to marriage unless there is a separate house—even though that house is often attached to, or shares a courtyard with, the in-law's house. Even the parents of sons with city jobs feel it necessary to build houses in the village for their sons, for a variety of reasons. Perhaps it is out of custom that they do so, or perhaps parents would be afraid of losing face in the village if they did not engage in all the sacrifice and prestige involved in building a new house. It may also be to encourage the son and his new family to come home for frequent visits, and/or a signal that the son is expected to eventually come back to the village to take care of his aging parents.

Another testimony to the importance of a house in Ganglong is that the largest reason people reported going into debt was in order to build a new house.[18] Families in the process of building new houses consistently told of how they ate very simply for many years in order to save money for their new house. One Cuitai family lives extremely frugally because, they say, the new house has taken about all the financial (and physical—since they are doing much of the work themselves) resources they have. It cost 60,000 yuan in all. The head of household told me that if they want to eat meat, they go over to his cousin's (who is a butcher) for dinner; they cannot afford to buy meat themselves. This year alone they borrowed 10,000 yuan to finish building the house.[19]

The residential plot and housing layouts in Ganglong are the same as those found throughout northern, northeastern and north central areas of China. High brick walls separate each courtyard from the alleys, roads and other houses running along them. One large doorway leads out onto the road, and occasionally there might be a smaller door accessing the alley or relative's house on the other side. The courtyard, usually about twelve by twenty-four feet (but potentially anywhere from half this size to double this size), often contains flowering trees and shrubs, a small vegetable garden, a tool shed or two, cages for rabbits or fowl, and a stable if the family owns a draft animal. The main door to the house opens into the middle room, and there may be smaller outside doors to rooms on either side. Each room is usually an equal-sized rectangle (about 144 to 160 square feet) with large glass and screened windows facing out into the courtyard.

Most houses built in Ganglong in the last ten to fifteen years also have one smaller window high up in each room opposite the main windows, but there are no windows on the sides of the houses, making these houses fairly dark. Older houses have mud brick or cement floors, while newer ones tend to have more fashionable and easy-to-clean tile floors. Running water (only cold) is found in one room, the kitchen, and in many of the Ganglong villages, water may only be available once a day for an hour or so. Most families use a public outhouse maintained by the village, though some have built their own within their own courtyards.[20] Only the newest houses, and certainly not even all of them, have indoor bathing facilities.[21]

The oldest Ganglong house still occupied during my stay was a "mud" one built in 1952 in Baihu. Mud houses are built with bricks of hardened mud/clay and straw, with large wooden beams, wooden door and window frames. They generally have ceramic tile roofs, but before the 1970s may also have had straw and mud roofs. Until the late 1970s, most houses were mud houses or combination mud and brick and, from the 1980s on, virtually all new houses have been made of red or gray brick.[22] The vast majority of mud houses belong to older people who have long since built nice, new brick houses for their sons, but see no reason to spend all that money on a new house for themselves, especially when they have lived in mud houses all their lives. Interestingly, everyone - even young people with brick houses - admitted that the mud houses provide better insulation; they are cooler in the summer and warmer in the winter.

Table 4.4 shows village differences in housing among the 150 surveyed households. Almost half the houses in China as a whole contain some mud (or clay) in their structures, but our six villages follow Tianjin averages in having much fewer (*Zhongguo nongcun tongji nianjian*, 1996:296). It is not necessarily the case that the owners (or anyone) are actually living in these mud-

Table 4.4. Housing situation in the six survey villages.*

	Mean amount of housing space per person in sq. meters	Mean net value of housing assets in yuan	Number of mud houses among the 25 survey households+	Number of kang among the 25 households+	Mean year in which houses were built
Baihu	17.8 (5.8)	18,692 (15,736)	8	21	1983 (9.3)
Cuitai	18.0 (6.4)	29,936 (26,765)	5	22	1989 (4.7)
Yonghe	18.5 (10.2)**	25,880 (29,220)	6	27	1985 (7.5)
Langwo	18.9 (8.7)	23,979 (19,865)	8	31	1985 (8.2)
Niudian	15.7 (6.9)	16,770 (13,242)	9	31	1982 (9.9)
Wanjun	15.7 (5.0)	17,901 (17,841)	3	25++	1988 (5.0)

* Standard deviations in parentheses to the right side of the bolded means.

**These figures do not include household #112 in which there was one man with a 90 sq. meter house. If included, the average for Yonghe would be 21.3 and the standard deviation 17.5.

+ Indicated column figures are sums, while the other data in this table are averages.

++ Incomplete-based on 20 households only.

brick houses. In Cuitai, for example, all surveyed families lived in brick houses and rented out the older mud ones, but in Niudian and Langwo it was
common for families to use the old mud houses as chicken coops or for storage. It is very surprising to me that Wanjun had so few mud houses and that
it ranked second among villages for having the newest houses. As we have
seen and will continue to see later in this chapter, in almost every other way,
Wanjun is the village with the lowest living standards. My guess is that
Wanjun residents are all too aware of their poor reputation and have steadily and purposefully built new (though small) brick houses over the past
decade or so to attract new brides. This is perhaps also the case with Langwo,
which also has larger and newer houses than its recent status as "poor village" would indicate it should.

The presence of *kang* (hollow beds made of brick and connected to the
cooking stove so that the heat from the cooking fire will heat up the bed) can
be used as a general gauge of the age of houses-almost all houses from the
mid-80s and before have them. This is not always the case, though, as I came
across some new houses with built-in *kang*. Note that there are many more
kang in Niudian and Langwo, the two villages with the most land. People
who spend most of their time doing heavy agricultural work (but some doing
factory work, too) reported that the heat of the *kang*, even in the summer,
did wonders in alleviating their back pain.

Despite the larger houses in Langwo and Yonghe, they are worth less and
built less recently than Cuitai's. One reason for this is that there is a very lively market for older houses in Cuitai. With its central location, numerous factories and abundance of older, second houses no longer needed by Cuitai
natives, Cuitai has one of the largest populations of migrant workers and
families. Migrants to Cuitai can rent an older mud house for 20–30 yuan per
month, or even buy one for 2000–5000 yuan. The older brick houses go for
7000–10,000 yuan and many are sold to Cuitai natives who do not want to
go to the trouble of building their own house. Thus, Cuitai residents are
much more in touch with housing values, whereas in villages where the housing market is undeveloped, people really do not have a sense for what their
older houses might be worth. Owning two houses also accounts for the higher net housing values there. Interestingly, Baihu, with the same (if not better)
central location as Cuitai, lags far behind Cuitai across most housing indicators in Table 4.4.

With nine rooms, central heating and beautiful marble floors, the most
valuable house among the 150 households was in Cuitai. It cost 90,000 yuan
to build in 1994, and is certainly worth much more than that: the head of
household is a construction team manager and was able to get most of the
materials at cost. Still, in 1994 and 1995, most new houses cost
40,000–60,000 yuan, which is several years' income for most families. Having
to save up to build a house is not a new phenomenon: the average family

had to save for several years to buy the materials to build and furnish a mud house, even in 1952.[23] Today, families not only have to buy materials, they also have to hire laborers, as well as provide meals, drinks and cigarettes for the hired help. One family I interviewed had already started buying house-building materials in 1994 for their nine- year old son (who, if the marrying age stays where it is, will marry at 21 or 22)! Poorer families must either start earlier, put off building for several years, and/or must build smaller houses.

There are other possibilities for poorer families with good social relation-ships and connections to get houses built.[24] Borrowing from relatives and friends to build houses is very common, and poorer families with a son approaching marriage age will do just about anything they can to borrow enough to build a new house for the son. People with good reputations and relationships with more wealthy friends and relatives are able to borrow while those without such connections will have to keep slowly saving.[25]

Good relationships with village leaders are needed in some villages more than in others, as evidenced by the story of two residents, Gao and Cai, of Baihu. Gao sighed heavily and said that Party Secretary Li was not allowing people to build new houses unless people paid him off first. Cai said that his own brother had bought the bricks and other materials to build a new house four or five years ago, but the Party Secretary would not approve land for him to build on. Since this man's brother refuses to bribe Party Secretary Li, he has not been able to build his house.[26] From my experience, this blatant type of corruption was the exception rather than the rule in Ganglong.

Good relationships with village officials have other benefits in relation to house-building: if one is on good terms with the officials in charge, one is then more likely to be allotted a plot of land in a good location—a plot that is high and not prone to flooding, closer to one's fields or a paved road, and/or one that has some redeeming physical qualities. Residential plots still have to be applied for, and while there is generally not much choice in loca-tion, someone with a close relationship to a village official in charge is more likely to get a better location. Although few families invite a geomancer to inspect a house site these days, this practice does still exist in Ganglong. More common, however, is the perception that certain locations are unlucky and, if at all possible, people would like to avoid getting such plots.[27]

In addition to their practical use as shelter and as a symbolic indication of a family's financial and social resources, houses are also a way to stake out a seemingly permanent piece of village real estate. Although residential plots technically belong to the village, in practice a home is a piece of private real estate. As village land available for crops dwindles due to factory, school, housing and road construction, villagers can comfort themselves with the knowledge that—at least since Land Reform—one's house and the land it is built on truly belong to the family. In recent years this has become more explicit as new houses are built and the older ones are either sold or rented to fellow villagers or non-villagers who come to live and work in factories.

A word of caution is appropriate here in equating housing quality and size directly with well-being. Not all families elect to build homes up to the latest local standards. Instead, they might decide to send a child away to a better high school, technical school, or college, or invest extra savings in productive equipment or inventory for a private business. One family in Yonghe had a different idea about what to do about housing for their son: instead of building a house for their son when the time comes around, they will buy him a *shangpin fang*—a home built for sale by real estate developers. They said that building a house on one's own is much too time-consuming and tedious.[28] But there are at least three reasons this family can even contemplate such a move: one is that their son is in college and they believe he will get a job in the city where commercial housing has become more and more common and, second, they have the money. This is combined with their more modern mindset; they feel less obligated to build in the village where their son would be close by to take care of them. Perhaps they are hoping to move to the city when they need care. One should note that their first investment was in their son's college education.

The propensity to invest in education or production instead of housing was less common in the early years of reform when there was something of a housing boom. Observers largely credit this housing craze to excess cash made available by reform as well as the uncertainties of the reform: why should they invest in private productive means when it was not yet clear how long this would be tolerated or if these investments would be confiscated in some later movement against "capitalist elements"?

Although two of the southeast villages (Cuitai, Yonghe) had the most valuable houses and two of the northwest villages (Niudian and Wanjun) had the least valuable and smallest houses, we have seen a less obvious set of differences in this section between northwest and southeast villages. Due to the crucial importance of housing in attracting a potential bride, poorer households (and villages) are extra-sensitive to the importance of building new houses for their sons. This may explain why the generally poorer northwest villages had a better showing in the housing area than in income, expenditures and durables. In contrast, a southeast village like Baihu, which has a great central location, has less incentive to build houses because potential brides are perhaps attracted by other village attributes.

LOOKING TO THE FUTURE: PROVIDING CHILDREN WITH A BETTER LIFE

As alluded to in the last section, giving children a better life is one of the main impetuses for Ganglong people working long hours at often tedious work. Part of the reason for this is that children have been and continue to be the main source of physical and financial care for elderly rural Chinese. I was quite shocked to find that most children under twenty did not step foot into the fields once all year long, despite the fact that both parents might be working full time in off-farm positions only to have to labor a few more hours in the fields after work. Instead, in their spare time, the children were doing homework, watching TV or just relaxing. Only in a tiny minority of cases did the children even help out with chores at home while their parents toiled in the fields. Many parents did not want their children to help out at all; they felt that their children deserved a better, more leisurely lifestyle.

Ganglong kids have more and better clothes and leisure time, use newer bicycles and school supplies, and even get to use more expensive shampoo than their parents. When asking about expenditures on clothing, parents would often say that, except for yearly purchases of new socks, shoes and face towels for themselves, all other clothing was purchased for their children. Even more striking was the pocket money given to children, which was as high as five yuan per day. This sum can buy lots of candy, soda and popsicles, which is what the kids generally use it for.

Most parents pay close attention to their children's education, and the education in Ganglong is quite good. There are elementary schools (grades one through six) in four villages, and three or four more villages have schools for only the first and second grades so that the younger children do not have to walk very far in bad weather. There is a lower middle school (grades seven through nine) in Cuitai serving the whole township, though many children go to the one in the nearby market town, Shimiao. The students who go on to high school will either attend the one in Shimiao or, if they test into it, possibly the high school or one of the vocational schools located in the Jinghai county seat. The high schools and vocational schools, like college, are very costly—at least five thousand yuan per year for room and board. Parents often complained about the cost of schooling, even elementary school that costs between 300 to 500 yuan per year, including books and supplies. But only one or two ever said they did not think the schooling was worth it.

Cuitai and Yonghe parents spent the most money on schooling for their kids. One might think that for K-6 schooling, this discrepancy might be due to the different tuition for the various elementary schools. Cuitai's K-6 tuition is slightly more than the other schools, but not by hundreds of yuan as shown in Table 4.5. Also, Baihu children are schooled in the Cuitai elementary school and the Baihu schooling expenditures are much less. The unusually large amounts for Cuitai and Yonghe are in part due to the parents in those two villages paying extra tuition money because some of the children did not pass the tests required to get lower tuition rates. The other reason might be that parents in Cuitai and Yonghe spend more on school supplies (tuition and school supplies were listed together in one question on my survey). The northwest villages Langwo and Niudian spend less on tuition, books and pocket money for children who have not reached school age, though Wanjun has higher-than-expected figures for pocket money expenditures. The amounts of pocket money spent per child are especially startling when compared to some families in poorer parts of China who do not earn that much cash in a year.

Once they have finished the ninth grade, seven out of ten Langwo children go to work in factories, which accounts for the fact that only 50% of school age children are still in school there. Half the Wanjun children drop

Table 4.5. Mean annual tuition and school supplies expenditures, pocket money, and proportion of school-age children who are working.

	School expenditures, grades K-6*	School expenditures, grades 7-9	School expenditures, grades 10-13	Pocket money per child 0-7 years old	Proportion of 12 to 18 year olds working
Baihu	391 [18]	775 [2]	700 [1]	836 [8]	14% [7]
Cuitai	849 [7]	2,738 [4]	2,625 [6]	725 [9]	15% [13]
Yonghe	850 [7]	983 [6]	3,250 [1]	554 [9]	33% [15]
Langwo	286 [8]	100 [1]	0	440 [6]	70% [10]
Niudian	175 [8]	160 [5]	667 [3]	243 [6]	11% [9]
Wanjun	168 [4]	650 [1]	500 [1]	638 [5]	25% [8]

* Number of cases (children) in brackets.

out after the eighth grade but only half of these are actually working. Niudian children are the least likely to drop out of school to work, and Baihu and Cuitai children follow Niudian's lead. One third of Yonghe children in the 12–18 year old age bracket are working, no doubt a function of its large village-run factories which only hire Yonghe residents.

Physical health is another aspect of well-being closely linked to the future. I included two survey questions that reflected physical health: whether anyone in the household was seriously ill in the past year and how much money was spent on medicine and medical bills. Between 2 and 6 people were reported to be seriously ill in each village (between 2% and 7% of the population). Only later did I realize that what was "seriously ill" for one family might not be the same as for another. Medical bills were lowest in Langwo (household average 137.80 yuan for the year) and highest in Niudian (1171.20 yuan). Three elderly people in Niudian died that year and, prior to passing away, required costly doctor's visits and medicine. These circumstances account for the inordinately high figure in that village. Wanjun family medical bills were also quite high at 614.20 yuan.

In the survey villages we find that, except for Baihu (which is a five-minute walk from the township hospital), all the villages have at least one doctor in residence, while both Cuitai and Niudian have two.[29] Generally speaking, each village doctor has his or her own in-home clinic stocked with common herbal and western-style medicines. These doctors make house calls if necessary, though there is a Ganglong Township-run hospital in the township seat and a larger, better-equipped hospital in the nearby market town, Shimiao. The county hospital is about an hour away by bus and, for more serious cases, the ill or wounded might travel to one of the several large Tianjin hospitals about two hours away. Although people could go to other villages or to one of the nearby hospitals, most people will start with their village doctors first, because they know and trust them and because it will not cost as much as the hospital.[30] My impression is that health care is generally adequate for all but a few very seriously ill people who do not want to leave the comfort of home, family, and village. However, in one or two such cases, lack of funds was the major consideration cited in not obtaining needed health services.

Just like consumer durables, housing and food, the quality of schooling, goodies and necessities for the kids, and health care are quite dependent on having the cash to pay for them. The important life cycle rituals of marriage and funeral do not differ on this account. Aside from housing, the largest household expenditures are for marriages and funerals which, like housing, are public manifestations of wealth, filial ties, magnanimity, family solidarity and other social capital. Therefore, people will often go into debt to put on a marriage or funeral that, if done well, will gain them prestige in the community.[31] Marriages cost about 10,000 yuan, including the money and gifts given to the bride, the hiring of taxis, music, banquet, etc. that are all essential parts of a marriage in Ganglong. This of course does not include the cost of the house, which must be built and fully furnished. Funerals cost about 6,000 yuan; this includes the obligatory banquet for relatives, the music, hired Buddhist "monks" or "Daoists priests," etc.[32]

Future well-being, therefore, is very much related to how much money people earn and spend today.

LAND ASSETS, FARMING AND WELL-BEING

Recent studies on wealth and income in rural China have found that, in general, having use-rights to greater amounts of land (there is, as yet, no fully private farmland ownership in China) does not lead to higher incomes or wealth (Khan 1993:108; McKinley 1996:42, 125).[34] In Croll's (1994:99) summary of her many years studying rural China, she finds that land still does produce a large proportion of rural family food, though market sales contribute only a tiny fraction to family incomes. In Ganglong today, land is a complicated asset which one family may see as a liability while neighbors are willing and able to capitalize on their own landholdings. In this section I try to untangle the different aspects of landholdings and land use which render land an asset or a potential liability for village and its residents.

There are two basic orientations to the land, positive and negative, and these are usually tied to generation and/or experience. Younger people and those who have grown up without strong ties to the land are less eager to have it and farm it. Nineteen-year old Hong, a native of Cuitai, declared unequivocally that she would prefer to live in Cuitai the rest of her life. She went on to say that Daren, Fuguantun and Dingxiang would be okay too. Huoxing and Jinqiu were too far away and Hong did not want to go to any of the villages on the northwest of the river because they had too much land—which would mean that she might get stuck farming (Notes, Oct. 29, 1995). She added that she would not have a problem finding a husband in the places that she wanted. Hong expresses views typical of her generation: she does not want to work on the land.[35] As a woman, she has the ability to make sure that her time on the land is limited, if not altogether terminated, by marrying into a village with little land. Perhaps this is the one area where young men would envy their female peers.[36]

The views of Han, a 60+ year old Cuitai man, are quite different when it comes to the value of farm land, and reflect those of older Cuitai villagers: he is not happy that the new high school is going to occupy several acres of prime Cuitai land because he feels that the village cannot afford to lose any more land. As it is, the land in Cuitai is already over-used; he believes some should be left fallow every year. This is impossible, even without the new school.

Cuitai landholdings, as well as those of most of the other southeastern villages, are relatively small in relationship to the population, hence the concern on the part of older residents that landholdings are dwindling. Villagers from the northwest side of the river generally have more land, which means that they tend to spend more time farming, and eat more of what they have grown. (Recall the quote in Chapter Three about how people in Langwo were clamoring to contract extra land because if tilled well, it could make them a lot of money). Because of this, they have a more positive view of land, though it is safe to say that younger people in northwest villages are also more interested in opportunities that take them off the land.

Wen, a fifty-five year-old Langwo farmer, told me that he grew everything on my list of over 15 different non-vegetable crops, with the exception of rice and tobacco, neither of which are grown anymore in the whole township. In recent years Wen has begun to like farming more and more. He told me he does not want to be exploited (i.e. work in a rural enterprise) and does not want to exploit people (by being a private entrepreneur): by farming he avoids both. Wen said he wanted to contract 30 mu of land from the village, but the village would not let him.[37] He thinks this land "rental" is terrible and wishes that the government would let people buy land. Wen said he would eat sorghum—a coarse grain only consumed when nothing else is available—three meals a day in order to buy land.[38] Although Farmer Wen is certainly in the minority with some of his enthusiastic views on farming, his wish to own land is shared by many.

Table 4.6 below lays out the differences in land holdings, grain yields, and other aspects of land quality and quantity among the 150 families in our six survey villages. Whether one looks at per household or per capita land holdings, the three northwest villages, Niudian, Langwo and Wanjun all have significantly more land than the three southeast villages. The northwest villages also have land that is farther away from home, and different kinds of grain and oil crops. The more distant land is often too far away to be managed as well as it should be, and too far away to irrigate at reasonable cost. Add to this the fact that putting enough fertilizer and soil enhancers on it would not be cost effective, we begin to understand why northwest village land is less productive, as reflected in grain yields.

The amount of garden land varies among all the villages; the Grand Canal does not provide a meaningful separation point in this case. My impression is that the amount of garden land is set by the quality of the land, the proximity to village residential areas, and accessibility to irrigation sources. Township residents often commented on how good the Cuitai soil was, though Baihu, and Niudian also have good garden land. In order to ensure that everyone gets about as much similar quality of land as everyone else, all the land in Ganglong is divided up into usually four, but sometimes five or six, different grades based on quality. As villagers are quick to point out, there is still much disparity within the different grades, but unless people wanted twenty or so tiny little plots each, it is simply not feasible to make sure everyone has exactly the same amount of each grade of land. As it is, we see from Table 4.6 there are still four to six plots per person. When the garden land is added, the average total number of plots rises to five to eight per family. Economies of scale, which might result from agricultural mechanization are lost, and this is often cited as one of the main disadvantages of dismantling the commune system.[39]

Villages in the Jiangnan area (as well as other coastal regions), where there are a host of successful rural industries, have solved the problem of scale in many different concrete ways. The primary way they do this is by putting the land back together and employing a small number of people to do all the agricultural tasks. In Ganglong, a few villages also aspire to this, and Cuitai has come the closest to achieving almost full mechanization. Plowing and planting of both wheat and corn are done mechanically by a team of men hired by the village (mostly lower-level village officials, village electric repair people, etc.). Much of the wheat harvesting is also done by machines. Only those plots of land (very few in Cuitai) that are inaccessible by large tractors must be cultivated by manual labor. Interviews with other village leaders revealed that full mechanization was their main goal—if and when they could get the funds.

Table 4.6. Mean household landholdings, grain yields, numbers of, and distance to, farm plots in the six survey villages, 1995.

	Per house-hold arable land-holdings in mu	Grain yield in jin per mu	Per capita land holdings in mu	Garden land per household in mu	Number of plots of land per house-hold**	Distance to the farthest piece of land (li)	Number of other non-vegetable crops raised++
Baihu	3.66	436	1.08	0.20	4.67 [14]	3.23	1.21
	(2.86)	(152)	(.80)	(0.13)	(4.73)	(1.29)	(1.27)
Cuitai	3.63	565	0.98	0.27	4.60 [25]	2.21	0.88
	(1.50)	(88)	(.33)	(0.23)	(1.38)	(0.75)	(0.72)
Yonghe	5.23	663	1.45	0.49	6.13 [23]	2.68+	2.22
	(3.28)	(136)	(.88)	(0.24)	(1.98)	(0.85)	(1.10)
Langwo	8.33	514	2.29	0.52	6.17 [23]	5.88	3.09
	(5.69)	(103)	(1.66)	(0.50)	(3.14)	(2.03)	(1.77)
Niudian	8.12	483	2.07	0.25	6.32 [22]	6.90	2.45
	(5.42)	(104)	(1.10)	(0.14)	(1.81)	(2.49)	(1.57)
Wanjun	8.05	425	2.18	0.19	5.57 [3]	6.78	3.17
	(3.19)	(118)	(3.19)	(0.10)	(1.90)	(2.98)	(1.81)

* Standard deviations in parentheses on the bottom half of cell under the bolded means.
**Number of cases is in brackets to the right of the bolded mean. I did not start asking this question in Wanjun until the last three households; lower numbers of cases in other villages indicate families without any land at all. This only includes "grain land" and not garden land.
+ Distances for Yonghe omit three households with land in another township 20 or more li away. If included the mean distance would be 5.33 with a standard deviation of 7.09.
++ Other crops include grain and oil crops such as peanuts, sesame, sorghum, millet, beans (other than soya or string).

During 1994–1995, only Cuitai offered full agricultural services (mechanized plowing, planting and harvesting), though Yonghe and some of the other villages offered some plowing. One would have expected that with its successful factories, Yonghe would also be able to provide more extensive agricultural services to its residents, but it did not (at least as of 1995). The young Party Secretary Tan expressed his interest in purchasing the equipment, and hoped to do this within the next few years. Langwo and Niudian village officials also expressed their desire to buy agricultural equipment, but as yet have not. With all the land in Wanjun, much of it seemingly marginal, mechanical plowing and sowing could also be a big time and labor saver.

One former Party Secretary from Wanjun expressed great dissatisfaction with the fact that current Wanjun officials are not paying attention to agriculture. He said that Wanjun is really backward technologically. On his watch as Party Secretary he bought a large tractor that could be used for scale agriculture, but the current Party Secretary sold it.[40] While village officials prior to the reform period actually did have a more agricultural mindset which might be considered out of sync with "market socialism" and the needs of today's rural industry, there is still a point to be made about fully utilizing village land resources and reducing agricultural labor time.

For families that have one, two or even several members working in off-farm jobs, agricultural mechanization is a welcome relief. Presumably, mechanization would also benefit those people in the northwest villages, where land is so far away and the quality is poor.[41] But households which do not want to till some or all of the land allocated to them can let others use it (*zhuanrang*), though they may not sell or build on it. In the process of conducting the household surveys I found that some people let friends and relatives use their land with no compensation at all, while others expected to receive some of the harvest and/or be paid the nominal grain quotas associated with the land.[42] No one leased the land at market rates, although Baihu's Party Secretary did contract some Baihu land out to farmers across the border in Hebei. Of all the villages, Baihu was the one with the most families not tilling any land at all: eleven out of twenty-five families. Most of these families had lucrative private businesses. While many people in Cuitai also had private businesses and might otherwise have relinquished their land, the unified agricultural management by the village made it reasonable to keep: their agricultural work was minimal and the grain grown would have to be bought anyway.

This is the main reason why people continue to farm despite the long hours it demands. The grain and other food products raised on their land are the most tangible reasons for a family to keep and till land. Table 4.7 gives information on the productivity of land in its yuan cash value.

Crop expenses per mu include cash amounts spent on seed, fertilizer, pesticide, irrigation, plowing (many people hired local people to plow). I did not include the grain quota costs here, because in Jinghai County and all other Tianjin districts, it is very minimal: just 15 jin of corn per person. This fee translates into a cash value of about 50 yuan total annually for a four-per-son household. Crop income is cash income from actual sales of grains,

Table 4.7. Mean annual crop expenses, income and value of self-provided crop foods in yuan.*

	Crop expenses per mu in yuan	Crop cash income per mu in yuan	Value of self- provided crop foods in yuan per household	Average number of labor days spent in crop agriculture per household
Baihu	103 (73)	64 (66)	1106 (740)	65 (55)
Cuitai**	209 (67)	414 (387)	1360 (723)	99 (77)
Yonghe	164 (84)	236 (160)	1617 (683)	145 (72)
Langwo	111 (43)	136 (119)	1748 (747)	157 (114)
Niudian	79 (35)	148 (132)	1760 (973)	96 (68)
Wanjun	96 (64)	66 (51)	2083 (955)	79 (81)

*Standard deviations in parentheses next to bolded means.
** The crop income per mu and mean days spent doing crop work figures exclude one Cuitai family (Household #129) which had a crop income per mu of over 1000 yuan and worked over 600 person-days in crop agriculture. If they are included here, Cuitai's average crop income per mu would be 571 yuan per mu and the average number of days worked would be 120.

seeds, vegetables, fruits, stalks and other by-products and, in one case, flow-ers. In both Baihu and Wanjun, crop expenses per mu are more than crop income per mu, though Wanjun villagers tended to eat much more self-pro-vided food than Baihu residents. The high productivity of Cuitai (with or without the "outlier" family) is mainly due to the greenhouse vegetables which, jin for jin, have a much higher value than grain.

I initially assumed that factoring in labor costs would not make crop agri-culture nearly as profitable as off-farm work. But even in Baihu, where both the value of self-provided crops and income from crops is the smallest, farm-ing one's own land is still much more cost effective than buying grain on the free market.[43] Consequentially, Ganglong residents—along with those in many other rural areas in China—find it very difficult economically to leave the land completely. In a sense, they are tied to their off-farm jobs because there simply is not enough land to support a family by agriculture alone, and the non-farm wages are too meager to purchase all farm products on the free market.

There are reasons other than pure economic welfare for staying on the land. Despite new county rules which went into effect in 1996 and are sup-posed to concentrate more land in the hands of those who are willing and able to make the most of it agriculturally, most Ganglong villages still seem to distribute the land in a fairly egalitarian manner: plots continue to be small and spread apart.[44] The main reason echoed by people all over the township (and from most walks of life) is that in these are uncertain times: factories open and close with alarming frequency so there is a sense that no job is secure. Therefore, people consider their farmland a safeguard against hunger.

When all else fails, land means food, and thus it embodies a very tangible sense of future well-being.

Thus, although scholars may find that land is not a significant determinant of income (i.e. more land does not directly lead to more cash income), it nevertheless continues to be an important asset for older Ganglong residents. If nothing else, it is seen as insurance against future uncertainties. The younger generation—at least now when they are young—do not share this view. The middle-aged villagers are unsurprisingly ambivalent: although they would rather not do the hard work, it is still financially worthwhile to grow what they can for subsistence and use the precious cash from off-farm labor for goods and services they cannot provide themselves.[45]

VILLAGE INDUSTRY JOBS AND EMPLOYMENT

Since the reform era in China began, China scholars have commented upon the benefits of rural industrialization. Most often, however, these scholars have been studying rural industrialization in the Jiangnan area (the region just to the south of the Yangtze River), which leads the nation in rural industry profitability and scale. The broad definition of rural industry refers to enterprises operated at the township level and below, and includes collective, private, shareholding and international joint-venture enterprises. Rural industrial products can be heavy machinery and machine parts, processed agricultural goods, or even agricultural products themselves if they are grown in large-scale, semi-mechanized animal husbandry firms. One indicator of how important rural industry is to the people of Ganglong is that, of the 283 non-farm jobs held by interviewees in 1995, 50% were in rural industry. The next most common non-farm job was driver (9% of all jobs), however many of the drivers were also employed by rural enterprises.[46]

All of the recent work on rural inequality in China has emphasized the importance of wage income, especially from rural industry (and private enterprise), as the single most important cause of increasing household stratification in the countryside.[47] For our purposes here, such observations certainly point to considering higher levels of rural industrialization among the measures of villager well-being. In fact, Sjorberg and Zhang say unequivocally in their introduction, "the difference between poor and rich rural areas is mainly a result of rural industrialization." [48] What I hope to show in this section is that, although the story is much the same in Ganglong, down at the village level villager *experience* of rural industrial labor is not always as rosy as the numbers might indicate.

For the individual and the household, the positive aspects of working in rural industry are the goods and opportunities their cash income enables them to purchase. These include not only the consumer goods they desire, but also their very houses and the potential to broaden their social networks and access more information. It also provides them with an indoor environment more physically comfortable during extreme weather. Furthermore, especially for young people, a job in rural industry is a good excuse to escape arduous and virtually non-cash compensating agricultural labor—in addition to simply getting out of the house. Younger Ganglong residents generally look for factory work as soon as they leave school, though some teenagers may have to quit school early to go to work because their family needs the cash.[49] Further, depending on the enterprise, benefits can be quite lucrative. At one Yonghe factory, workers get periodic supplies of gloves, laundry detergent, sugar, soap, towels, food at the major holidays, and cash bonuses.[50] Almost all factories periodically give out towels, laundry detergent and work gloves to workers.

Jobs in rural industry do not attract everyone, however. There are people who feel suffocated by the strict time requirements. One Hao in his mid-twenties from Niudian told me:

> I have no desire to work in a factory where people boss me around all day, where the hours are long and pay is little. So I stay at home and put together door and window frames for people when there is work, and farm when there is not any work. I have made about 4000–5000 yuan this year, which is better than working in a factory, especially since I have only worked five months at the carpentry.[51]

Many workers I interviewed really despise the Dingxiang automobile tire factory because it has three-shifts and everyone must rotate to the next shift once a month. Workers complain that by the time they finally get used to working nights, they have to go to mornings, and they are perpetually tired.[52] One woman who works there said that the one good thing about the Dingxiang factory is that, because of the three-shift policy, there is no mandatory overtime. This confession brings us to another drawback with working in rural industry: long hours and tedious work. This same woman's son has worked at the big factory in Dingxiang for the past seven years. He told me that no one over 30 years old works there because people that "old" are no longer able to do the hard work.[53]

Similarly, another woman, Fan, works in a new township factory that makes steel rods. She says that she had been very healthy until she started working at this job where the hours are really long—more than eleven hours a day and, unlike most other factories, workers at the rod factory are not allowed to go home for lunch. There are only two shifts, a night one and a day one.[54]

Despite the hard work, factory pay is usually not very good, usually between 200–300 yuan per month for six to seven day workweeks. To most workers in Ganglong factories, that level of pay would be fine if it were actually paid—or if it were paid on time. One of the biggest problems with rural industries all over China is the triangular debt: Factory A owes money to

Factory B for products delivered, but Factory A cannot pay because Factory C in turn owes them money. The result is that employees often work for months without pay in a vicious circle where, if they quit, they will never receive their back pay, so they continue working (certainly with little enthusiasm) and borrow money to make ends meet.

One woman who had not been paid for months of work at one rural enterprise quit and subsequently found a job in a pickled vegetable factory right in her home village, Wanjun, while her husband stoked the furnace in a factory in Shimiao. Both jobs involve backbreaking physical labor. The striking feature with both of their new jobs is that they are paid yearly: she said herself that for most of the year they have no money and have to borrow at least two times a year. They have no savings to speak of. Her two sisters send a total of about 1000 yuan per year to help out.[55]

This is typical of how some rural industries in Ganglong have developed clever ways to keep newly-trained workers from leaving once they find out how hard the work is: they request down payments or withhold wages until a worker has worked for a specified length of time. As one parent testified:

> My son quit the factory because they only gave one month of pay for every 3 months he worked. The factory is afraid that if they give workers wages as they earn it, the employees would run away with the skills. After working there for two years, they still kept 100 yuan of back wages when my son quit. If, before quitting, you worked there less time they would keep even more...If I could write, I would write a letter to the government about this.[56]

In an even more creative move to increase its operating budget, one factory required that its employees invest in it as a condition of continued employment. Li works as a marketing agent for this same factory in Shimiao. Just this year he gave them 5000 yuan as shares in the factory. Everyone had to invest: regular workers gave 2000 yuan each and the factory manager gave 10,000 yuan. The regular workers who did not want to buy shares got fired. If managerial staff could not come up with enough money to buy these shares, the factory would take it out of their pay. Li did not know the details regarding his investment - for example, what percentage 5000 yuan in shares would buy or how much in dividends they could expect at the end of this year.[57]

I should point out that most of the delayed wages, forced down-payments or share purchase strategies are found in village-level enterprises. Generally speaking, township-run enterprises have better and more timely wages and benefits. There are not many township-run jobs in the Ganglong/Shimiao area, but they are coveted. Thus many people—younger people especially—try to combat the insecurities of rural industry by trying to find more secure township-level employment, or better yet, employment in

state-run industry. Children who have mothers with non-agricultural residency are automatically assigned these kinds of jobs with good benefits.[58]

A more simple solution to the problem of keeping down costs is to hire
people from areas much poorer than in Baihu, so that they will accept lower
pay and not complain about the work. We saw in the previous chapter that
most villages had a small group of migrants mostly from Heilongjiang, poor
areas of Hebei, Henan, Shandong and even Sichuan. These are people who
have no possibility of cash income in their hometowns, so they are willing to
put up with almost any conditions.

In addition to the low and delayed pay and long hours, poor working
conditions abound, health care is totally absent, and only a small minority of
upper-level management positions qualify for the limited retirement benefits.
A current factory manager in Yonghe says that if he stays in a management
position for ten years or more, his retirement pay will be 20 yuan a month,
at least at the current rate.[59] In the Jiangnan area rural industries, on the other
hand, all workers, not just those in management, reportedly should all be
able to get retirement benefits and keep their health insurance when they
retire—men at age sixty and women at age 55 (May 27, 1995, Tianjin City
Radio Broadcast).

Not one of the twenty or more village-level factories I visited had heat in
the main rooms where work was done. The daytime temperature got down
to nine degrees Fahrenheit during the winter I lived there, so it could be very,
very cold at work. At one car parts factory I visited, employees were working
at lathes without any eye protection.

Table 4.8 shows some basic information about rural industry laborers.
With the exception of Niudian and Wanjun (with 14 and 18 people total
working in factories), on average about one person in every household I surveyed worked in a factory.[60] Langwo had the highest number, one reason
being that households there are larger and have more grown children living
at home. Younger people tend to work at factories while their parents stay
home, work the land, and take care of grandchildren.

With respect to the ratio of people working in the home village, Baihu
has the lowest. This reflects the weakness of rural industry in Baihu despite its
prime southeast location and proximity to the main road. Cuitai, Yonghe and
Niudian do provide more jobs in the home village for residents; in all three
villages over 50% of factory workers work in their home villages. Laborers in
these three villages, however, pay a price for being so close: they work longer
days than their counterparts in the other three villages surveyed. Cuitai and
Niudian workers are the best compensated as far as monthly salaries go.
Cuitai annual and semi-annual income is the lowest—much lower than the
other villages. This is less an indication of low bonuses than that Cuitai workers have jobs which consistently pay by the month rather than one or two
times a year. Yonghe, on the other hand, has very good annual bonuses (that

Table 4.8. Basic indicators for household members working in rural industry.

	# Factory workers	Ratio working in home village	Ratio female factory workers	Mean # hours worked per day	Mean monthly salary in yuan	Mean yearly payments in yuan*	Mean age
Baihu	24	21%	67%	9.57	274	217	34
Cuitai	24	54%	42%	10.25	314	49	38
Yonghe	22	68%	27%	11.12	256	565	34
Niudian	14	57%	50%	11.65	288	286	40
Langwo	31	29%	61%	9.97	261	121	33
Wanjun	18	28%	78%	8.57	203	283	31

*Yearly payments include bonuses and factory wages that are paid only on an annual or semi-annual basis.

Table 4.9. Human capital indicators of all people aged 14 through 55, 1995.*

	Years of education	Employ-ment skill level**	Number of village-level and higher former or present cadres	Specialized training level	Years on the job	Age
Baihu	7.23 (55)	1.45 (42)	6	2.73 (26)	6.75 (40)	33
Cuitai	6.77 (67)	1.33 (42)	8	2.15 (20)	8.47 (45)	34
Yonghe	5.99 (61)	1.59 (41)	4	2.07 (15)	6.06 (38)	33
Langwo	5.76 (58)	1.32 (41)	15	2.33 (12)	5.67 (42)	34
Niudian	6.56 (56)	1.59 (32)	1	2.63 (16)	11.33 (32)	33
Wanjun	5.48 (73)	1.26 (42)	9	2.06 (17)	4.72 (43)	37

* Number of cases in parentheses.
** Employment skill level is for the current job only.

is, at least, in the year I conducted the surveys: in years when profits are low, so are the bonuses), though their monthly wages are middling. Wanjun workers (almost all women) receive the lowest monthly salaries and often their pay is several months late.

Looking at the figures for female factory workers, it might be tempting to conclude that Cuitai and Yonghe are not as progressive as the other villages when it comes to female workers. Not so. The factory jobs employing higher proportions of women in the other villages tend to be low-skill, low-paying pickled vegetable factory jobs in which women outnumber men. When all non-farm jobs are considered, the gender gap in all the villages is about the same: with the exception of Yonghe which has a low proportion of female workers, the ratio of female workers in rural industry hovers around 40%.[61] My suspicion is that in the primarily heavy industry factories in Yonghe, the more traditional division of labor is present whereby men are seen as more fit to engage in heavy industry (while women are targeted for light industry, electronics and textiles).[62]

To summarize how workers at Ganglong area factories actually feel about their jobs, it is probably safe to say that they like the cash, but (much like workers anywhere) they would like higher wages, wages paid on time with no unfair payment conditions, shorter hours, better work conditions, health care and retirement benefits. Still, for most people who do not have the mind for, or interest in, private business or agriculture, the cash from rural industrial jobs outweighs the many problems they face.

However, in weighing the pros and cons of rural industry for Ganglong township residents, another aspect must be considered: the benefits accruing to the village as a whole from having rural industry located there. These benefits might be as simple as convenience; the parents who work in their home village are able to get home for lunch quickly and easily to eat with their schoolage children. This possibility is especially appreciated during the rainy season when travel is slow and messy.

Whiting (1993 and 2001) finds that rural industry in the Jiangnan region results in such benefits as more village welfare expenditures and higher individual incomes. Nee (1996), Knight and Song (1992) and Ho (1994) uncover decreasing income inequality in the Jiangnan areas where rural industry is strong. But other positive aspects of having rural industry in one's own village are highly dependent on the success of these enterprises: How are the profits divided? Are they used on schools, roads, lighting, water supply, unified agricultural services, or emergency funds for individuals and families in need? Simply having rural industry, even very successful factories, does not necessarily mean that villagers will actually be better off than counterparts in villages without industry, or that more factories are better. It is not surprising, then, that while Knight and Song (1992) and Ho (1994) find the same decreasing inequality for *households* where collective rural industry has taken root, they note that rural industry has given rise to income stratification among *villages*.[63] This is seems to be happening in Ganglong township.

The most important single factor in determining whether collective village industry will trickle down to each villager is the quality of village leadership: good leadership results in successful industries and distributes the profits in a way advantageous to village residents (and most likely to themselves as well).[64] Knight and Song (1992) provide a list of the factors leading to successful village industry, in which village leader initiative is at the top. But several of the other items on this list are also largely contingent on village leadership: infrastructure, transport facilities, and access to funds. To this list, I add the following aspects of leadership quality: leader education, support and respect from village residents, and good ties with township and other non-village individuals, enterprises and government institutions. Ample tenure is also very important; a party secretary or leadership team cannot do well if they are only in power for a year or two.

Generally speaking, the younger the working-age person, the more education that person will have which, in part, explains Wanjun's comparatively low educational levels.[65] Employment skill level runs from zero (unskilled manual labor) to four (highly educated such as health care workers and middle school teachers). Niudian has surprisingly high employment skill and specialized training levels. This is due to there being an unusually high proportion of teachers and doctors in the survey sample. In addition, several people in the Niudian sample had worked for years in Tianjin urban factories (hence the extremely high job tenure level), where they also received specialized training.[66] Training levels are from one to three: one is manual labor training in construction (or the hellish job of furnace stoking); two includes training as an artisan, cook or tailor; three is for machine repair, veterinary, medical, teacher and party school training.

Cuitai people have a lower employment skill level than their education and years on the job would imply. Cuitai does, however, have a large number of past and present village and township-level cadres, but not as many as Langwo—with the smallest population of the six villages. This is a vestige of Langwo's revolutionary vigor in the 1940s and 50s. Note that Baihu and Niudian have fairly high levels along all human capital indicators. Unfortunately, these abilities do not seem to be utilized in collective rural industry or any other form of activity which might benefit the village at large. Baihu and Niudian residents use their talents more in private business or in the state enterprise sector. Wanjun, unsurprisingly, has the lowest levels of all the human capital indicators.

More difficult to document than the existence of rural industry or the extent of a village's human capital endowments is the complex process of cumulative causation whereby some villages seem to be locked into virtuous cycles of prosperity while others are plagued by vicious cycles of stagnation and poverty. This is absolutely crucial to village development. The question of how and why the Ganglong villages arrived at where they are today will be taken up in Chapter Six.

To summarize this section on employment and rural industry, we have found that although rural industrial and other off-farm labor provides important cash-making sources which families can spend on things important to them (e.g. children, status symbols, labor-saving devices, etc.), it by no means comes easily. And in some cases, village governments do not even get the compensation they deserve due to enterprise fiscal irresponsibility, debt-triangle problems or simply greediness on the part of enterprise managers. For villagers working in village-run enterprises in their home villages, their appeals to village leaders (who have some say in enterprise decision-making about the fairness of "collective" industries) may still have an impact on getting fair pay, better working conditions and actually getting their pay on time. Such appeals are virtually impossible to make to managers of enterprises outside one's village.

CONCLUSION: WELL-BEING IN GANGLONG

Without a doubt there are other more personal elements in well-being (such as inter-familial and inter-village relationships, mental health, savings, etc.) which I was not able to capture in these surveys.[67] One other aspect which people repeatedly mentioned as being important to them is their preference for most families having just about the same level of prosperity. It was very unsettling for Ganglong residents to see people who were either very wealthy or very poor.

A great deal of evidence from developing countries in recent years shows that in households and localities where women have higher status and control over income, levels of well-being are higher than in areas where women have lower status.[68] Mainly, this is because women use the income they control in ways much different from men: mothers with income to spend tend to give children more and better food, clothing and education than men do.[69] I can say from the detailed information I collected on household consumption that the largest non-food, non-durable item expenditures were on liquor and cigarettes, sometimes amounting to thousands of yuan per year. Since the vast majority of Ganglong women neither smoke nor drink, this is a sliver of evidence that men who like to smoke and drink might be creating the spending patterns for those households.[70] At the same time, I have no evidence that such expenditures were at the expense of a child's schooling, food or clothing. The question of whether there are significant village differences between male and female control of income in China, and differential spending, must be left to future research.

Overall, however, the survey results discussed throughout this chapter give a good idea of what constitutes prosperity for most Ganglong residents.

Like most people around the world, the basic concerns of food, housing, jobs and their children's future are high priorities. Yet for most Ganglong families, the issue is not basic needs, but the desire for better quality foods, housing, jobs and education, labor-saving and luxury items such as refrigerators, color TVs, VCRs, gold jewelry, leather clothes and vacations. At the same time, many Ganglong families, will have to wait many years to—or perhaps will never—enjoy such luxuries.

Generally speaking, the southeast villages of Cuitai, Yonghe and Baihu are doing better than their northwest counterparts when it comes to food and durable goods, housing and pay from off-farm jobs. The northwest villagers spend more time in the fields and get smaller grain yields, though the fact that they have more land still gives them greater grain harvests which can then be sold or fed to livestock. Wanjun consistently ranks at the bottom of the indicators of prosperity (except for housing), while Langwo—the "poor" village—seems to be doing quite well for itself. Niudian is perhaps the most "agricultural" village occupationally, in that people there have the fewest off-farm jobs. Surprisingly, Niudian residents are not far behind on other indicators the way Wanjun is. Baihu shows very mixed results: it is on top for per capita expenditures and children's pocket money, but has a very poor record of providing jobs and services to its residents despite the seeming high levels of household spending. Yonghe people seem to work hard and save their money rather than spending it on consumption. Although Yonghe has factories that are doing very well, it lags behind by not providing labor-saving agricultural services to its residents–many of whom are workers in Yonghe's own factories and who spend very long hours on the job. Overall, the village coming out on or near the top in most categories is Cuitai. That the southeast villages seem to consistently have more of what villagers identified as well-being, and whether this holds true for the rest of the non-surveyed villages in the township, are among the main topics of the next chapter.

Having shown, then, that aggregate household information from each village does indicate that the villages have unique characteristics, the task of Chapter Five is to use the criteria of well-being identified here to establish that village-level data from the annual accountant records do indeed reflect aspects of well-being in Ganglong. This household-village link will allow village comparisons - even without detailed household data.

NOTES

[1] In fact, the official calculation for net village income is calculated this way: gross village income minus expenses, where expenses are production and operating costs. The figure "distributable income" (*nongmin suode*) which is divided by population to get per capita income takes net income and subtracts taxes, rural industry fees (*xiangcun qiye shangjiao youguan bumen*), "enterprise funds" (*qiye*

gexiang jijin) and township and village fees (*xiangcun tongchou ji tiliu*). This information comes from notes on the calculations from 1993 village accountant records located in the Ganglong Township Archives.

[2] Similarly, Yang (1994) notes in a study of a village Xindu County, Sichuan, that although there was a prosperous factory there, most of the workers were from other villages, and only the managers and shareholders of the factory benefited by its existence. This prompted villagers to complain that the visibility of that one successful factory made outsiders (including government officials) ignore the poor conditions. Villagers said, "People look at the factory and think the village is rich. But it has nothing to do with us" (Yang 1994:169–170).

[3] A special issue of Chinese Peasant (*Zhongguo nongmin*) Magazine from January, 1995, gave the following list of the 1993 minimum criteria for determining whether a village was a *xiaokangcun*: gross per capita income of 1100 yuan, gini coefficient of 0.3 to 0.4, Engels coefficient of less than 50, intake of protein of 75 grams per person per day, 70 yuan spent on clothing per person per year, and houses built with steel and/or wood frames, 70 television sets per 100 households, 10% of consumption for services, life expectancy of 70 years, 8 years of education for adults of working age, health care availability of 90% (but details of what this means are not given), 70% of households have a telephone, 95% of households have electricity, less than 20 criminal cases per 10,000 people per year. By these standards, none of the Ganglong villages would qualify.

[4] "Worthiness," as I found out, is not always dependent on the actual conditions in the villages, but instead is tweaked by a given village leadership's desire to be a *xiaokangcun*. There were more than a few Ganglong villages awarded the "*xiaokangcun*" title whose qualifications I found lacking. In particular, I was surprised at Gaoduizi's possession of this title. When I asked the township official in charge of overall village economic matters about this, he said that Gaoduizi inflated many of the relevant numbers. What he did not explain was why, knowing this, the township still awarded Gaoduizi the title. I suspect that there are probably county quotas for township proportions of *xiaokangcun*, and the township conveniently overlooked the fact that Gaoduizi was not up to the standard.

[5] See Partha Dasgupta's *An Inquiry into Well-Being and Destitution* (1993) for one of the most thorough and thoughtful recent explorations of well-being. Among the other more common indicators of well-being, Dasgupta explores and compares political and civic freedoms across several countries.

[6] In a recent article and book Khan and Riskin (1998 and 2001) compare the 1988 data McKinley used (and which they themselves also analyzed and wrote extensively about) with the latest resurvey done in 1995. They found that the distribution of rural income was more unequal in 1995 than in 1988 and that the main reasons for this were non-farm wages from industry, private business and property income.

[7] The figures for Yonghe exclude Household #117. This family made over 200,000 yuan in net profits from a private factory—over four times the next highest household income reported in all the surveys. If included, Yonghe's average household income and expenditures would be 21,034 yuan and 16,721 yuan, respectively and the household per capita income would be 5,397 yuan. Wealth figures are also affected because of the worth of their costly factory assets. If included,

household wealth would be 58,278 yuan and per capita wealth would be 14,499 yuan.

8 Unfortunately I do not have savings information. While at first, I did ask households about how much savings they had, after sensing a large degree of discomfort on the part of interviewees, I decided that it was not worth asking if it risked establishing a good working relationship with them.

9 Although my calculation of wealth generally follows McKinley's, I have made some changes. I did not ask directly about financial assets but believe that using household income instead is reasonable and well-founded. One of McKinley's principal findings is that "the level of income . . . is the main determinant of a household's financial assets" (1996:85).

Whereas McKinley's definition of wealth includes the value of all consumer durables, furniture, agricultural hand tools, etc., I did not include these. This is mainly because I did not ask about the value of these goods unless they were bought in the year covered by the survey (and therefore were part of household expenditures). I do use McKinley's method of calculating land and housing value. Land value adds all income from landholdings (both for market sales and home consumption), divided by the total amount of household landholdings. This number is then divided by 4 (see McKinley, 1996:102–103 for further explanation). Net housing value is the current value of the house minus housing-related debt (1996:73).

10 The quality of some of the pickled vegetable factories' products leave a little to be desired and I ran across many people who would only purchase established brands. Someone gave me several packets from a local factory, but when I opened them it turned out that they had gone bad—which should be close to impossible for pickled goods!

11 Although they described themselves as eating a vegetarian diet (*chi su*), I discovered that this did not always mean what I (a vegetarian of almost 20 years) thought it did. The Cuitai Party Secretary's son was described to me as a vegetarian by his mother, but I saw him eating ribs one night. When I asked about it, the reply was that yes he was a vegetarian and he ate ribs!

12 Household #46, May 11, 1995.

13 I use the per 100 households for comparison purposes: durables are listed this way in national statistics.

14 The alternative to gas stove cooking is burning corncobs and stalks in a hearth of mud or brick built right into the house. Generally speaking, younger people in the semi-agricultural villages are more likely to use gas stoves exclusively, but for some things like unleavened bread (*laobing*) and corn porridge, the larger wok-hearths are preferred.

15 Although I generally agree that this is true in Ganglong, there are certainly families who decide to use their networks for purposes other than house-building. This means that their networks might be more extensive than the condition of their house would suggest. Also, I came across some families who had one relative willing to put up all the money for their house. This one strong relationship replaces the need for a larger, more complex set of relationships with neighbors—at least in the house-building context.

16 Household #129, Nov. 26, 1995.

[17] A relative suggested that since Niu will soon finish building his new house, he should try to find his wife, but Niu replied, "I'm not going to look for that fucking wife" (Household #44 notes, May 10, 1995).

[18] Croll (1994:41) also found that house-building and house repair was "one of the largest and most recent expenses and cause of debt for nearly all households" in the Henan villages she studied in 1987.

[19] Household #132, Nov. 27, 1995.

[20] One home I visited used its horse stable as a latrine. Not one of the homes I visited had a fixed place for relieving bladder and bowels *inside* the house, nor did I ever run across a flush toilet, even in the largest township and village factories. Chamber pots are used at night.

[21] There is a bathhouse open to the public on Sundays at a state-run factory in the nearby Shimiao market town. Many people have their own solar-heated plastic bags for outside showers during the summer, but it is only in the past few years that a very few families have installed bathing facilities in their homes. The old boiled water-and-basin method is what most people—including me during my stay in Ganglong—still use.

[22] I found only one family that had built a mud house in the 1990s. By the household head's own admission (as well as by other villagers), he was very nostalgic for the Mao years, when he said officials were hard-working and honest and people lived simply. This man, in his fifties, engaged exclusively in agriculture and his new mud house consisted only of two rooms—the smallest recently-built house in my sample, or that I had heard of.

[23] One of the benefits of the commune system was that house-building was done by relatives and friends in the village, for which only meals and drinks had to be provided. After the dissolution of the commune, village leaders were no longer willing or able to harness the labor for house-building and for-profit construction teams started to emerge.

[24] Again, Wilson (1994) explores in great detail how social relationships in a suburban Shanghai village are used in house building and marriages, not just for poor families, but for all families.

[25] Social relationships were just as important during the commune years when a family wanting to build a house would apply to village officials, who would then organize the building team. At that time people with "bad" class backgrounds, even if they had collected all the necessary materials to build a house, could expect either long delays or no help whatsoever in getting their houses built.

[26] Baihu notes, May 5&13, 1995.

[27] This point was brought home very well in an interview with a twenty-eight year old woman in Yonghe Household #115. According to village superstition, all the houses on her alley have bad luck. She went on to cite four or five cases of people and even one child living in this alley who had died young (including her mother-in-law) or who had had severe illnesses. Right during our interview, their dog frothed at the mouth, vomited and within minutes rolled over and died right in front of our very eyes. When I asked her if she believed in this "superstition" she said that she half-believed it. Later, another Yonghe villager told me that this woman herself was extremely sick and almost died a few years ago.

[28] Household #109, Nov.11, 1995.

29 Information about doctors is not from the household surveys but represents absolute village totals in 1995 from the village-level surveys.

30 It would have been more appropriate to gather systematic qualitative types of information for this period, such as which villages had good doctors and sources of medicine, etc., which had the best teachers and schools, etc., but the problem of criteria for such normative assessments made it unfeasible.

31 Wilson (1994) discusses the social capital dimensions of weddings at length in Chapter Eight.

32 I put "monks" and "Daoist priests" in quotes because at two of the funerals I witnessed, there were people who dressed in the appropriate clothes and went through some of the Buddhist or Daoist rituals, but were not actually monks or Daoist priests.

33 I have decided not to discuss livestock as an element of well-being. They only make a significant difference to households if they are raised on a large scale. Although there were a few families in my surveys that did this, they were a small minority. Moreover, the income and expenditures associated with animal husbandry is reflected in the survey statistics for total household expenditures and the value of all livestock is included in survey wealth figures as household assets.

34 McKinley (1996:44) says that once geographical factors are adjusted for (he uses only provincial dummy variables to do this!!), land does become significant, but still it is one of the least significant in his model (where Communist Party membership and occupation were most important).

35 I helped Hong's family out at wheat harvest. Hong spent about ten minutes there in high heels, obviously not at all adept at the very arduous work. Later she said that her older sister, brother and sister-in-law take care of most of the agricultural work in her family.

36 Again, see Lavely (1991) for more about women's mobility via marriage.

37 I received a letter from Wen in the fall of 1998 happily notifying me that he now contracts and manages 30 mu of village land under the new county policy.

38 Household #93, November 5, 1995.

39 Whether scale farming is indeed something that China should strive for is addressed in Prosterman, Roy, and Li (1998) and, in the context of very poor rural areas where land is scarce, by Pennarz (1998).

40 Household #11, April 15, 1995.

41 As a matter of fact, the Party Secretary of Ganglong township told me that he was negotiating a deal with five of the northwest villages to create a 3000 mu township farm on that low-yield land. The township plan is to use township machinery to plow, plant and harvest the wheat that was grown on that land. The county would arrange it so that the nearby Ziya River would have enough water for irrigation. They would then contract it out to villagers in those villages for about 30 yuan per mu/year. Basically, the villagers would just have to add fertilizer and take care of bagging the harvest. The Party Secretary was really enthusiastic about this idea and said it would bring in more money than most of the township enterprises now did. But many people are unhappy about this, and several meetings were held to try to get the opposing parties to agree. In the meantime, much of that low-yield land lies in waste because people just do not have the time or resources to work it.

[42] In 1995, as in all preceeding years, there were grain quotas—a certain amount of grain which had to be sold to the state below market price. In Tianjin municipality, these quotas are very nominal. In Ganglong, the annual quota is 15 jin of corn per person, which is really very small, especially when compared to nearby Hebei quotas (Hebei has very hefty quotas on wheat, sesame, peanuts, cotton, millet and other crops, and account for a hefty chunk of annual income). There are also relatively small agricultural taxes on land, usually paid with the money made from the quota corn sales. This is why many of the people I interviewed had no idea how much the agricultural tax actually was; they had never actually paid any money.

[43] I figured this by a very crude method, using Baihu as worst-case scenario. If the average Baihu family has 3.66 mu of land and is losing 39 yuan per mu (the average Baihu crop income minus crop expenses per mu), then this amounts to only 142.74 yuan. I subtracted this figure from the average cash value of self-provided food (1,106 yuan), which comes to 963.26 yuan. Then, I divided this amount by the average number of days worked in agriculture in Baihu (65), and the result was 14.8 yuan per day—more than the average factory job provides. Since most agricultural work in Baihu is done after off-farm working hours, there is no need to subtract lost wages because no wages are being lost to farm work.

Additionally, farm work is cost-effective in the sense that it can, for the most part, be done part-time by elders unable to work full-time in off-farm labor or after regular job hours. In other words, crop cultivation is extra income rather than a substitute for factory income. If people purchased their grain they would have to spend almost three months of their precious factory wages on grain (average 941 yuan per household annually). However, the extra hours might not be worth it or possible for some people in Baihu, especially those kept very busy by private businesses or without elders to help them. No wonder Baihu has the most households that have given up their land altogether.

[44] Since the new policy land redistributions were carried out when I was still in Ganglong, I was able to ask village officials and residents about them.

[45] When I say "middle-aged" I mean people roughly between 35 and 50. Perhaps their ambivalence has to do with their place in the life cycle—worried about their own retirement—or the fact that they were old enough during the tumultuous sixties to understand that political winds do come and go and that the land can always provide stability and food when everything else crumbles.

[46] If both types of private business activities (peddling to rotating markets and fixed location stores and businesses) are taken together, however, these are the second most common non-farm jobs (9%).

[47] Khan and Riskin (1998 and 2001); Riskin (1996a); McKinley (1996); Khan et al (1993); Knight and Song (1992); Ho (1994). Khan (1993) notes that in comparative perspective, rural Chinese household income from wage labor is an important contributor to overall prosperity while, in other countries, rural wage labor is correlated with poverty.

[48] Sjorberg and Zhang (1998:12). Cheng (1996) provides evidence, however, that in heavily grain-producing areas differences in *crop* income (rather than non-farm income) are the major source of inequality.

⁴⁹ In Langwo, a father's debilitating accident prevented him from returning to work. Since his injuries are most likely life-long, his fourteen-year-old daughter was forced to leave school and start earning money for the household (Household #96, Nov. 6, 1995).

⁵⁰ Household #111, Nov. 17, 1995.

⁵¹ Household #81, Nov.11, 1995.

⁵² Household #79, October 31, 1995.

⁵³ Household #92, Nov. 5, 1995.

⁵⁴ Household #144, Dec. 2, 1995.

⁵⁵ Household #1 April 9, 1995.

⁵⁶ Household #34, May 6, 1995.

⁵⁷ Household #133, Nov. 28, 1995.

⁵⁸ Non-agricultural residency can also be bought for a price. In one Cuitai family, the oldest daughter works at a hotel in Tianjin and makes 700 yuan per month. She has agricultural residency in Cuitai, but is planning to buy a non-agricultural residency permit so that she can get benefits such as retirement and health care. Her father thinks it is not worth it because things are changing so much that spending 20,000 yuan now may not get her anything in the future (Household #129, Nov. 26, 1995). Twenty thousand yuan is a hefty sum for, as the woman's father noted, uncertain benefits.

⁵⁹ Household #111, Nov. 17, 1995.

⁶⁰ The figures here include factory managers (5) and regular factory workers (114) factory technicians (4) and accountants (8).

⁶¹ As mentioned earlier, about 50% of the total (283) non-farm jobs found in the survey are in rural industry. The other types of jobs, from most numerous down, are drivers (24), roving peddlers (19), construction workers (17), self-employed people with a fixed location business (12 - owners of beauty shops, restaurants, etc.), current village and township cadres (10), service workers in restaurants, etc. (9), train station dock workers (8), teachers (7), bank and credit co-op clerks (7), a few artisans and health care workers.

The lowest proportion of women in non-farm jobs is in Yonghe (27%), while Langwo has the highest proportion (42%). Monthly salaries even out a bit if all off-farm labor is taken into account, ranging from 240 to 305 yuan per month. Baihu still provides the fewest off-farm jobs for its residents (only 12%), while Yonghe provides half the off-farm jobs to its own villagers who, again, do pay the price of proximity in longer hours.

⁶² On the other hand, it turns out that the gender gap with regard to schooling is quite large and does not really correspond to the figures for ratio of women working. Of all working-age people surveyed (14–55 years olds), the largest gap was in Niudian, where men had an average of 7.68 years of schooling but women only had 5.66. The lowest gender gap was in Baihu: men 7.68 years and women 6.76 years. When we take into account that Niudian is the most traditional agricultural village and Baihu is the most urbanized, these figures make more sense.

⁶³ Rozelle (1994a) also finds that rural industrialization was responsible for increasing inequality among 40 villages in two Jiangsu townships.

⁶⁴ See Wilson (1994) for a more detailed discussion of the delicate balancing act between village leaders' own interests and village interests.

[65] Note that according to the educational criteria of *xiaokangcun* (footnote #4), none of the six villages should count as a "prosperous" village. This, despite the fact that Cuitai was probably the best off across the board of all Ganglong villages and that at least twelve of the twenty-three villages were deemed to be *xiaokang-cun* by 1995.

[66] The families of these men (I ran across no women in these jobs) generally stay in the village in order to keep the land and because the wife and children have rural residency.

[67] One other factor I did not pursue here was Chayanov's life-cycle theory of household well-being, whereby households with more young children and elder dependents will almost always be less well-off than those with grown children still living at home (who can bring in a full salary or in other ways work for the family benefit). Recent research (Selden 1993 and Unger 1994) indicates this should be a very important reason for inequality. Baihu and Yonghe had the highest proportion (both 27%) of children under 20, while Wanjun and Langwo had the lowest proportions (15% and 19%, respectively). Cuitai and Baihu had the lowest proportion of people over 65 years of age (4% and 7%, respectively); the other four villages had between 10% and 12%. By these figures alone, Baihu should be doing the worst, followed by Yonghe. This does not seem to be the case: even Baihu's higher levels of stratification cannot be traced to the life-cycle effects, though I believe this theory in general to be quite powerful.

[68] Blumberg, Rakowski, Tinker and Monteon (1995).

[69] Blumberg (1988); Engle (1995).

[70] On the other hand, not all men smoked or drank in such large amounts, and these expenditures on cigarettes and liquor were often for gift-giving. Less frequently these expenditures were offset by hair care and makeup product purchases by household women.

CHAPTER 5.

HOUSEHOLD-VILLAGE LINKS AND THE OTHER SEVENTEEN GANGLONG VILLAGES

OVER AND OVER AGAIN IN CHAPTER FOUR WE SAW SIZABLE DIFFERENCES between the villages on the southeast of the Grand Canal and those on the northwest: southeast villagers had more disposable cash on hand, spent more on fruits and vegetables, and ate less low-nutrient grains. They had more consumer durables, better paying jobs, bigger, more modern and expensive houses, less land (and therefore less time spent in agricultural labor), but reaped higher grain yields. They had higher educational levels and spent more on their children. In short, they had more of what township residents consider the elements of well-being.

In this chapter, I build on the local conceptions of well-being from household surveys in the six villages to show that there is a close relationship between the household-level data and village-level accountant record data. To this end I compile a correlation table for corresponding measures of well-being; it matches my household survey data against village-level data from the 1994 village accountant records. I do this because I want to know which potential village-level indicators are likely to give me the most accurate information about well-being levels in the other Ganglong villages for which I do not have any household surveys. The high correlations between household and village-level data, in the consumer durables category especially, indicate that using consumer durable information from the village data as a proxy for well-being is quite reasonable. From there, I move on to rank all the Ganglong villages with respect to well-being. Despite a very few exceptions, two starkly contrasting groups of villages emerge from this comparison: the northwest (which has lower levels of the components of well-being) versus southeast (which has higher levels).

In addition, later in this chapter I untangle "northwest" and "southeast" in a bit more detail, exposing the few exceptions to these two, rather bulky, categories. My first task, however, is to convince readers that assessing well-being by using village-level data is legitimate, especially given my earlier comments on how per capita village income bears virtually no indication of actual living standards in many villages. The method, if not the findings, unfolded in this chapter are meant as a potentially fruitful method for other researchers to decide which of the many data in the village accountant records best reflect village socioeconomic conditions.

THE HOUSEHOLD-VILLAGE CONNECTION

Even documents from the Ganglong archives themselves indicate that the village accountant records may not be as reliable as they could or should be.[1] In order to test the idea that there was indeed a correspondence between what I found in the household surveys and what was recorded in the village accountant records, I set up a small database for the six villages. On the one hand, this database included village averages for the main measures of prosperity calculated from the twenty-five households in each village (e.g. average total income, average total expenses, average number of consumer durables, average quantities of food and housing). But it also contained relevant variables for these same six villages from the village accountant records (e.g. averages for village per capita income, household durables, housing, grain yields, and other variables). I then ran correlations between the household survey and village accountant record variables. Table 5.1 gives a few of the more important correlation findings.[2]

In Chapter Four, several components of household well-being were identified, including consumer durables, food consumption, household income (especially nonfarm income), household expenditures, value of land as measured in value of production for self-consumption and/or cash sales, and household wealth (i.e. household income plus net value of housing). All of these elements of household well-being, in addition to the amount of land per capita and grain yield, can be found in the leftmost vertical column in Table 5.1. The relationships between these variables from the household surveys (vertical-left) and similar ones from the village surveys (horizontal-top) reveal several things.

First, the high and significant correlations between village-level consumer durables and several of the household-level indicators of well-being lead me to conclude that 1) there is a larger, more general, significance to household well-being in the number of consumer durables owned by households, and that 2) village-level measures do indeed have a strong relationship to household well-being. The other village-level income measures (such as per capita income, gross income per household, and industrial income per household) also show high and significant correlations with household indi-

Table 5.1. Correlation coefficients for indicators of well-being from the household surveys (horizontal) and accountant record data (vertical) for 1994.

Accountant records> / Household survey \/	Consumer durables+	Washing machines	TVs	Gross village income per household	Per capita income (net)	Gross industrial income per household	Estimated private business income per capita	Land in mu Per capita	Grain yield in jin per mu
Consumer durables	.8579*	.9058*	.8369*	.9558**	.9297**	.9308**	.7040	-.6319	.9060*
Washing machines	.7621	.8504*	.6235	.8863*	.7327	.7750	.7197	-.6179	.8577*
TVs	.1150	.4441	.4425	.5168	.6356	.7446	.0346	.1678	.3630
Yuan value of food consumed	.8904*	.9365**	.6595	.7827	.6468	.6822	.8279*	-.5094	.5884
Land value per mu	.7830	.8038	.9486**	.8407*	.9647**	.9492**	.6732	-.5937	.7727
Land in mu per capita	-.9199**	-.8780*	-.7350	-.8028	-.6925	-.6921	-.8870*	.7560	-.7310
Grain yield in jin per mu	.5235	.4839	-.7350	.3088	.5754	.5523	.5476	-.2383	.0830
Nonfarm income	.8107*	.5544	.6441	.4511	.4141	.3405	.8972*	-.9248**	.4839
Household income	.5109	.6807	.7714	.6556	.7380	.8328*	.6464	-.4838	.5452
Household expenditures	.9603**	.9211*	.7044	.8833*	.7676	.7329	.7403	-.5888	.7904
Household wealth	.8716*	.7041	.9233**	.6394	.8132*	.7124	.7197	-.5986	.5414

* Significant to the .05 level (2-tailed test).

** Significant to the .01 level (2-tailed test).

+Consumer durables for both household and village-level surveys include fans, TVs, washing machines, refrigerators and motorcycles. All these variables are in units per 100 households.

cators of well-being. However, this result needs some qualification, and will be discussed further below.

Remembering that household expenditures (all cash outlays) are a better indicator of household income and resources than reported household income, we should be especially interested in looking at which of the village-level variables correlate to household expenditures. It turns out that household expenditures correlate most highly with the number of consumer durables per village, and with washing machines in particular. Household expenditures also correlate fairly highly with gross village per capita income, but correlations with the other village measures are insignificant.

Interestingly, the correlation between specific household survey and village survey consumer variables (such as TVs and washing machines) are not as strong as the more general "durables" category.[3] Additionally, specific village-level durables have relationships with household survey well-being variables even when the general consumer durable category does not. For example, the number of TVs reported in the villages is related significantly to the survey variable for household wealth, while the number of washing machines in each village is strongly related to the yuan value of food consumed. In both cases, no other village-level consumer durable measure was correlated to a significant degree. Thus, although the numbers of TVs and washing machines reported in the villages might not correlate strongly with the number of TVs and washing machines owned by households in the survey, the high correlations with other household well-being measures indicate that each village-level durable variable may still represent other aspects of well-being. Aggregating them in a generic durables category dilutes this part of their meaning.[4]

There are some relationships between household and village-level variables which seemingly should be present but are not: the grain yields calculated from the household surveys has an extremely weak correlation to the grain yields recorded at the village level (coefficient =.08). This shows that local cadres are either truly ignorant of agricultural conditions in their villages, they simply do not care enough about grain harvests to do a better job, they do not have a good idea about how much land people are letting go to waste and/or they are manipulating the figures a bit.[5] Having met and talked to the majority of accountants who compile these yearly village records, I lean toward the former explanations rather than self-conscious number manipulation—at least in regard to grain statistics.

The value of food consumed by households, in addition to being highly correlated with village figures for numbers of consumer durables—especially washing machines—is also strongly related to the estimated village income from private enterprise (per capita). Household survey calculations for land holdings per capita are inversely correlated to all village-level indicators in the table, with the predictable exception of village land per capita figures. This corroborates the observations made in previous chapters that the more land one has, the less well off one is. The value of household landholdings, like consumer durables, is also very highly correlated with village measures for durables gross, net, and industrial income and would seem to strengthen the case for using these village-level variables as proxies for well-being. However, further evidence shown below brings this conclusion into doubt.

Note also that non-farm income, household income and household expenditures are *not* significantly related to village per capita income.[6] This supports the fact that the most widely-used measures of income at the village-level are not able to capture income from non-farm jobs in other villages or income from private enterprise. On the other hand, since village per capita income figures are so highly correlated with household consumer durables, land value and, to a lesser extent, household wealth, it would seem that village per capita income figures do reflect certain other aspects of household well-being. On further examination of the data, however, I found this to be true only in the two most industrial villages, Cuitai and Yonghe.

As discussed in Chapter Four, the villages with strong village industry tended to have official per capita incomes more indicative of their residents' actual socioeconomic conditions. In actuality, those strong correlations between village per capita income figures and household variables only hold for Cuitai and Yonghe, the two most industrialized villages in my six-village sample. Also, unsurprisingly, it turns out that the more industrialized villages have higher land and net housing values because there is less land per capita in those villages, no doubt making existing more valuable. When Cuitai and Yonghe are left out of the equation, correlations between village per capita income and industrial income become insignificant in relation to all household variables. Table 5.2 reports the correlations without the two villages with the strongest rural industries, Yonghe and Cuitai.[7]

Leaving Cuitai and Yonghe out of the correlation equation still led to some results similar to those in Table 5.1: strong correlations persisted between village-level numbers of durables and household survey expenditures (0.973*) and village-level washing machines and the value of food consumed (0.965*) from the household survey. This exciting result gives more weight to the use of the village-level consumer durables data as a reasonable substitute for household expenditure information, and can be used for the other seventeen villages of Ganglong for which there is no household survey data. The strong relationships between household survey consumer durables and land value with the village-level data for gross, per capita and industrial income disappear when Yonghe and Cuitai are removed from the equation. Again, those strong relationships only occurred because of the high levels of industrialization of those two villages.[8]

Other new and significant correlations appear when Yonghe and Cuitai are eliminated. Village-level information about private entrepreneurial

Table 5.2. Correlation coefficients for indicators of well-being from the 150 sample households (horizontal) and accountant record data (vertical) for 1994, leaving out the villages with the strongest village industries (Cuitai and Yonghe).

Accountant records >> / Household survey ∨	Consumer durables	Washing machines	TVs	Gross village income per household	Income per capita (net)	Industrial income per household	Estimated private business income per capita	Land in mu per capita	Grain yield in jin per mu
Consumer durables	.7168	.7898	.6611	.7643	.3057	.4404	.9888*	-.5592	.7938
Washing machines	.6110	.7304	.5982	.7444	.1873	.4515	.9940**	-.5569	.7411
TVs	-.8069	-.1609	-.9530*	-.2455	-.1803	.5171	-.4006	.8164	-.8795
Yuan value of food consumed	.8484	.9650*	.5656	.9825*	.7201	.5769	.8013	-.2671	.6816
Land value	.1844	.3712	.3565	.3675	-.2797	.3315	.8604	-.5369	.4987
Land in mu per capita	-.8627	-.7732	-.8067	-.8122	-.3952	-.2859	-.9471	.6646	-.9025
Grain yield in jin per mu	-.1040	.0326	-.4977	.0094	.5958	.1646	-.6912	.7874	-.5587
Nonfarm income	.8326	.4140	.9808*	.4819	.1263	-.1933	.8052	-.9061	.9973**
Household income	-.3356	.1504	-.2210	.1022	-.4274	.5017	.4805	-.0465	-.0665
Household expenditures	.9732*	.8500	.7418	.8921	.7357	.3031	.7141	-.4082	.8008
Household wealth	.7355	.2248	.5852	.2989	.6203	-.3318	-.0203	-.2414	.4827

+ Consumer durables for both household and village-level surveys include fans, TVs, washing machines, refrigerators and motorcycles. All these variables are in units per 100 households.

* Significant to the .05 level (2-tailed test).

** Significant to the .01 level (2-tailed test).

income (which I estimated myself; see endnote #2 this chapter) is highly correlated with both aggregated consumer durables and washing machines; the
value of food consumed is strongly related to village gross income per capita; and household non-farm income is significantly correlated to village grain
yields and TVs.[9] And this result makes sense: more income from private enterprise will be reflected in consumption patterns.

The lesson from all this is that if household expenditures give us the best
indication of a household's well-being, then the aggregate per household
number of the five consumer durables (washing machines in particular) is the
village-level indicator of well-being at that level. The importance of consumer
goods in assessing the overall level of household prosperity has also been
studied and by Selden (1985). In a household survey in Wugong, a village in
Raoyang County, Hebei Province, Selden discovered an observable link
between household income and the then five most important durable
goods—bicycles, sewing machines, watches, clocks and radios.[10]

In addition to consumer durables, other village-level indicators may be
still be informative, although (as I discovered) great caution must be exer-
cised when using them: high degrees of rural industrialization in Yonghe and
Cuitai led to overestimated relationships between village-level income figures
and household data. This finding helps to confirm the problem of village-
level income figures in general, as discussed at the beginning of Chapter
Four. Although village per capita income in the Ganglong villages might be
more indicative of the strength of village collective industry, this relationship
is not very reliable. Dingxiang, with a reported gross industrial income of 130
million yuan per year (about US$ 16 million) reports a per capita income of
only about twice that of the next closest village, Cuitai. Cuitai's gross industrial income is just over 4 million yuan, almost 33 times less than Dingxiang,
but Cuitai's reported income is only half that of Dingxiang. Where did the
rest of Dingxiang's income go? Certainly not into infrastructure, investment
or taxes—at least not according to official figures.[11] Per capita village income,
therefore, cannot even be used as an approximate measure of the strength
of collective industry.[12] This makes the significance of consumer durables as
measures of well-being all the more poignant.

BRINGING IN THE OTHER GANGLONG VILLAGES

We saw in the last chapter that the three southeast villages had more consumer durables than the northwest villages. Looking at Table 5.3, this holds
true when the other seventeen villages are factored in using the village-level
accountant data. The strong trend showing villages on the southeast of the
Grand Canal having more consumer durables than the villages on the northwest continues and this is consistent over all items.

The difference between the numbers of fans and washing machines in
the northwest and southeast is the most striking and, from the discussion

above, indicates a basic disparity in living standards between northeast and southeast villages. For fans, washing machines and motorcycles, the southeast villages outnumber even the Tianjin averages. Poorer inland areas tend to lower the national average, although the high Tianjin averages most likely point to the fact that consumer durables are more common in the larger urban areas. Despite a strong showing from southeast Ganglong villages, aggregate Ganglong township figures are almost all lower than Tianjin averages, a reminder that it is an area of mediocre standing in respect to other Tianjin areas, both urban and rural.

Table 5.3. Average number of consumer durables per 100 households, 1994: averages for Ganglong villages, Tianjin and nation.*

	TVs**	Fans	Washing machines	Refrigerators	Motorcycles
Ganglong Township average	95 (32)	111	52	14	5
Ganglong Northwest	89 (28)	92	41	11	4
Ganglong Southeast	101 (36)	130	65	17	6
Tianjin average	115 (47)	112	61	25	5
China average	75 (14)	81	15	4	3

* Sources: Ganglong data from village accountant records hand copied from Ganglong township archives. National and Tianjin data from *Zhongguo nongcun tongji nianjian*, 1995
** Number of color TVs in parentheses.

Table 5.4. Comparison of Ganglong northwest and southeast villages over several socioeconomic measures, 1994.*

	Northwest villages	Southeast villages
Percentage of households living in mud houses	10% (12%)	5% (6%)
Number of new rooms per village	9 (5)	19 (21)
GVIO per capita in yuan**	4,172 (4,539)	9,696 (12,456)
Per capita village income in yuan	976 (221)	1,237 (558)
Per capita funds for public welfare in yuan	45 (62)	107 (107)
Arable land per capita	2.21 (0.1)	1.52 (0.5)
Grain yield in jin per mu	488 (75)	517 (78)
Grain output in jin per capita	732 (178)	587 (186)
Total number of doctors in the NW and SE	7	16

Sources: Ganglong Township archives. The number of doctors comes from village surveys done winter 1994-1995. National and Tianjin data from *Zhongguo nongcun tongji nianjian*, 1995 (p.302). Standard deviations in parentheses.
** GVIO prices for 1994 were reportedly the same as GVIO at 1990 fixed prices. The GVIO and social welfare figures here do not include Dingxiang (SE) because it is such an outlier. If included, per capita GVIO for southeast villages would be 33,865 yuan (SD=81,025) and social welfare per capita 262 yuan (SD=524).

This trend—southeast villages doing better than the northeast ones— continues across almost every possible measure of prosperity. While the village-level data for grain harvests and grain yields, per capita gross value of industrial output (GVIO) might not be reliable as absolute reflections of well-being, important information can still be gleaned from looking at these data from the standpoint of northwest and southeast. The accountants from the northwest villages and southeast villages consistently quoted figures indicating that northwest villages were poorer than the southeast villages. Table 5.4 further demonstrates the socioeconomic disparities between southeast and northwest villages.

The difference in gross value of industrial output per capita (GVIO) between the northwest and southeast villages in the township is stark. Again, it would have been more pronounced if the one "outlier" village, Dingxiang, which had a per capita GVIO of 275,553 yuan—almost seven times the amount of the next closest village—had been included. Even without Dingxiang in the equation, the per capita GVIO in the southeast is still more than twice that of the northwest, showing the strength of rural industry there. The southeastern villages spend more money on public welfare projects, in part, because revenues from rural industries can be used for that purpose. The variation among villages in the northeast is less than that in the southeast, evidenced by their standard deviations, over all the indicators except for the two housing measures.

Strangely, the average per capita income figures are not all that different whether or not Dingxiang is taken into consideration. It is a well-known fact that reported per capita income figures are tampered with a bit for political and taxation purposes—yet another reason that per capita income figures are not a good gauge of villagers' actual living standards. I was told by several of the village party secretaries and/or accountants that they lowered the village per capita income figures registered in the annual accountant records. In fact, Dingxiang's Party Secretary told me that his village's per capita income for 1994 should actually have been about 2,500 yuan (they reported 1619 yuan); and surely it was even higher than this.[13]

RANKING THE VILLAGES

I have stressed the differences between the villages on the northwest and southeast of the Grand Canal several times this chapter and last. This divide will be the basis for categorizing villages further into four groups: those doing well and those doing poorly within the northwest and the southeast village split. This will make it possible to locate specific villages (instead of faceless averages and statistics) and explain why they are not performing as well as the others—or why they are doing better.

In order to begin ranking the villages, measures of prosperity must be selected. From the discussion earlier in this chapter, the village-level measure of durable goods is an obvious choice because of the highly significant correlations with the household well-being indicators. Similarly, I use village gross per capita income, which is highly correlated with household food consumption and (less significantly) household expenditures. Because estimated village per capita income from private enterprise is strongly correlated with

both household consumer durables in the villages without strong rural industry and value of food consumed when all villages are factored in, I include
this measure as well.

Together, the three indicators offer a fairly well-rounded view of village
development levels: gross income ostensibly represents income from aggregate agricultural and rural industrial activities but does not include private
business income; durables measure levels of household prosperity in each village more directly. I combine the z-scores (standardized versions of variables
which can be compared over otherwise incommensurate units—in this case
consumer durables and yuan) of the three variables into an overall rank,
which can be found in Table 5.5.

Table 5.5. Village ranking according to village gross income per capita, private
business lincome per capita and mean number of the five consumer durables
per 100 households, 1994.*

Southeast villages		Northwest villages	
	Overall rank (and Z score)		Overall Rank (and Z score)
Baihu	8 (.80)	Kuihua	18 (-1.30)
Cuitai	1 (3.84)	Langwo	16 (-.95)
Daren	3 (2.02)	Lizhuang	22 (-2.43)
Dingxiang	2 (2.65)	Lujiatun	14 (-.23)
Fuguantun	6 (1.03)	Niudian	15 (-.80)
Gaoduizi	19 (-1.41)	Panzhuangzi	21 (-2.24)
Huoxing	13 (-.16)	Quanjiakou	9 (.51)
Jinqiu	5 (1.23)	Sanxiaotun	4 (1.33)
Yonghe	7 (.98)	Sunjiazhuang	12 (-.05)
Xiaobaotun	11 (.29)	Wanjun	17 (-.98)
Xiayuan	10 (.44)	Wuguantun	20 (-1.80)
		Yangcun	23 (-2.75)

*These rankings were obtained by turning values into z-scores and then adding them together.
Actual z-scores for the overall ranking are in parentheses.

Table 5.6. Categorization of Ganglong villages with respect to well-being by
location and rank.

	Southeast	Northwest
Good	Cuitai, Dingxiang, Daren, Jinqiu, Fuguantun, Yonghe, Baihu, Xiayuan, Xiaobaotun	Sanxiaotun, Quanjiakou
Poor	Huoxing, Gaoduizi	Sunjiazhuang, Lujiatun, Niudian, Langwo, Wanjun, Kuihua, Wuguantun, Panzhuangzi, Lizhuang, Yangcun

A brief glance at this table finds, again, that southeast villages' ranks are
generally higher (evidenced by lower numbers: one is the highest rank and
twenty-three is the lowest with respect to this well-being index) and north-

west villages' are usually lower. On the whole, the rankings generally conform to my subjective impressions, as well as ethnographic and other quantitative data.

Table 5.6 proceeds to shows a simple four-category classification of all twenty-three Ganglong villages on the basis of their z-score ranking from the previous table (they are in order from best to worst within each column). I have classified the villages into "good" and "poor" according to whether they were above or below the median (-.046) for all the villages using the ranking criteria above. Thus, the "good" villages are above the median in their overall z-scores while the "poor" villages are below the median. The shortcoming of this type of classification is that one cannot see the magnitude of the differences, for example, that Cuitai is well ahead of Dingxiang, which is right below Cuitai. But it does highlight a few discrepancies: how is it that Sanxiaotun and Quanjiakou (in 4th and 9th place overall) are doing so well, while all the other northwest villages are below the median? And what happened to Huoxing and Gaoduizi in the southeast?

Notice that although there is a strong tendency for southeast villages to be doing better than northwest villages, the geographic divide does not provide an absolute indication of what the socioeconomic characteristics of Ganglong villages are in 1994. More explaining needs to be done, and this will follow in the next chapter.

CONCLUSION

This chapter represents the critical passing-of-the-wand segment of my methodological relay race. The major task of this chapter was to demonstrate the links between household well-being (as defined in Chapter Four) and village-level indicators of prosperity. The findings of this chapter—that there are indeed strong relationships between household-level and village-level measures—allow me to bring the other seventeen Ganglong villages into the comparative picture, highlight some anomalies, and set the stage for exploring the determinants of village socioeconomic status in Chapter Six.

NOTES

[1] One archival document discusses statistics and archival records in the commune. It cites the brigades "which have done good, timely work in filling in their annual reports: Xiaobaotun, Cuitai, Fuguantun, Yangcun, Wanjun, Daren, Kuihua, Quanjiakou and Huoxing." The report then goes on to mention (not by name) the problems some brigades and teams have in doing their reports:

> They do not report in a timely manner and the commune has to keep asking them for their reports. Some are irresponsible and wanton in filling in their village reports; some leaders cheat their superiors by over-reporting the amount of crops planted to get more fertilizer; some cadres think that archive document work is unimportant; others roll the documents up, wrap

them in paper and throw them wherever there's space. Then, when they need to find one, they have to unwrap piles of them which not only wastes time but leads to losses in Party work (Ganglong Document #31-4 1974:36–38).

[2] Estimates of per capita income from private business and/or private industry per village are based on information given to me on the number and type of private enterprises in each village by village officials during the village-level surveys. I set a fixed annual income for each type of enterprise based on information I have for similar enterprises covered in the household surveys. For example, in every village there are small convenience shops. For all the shops in all the villages, I set annual net income to 10,000 yuan. Certainly this may be too low or too high for some shops, but the alternative would have been to visit every entrepreneur in the township—obviously not feasible. For the private industrial enterprises, I assumed a net income of 5,000 yuan for every worker or 10,000 yuan for every partner depending on the information I had. Large-scale animal husbandry outfits are also included in these figures for private enterprise.

[3] TVs in the household survey and in the 1994 records have a correlation coefficient of only .4425. Since there were only two families without a TV in the household sample, the differences between villages are really related most closely to the number of young couples just married but still living with the husband's parents. Each set of couples in the same household had their own TV and therefore the number per household is two.

It makes sense that TVs, washing machines and fans are best related to the other measures of prosperity because they are considered the most practical items: if a family has the money, they will certainly purchase these before, say, refrigerators or motorcycles which are considered more of a luxury.

[4] The high correlations between TVs and wealth, washing machines and value of food consumed do not hold within the household survey itself, as can be seen in the correlation matrix of the main determinants of well-being in Appendix B. Because we know that village-level numbers of TVs, for example, do not correspond to household numbers, this should not be surprising.

[5] Since I asked how much land was devoted to each crop and then how much of each crop was harvested, and how much was lost to natural disaster and poor management, I believe my figures to be much more accurate than those of the village accountants.

[6] This is true even if the village-level measure for per capita income is recalculated as per-household income.

[7] Yonghe and Cuitai have village industrial incomes per household greater than 7,080 yuan and GVIOs of over 20,000 yuan per household. The next closest village for industrial income per household is Niudian with 5,800 yuan; for GVIO per household, Langwo has 18,000 yuan. These two cases will be discussed later in this chapter.

[8] I also tried using Gross Value of Industrial Output (GVIO) and Gross Value of Material Output (GVMO), both per capita and per household, as well as net industrial income in place of the per capita gross industrial income figures, but none correlated any more strongly with the important household variables. I decided on the industrial income variable because it had a high correlation with

one measure of well-being—meat consumption. However, the GVIO and GVMO variables *did* correlate strongly with household survey per capita grain output, both in correlations calculated with and without the two industrialized villages.

[9] The seemingly anomalous inverse correlation between household numbers of TVs with village data can be explained by further dividing the category of TVs into black and white TVs and color TVs. This separation shows that only the household number of *black and white* televisions is negatively correlated with the village number of consumer durables (-0.96). Higher numbers of black and white TVs indicate fewer resources to buy color TVs. Therefore, one would expect fewer numbers of other durables in these same households. In contrast, household numbers of color TVs are positively, though not significantly, correlated with village data for color TVs (.31).

[10] Selden (1985:197). Color televisions are an important indicator of prosperity, a fact noted by Ke Bingsheng (1996) in his look at regional rural inequality. Along with color TVs, Ke uses per capita income and meat consumption to give a basic look at inequality. Lu Hanlong (2000:138–139) also found that consumer durables in the urban Shanghai context were closely related to household income, occupational prestige and quality of housing.

[11] While in some localities village cadre bonuses may be linked to their rural industrial output or income (which gives them incentives to inflate industry figures), cadres in the Ganglong villages with really successful industries have constraints which lead them to underreport. Township revenues are derived in part from taxes on village industries: the more profitable a village industry, the more it is taxed. But additionally, the more profitable, the more can be siphoned off for cadre use. This institutional environment pushes cadres in villages with successful enterprises to siphon off what they can, thereby under-reporting industrial and overall village income, which in turn decreases their taxes. My hunch is that Dingxiang village income is lining the pockets of village and township cadres who actively or passively permit this to happen. The amount Dingxiang can extract is, no doubt, more than any bonus they might receive for high industrial performance. Their counterparts in villages with more modestly performing industries would be better off over-reporting industrial income and collecting potential township bonuses because there is not much/any to siphon off in their industries.

[12] Nor are the reported figures for industry reliable (see Ho 1994:225). There is a widely-recognized practice among villages with collective village rural industries to have two sets of accounting books: one for internal use and the one upon which accountant records are based. Unfortunately, I did not have access to the accounting figures for internal use. Those for external use are reportedly quite unreliable (Personal communication with Scott Rozelle, May, 1996 and Loren Brandt September, 1998).

[13] Others report that per capita income figures are often pushed upward because village cadre remuneration is tied to it. This appeared to be the case in some of the poorer villages, such as Gaoduizi.

CHAPTER 6.

BACK TO THE FUTURE: VILLAGE WELL-BEING IN THE 1990S

I N THIS CHAPTER I EXAMINE SEVERAL INTER-CONNECTED PROCESSES THAT HAVE STRUC-tured contemporary village socioeconomic inequality in Ganglong Township. Some of these processes go back decades—and perhaps even centuries. I am not suggesting that these historical determinants are the *only* important determinants of well-being in 1994; there are surely other historical and contemporary factors which may be as strong as the ones I outline and test in this chapter.[1] Having said this, however, I believe that the explanation I unfold below for why some villages are doing better than others is an important contribution to comparative development studies in rural China, providing food for thought for those interested in post-socialist transitions and socioeconomic development in particular. Key concepts from economic sociology—institutions, institutional inertia, path dependence and social and human capital—are very useful in explaining how many macro-level policies and processes are articulated, often in unexpected ways, at the grassroots level.

I contend that the three main determinants of contemporary village socioeconomic performance in Ganglong are 1) geographic location and land holdings; 2) economic activities of each village in the precollectivization years; 3) social features such as lineage structure, social and human capital. Having demonstrated in Chapter Five that the village-level account record information for consumer durables can be used as approximate measures of village and villager well-being in 1994, I now proceed to examine the relationship between village socioeconomic status in 1994 and the historical determinants (variables) using both archival evidence and statistical methods. To this end, I first lay out the determinants (independent variables) in narrative terms, and then go on to explore the statistical findings (multiple regression).

VILLAGE LOCATION IN RELATION TO THE GRAND CANAL, ROADS, RAIL AND SHIMIAO MARKET

Although the rankings of the villages doing well and doing poorly in 1994 do not fall exclusively into a northwest/southeast dichotomy, from the observations in Chapters Four and Five it is clear that the relationship between village well-being and geographic location vis-a-vis the Southern Grand Canal is very meaningful. The northwest-southeast divide is an over-arching category which may include several distinct aspects: land quality, quantity and, more importantly I believe, access to transport links and markets which made it more lucrative for southeast villagers to engage in sidelines industries—at least in the years before paved roads and bridges over the river were built. First I will address the latter, proximity to market, which I assert is a key determinant of "northwest" and "southeast" socioeconomic disparities between villages on either side of the river.

Following Skinner's (1964) theory of the traditional rural periodic market and, in particular, the importance of area residents' access to it, the closest market for most Ganglong villages was at Shimiao on the southeast side of the river.[2] In 1912, the Tianjin-Pukou railroad began full operations and included a station in Shimiao, linking the whole area to important cities such as Tianjin and Beijing to the north and Nanjing and Shanghai to the south.[3] In 1966, the former dirt road running through Jinghai was paved over and became the Beijing-Fuzhou road.[4] Anyone from the twenty-three villages of present-day Ganglong wishing to sell produce, handicrafts or other goods to the larger urban coastal areas of Tianjin, Beijing, Nanjing and Shanghai would first have to get to Shimiao. Otherwise they would have to sell their goods through middlemen in the Changxi market on the northwest side of the river.

Today, with buses, bicycles and bridges, the problem of market access would no longer seem to be a barrier. However, after one has walked through the summer muds, it becomes clear that getting to a house on the other side of the village is a challenge, never mind getting to market with a large basket, bag, cart or even tractor full of things to sell from a village farther away. Before the late 1960s, when no bridges connected the northwest villages to the southeastern ones, the problem of market access for the northwestern villages was even more serious.

The northwest villages located just across the river from Shimiao (Quanjiakou, Sanxiaotun, Sunjiazhuang) are all very small, in terms of both land and population. To make a living, many residents of these three villages operated (and in very few cases, owned) boats going from the northwest to southeast, though they may have farmed a bit as well. The people in these three villages were therefore fairly well able to access the Shimiao market by foot and boat, whereas it would take them much longer to get to the Changxi market on their own northwest side of the river over dirt or mud paths. People from other northwestern villages, on the other hand, first had to get to these three villages, pay the fare, and load themselves and any goods they wanted to sell (and/or market purchases) into the boats to cross the river. Of necessity, large carts had to take a 10 *li* detour over the only existing bridge in the area—across the border in Qing County to the west of the township. Today, a round-trip market visit to Shimiao from the furthest northwestern villages can be done by bicycle in just over an hour, whereas it took the whole day before the bridges were built.

There are precollectivization (and pre-bridge) patterns whereby southeast villagers made their living in large part from handicrafts, commerce and transport while northwest villagers depended mainly on crop agriculture. These patterns are due primarily to the difficult market and transport link access ("transaction costs" in Coase's language), and they have continued to the present. People living in those villages closest to Shimiao market were much better positioned (literally) to take advantage of market and transport proximity and could more readily network with people from other villages and localities.[5] This, in turn, might have led to further economic, social or even political opportunities.[6] Undoubtedly, this trend will become less apparent in many villages as time goes on. For now at least, the remnants of this cross-river division of labor still influence village development, through pre-collectivization human capital endowments and subsequent social capital transfers from generation to generation (to be discussed below). Thus, even though there are roads and bridges connecting the northwest villages with the Shimiao market town today, the legacy of years when movement between the northwest villages and market towns was much more inconvenient is still observable.

What evidence is there for this cross-river division of labor? Although there is no village accountant record information on economic activities other than farming until the 1960's, grain output figures for the pre-collectivization years 1949–1953 provide a hint about staple grain production. Staple grain production figures in turn may indicate subsistence production with little or no non-agricultural income. My reasoning is as follows: a village able to produce enough grain per capita to sustain its residents food-wise may be considered a primarily agriculturally-based village. The inverse is also true: in a village unable to feed its residents purely from its own crops, people must support themselves through other activities.[7]

Twelve of the Ganglong villages were able to average at least 243 jin (about 220 pounds) of grain per capita, which was the average for all villages. In the 1960's a standard consumption level of 265 jin per adult annually was set in Ganglong, though most people at the time thought one jin per day per person was an ideal amount. For the twelve villages able to produce above standard, or very close to standard, levels of grain also tended to be the largest in arable land terms. They often had more draft animals per capita, but did not necessarily have higher land/labor ratios. Another important feature these villages share is that, with three exceptions, they are all northwest villages. The people in these twelve villages found it possible to sustain themselves by grain agriculture alone at least from 1949–1953, and presumably before then. The other eleven villages could not. In terms of northwest and southeast, the villages' ability to sustain their populations with agriculture can be found in Table 6.1.

Table 6.1. Categorization of Ganglong villages by location and grain production, 1949-1953.

	Southeast	Northwest
Under-producers of grain	Baihu, Cuitai, Daren, Dingxiang, Fuguantun, Gaoduizi, Jinqiu, Xiayuan	Quanjiakou, Sanxiaotun, Sunjiazhuang
Self-sufficient in grain	Huoxing, Yonghe, Xiaobaotun	Kuihua, Langwo, Lizhuang, Lujiatun, Niudian, Panzhuangzi, Wanjun, Wuguantun, Yangcun

Note the striking similarity of this table to Table 5.6 in Chapter Five, which presents a categorization of the villages by socioeconomic ranking criteria and location. Surprisingly, the *under*-producers of staple crops in the pre-collectivization period—villages that necessarily engaged in non-staple crop economic activities in order to feed themselves, are generally those which are doing the best in 1994–1995. Conversely, those villages self-sufficient (or nearly so) in staple crop production pre-1953 tend to be those doing poorly in 1994–1995.

Further evidence of the main types of precollectivization village economic activities comes from village-level interviews, as well as conversations with village officials and residents. Table 6.2 summarizes the economic activities other than grain production in the twenty-three villages that now make up Ganglong. Ironsmithing, carpentry, oil processing, fluffing cotton, and making fireworks were reported in a few northwest villages before collectivization, but did not occupy large segments of the labor force in those villages—simply a family or two. Small-scale peddling was certainly present in all villages, but in villages shown in Table 6.2, the proportion of people engaged in peddling was reported to be substantial.

Broadly speaking, the villages more oriented toward the market in the precollectivization era—those nearer to the markets of Shimiao and Changxi—today have healthier rural industries and private commercial activities.[8] Historically, the major producers of grain were less likely to be engaged

Table 6.2. Year-round non-grain crop agricultural activities in Ganglong villages prior to collectivization.

Activity	Southeast	Northwest
Mat/hat weaving	Daren, Dingxiang	Langwo
Fishing and selling fish	Gaoduizi, Baihu	
Vegetable/ fruit production for market	Cuitai, Yonghe, Xiayuan	
Dofu and pastry making	Huoxing	
Vegetable oil processing	Jinqiu	Panzhuangzi
Transport – Boat and ox-cart	Xiayuan	Quanjiakou, Sanxiaotun
Pickled vegetables	Yonghe	
Raising and selling chickens and eggs	Dingxiang	
Construction	Baihu	
Full-time peddling	Cuitai, Daren, Fuguantun, Xiayuan, Gaoduizi	

in commerce, due primarily to transport barriers to market. Somewhere in time, certainly long before 1949, a division of labor occurred whereby villages took advantage of their comparative advantages vis-a-vis Shimiao market: the southeast chiefly concentrated on production and/or sales for market while the northwest villages generally produced staple foods. Why this outcome has persisted over time will be discussed in the next two sections on land holdings, and human and social capital.

INITIAL LAND ASSETS AND SUBSEQUENT ADJUSTMENTS

The initial post-Liberation village endowment of land (in the precollectivist years 1949–1953) is closely linked to village and villager well-being today. The more land given per capita, the more villagers were likely to engage in subsistence grain production and have less incentive—and, as we saw above, fewer opportunities—actively to participate in rural markets of the time. More land at Liberation generally means more land today. Today, higher land-labor ratios make it more likely that village residents work longer hours in agricultural work, and less likely that a village has viable rural industries. Subsequently, these villagers will be poorer—compared to residents of villages with smaller land-to-population ratios. Why villages have the differing amounts of land that they do, particularly in relation to their populations, requires a probe into history.[9]

At Land Reform, which occurred in the Ganglong villages between 1948 and 1951, land that previously had been privately owned and/or tilled by people living in a particular village was given outright to the tillers (hence the "Land-to-the-Tiller" policy).[10] The landholdings of rich peasants or landlord lands were redistributed among village residents who previously had little or no land of their own.[11] Thus, the amount of land upon which village residents worked pre-Land Reform would become the amount of land belonging to the village when collectivization policies began.

Village land was readjusted, mostly in minor ways, over the first decade of Communist rule. The most drastic changes to village landholdings occurred in 1961; at that time Qing and Jinghai counties were separated once again after the Great Leap Forward when they were combined to form a huge commune.[12] The last important land adjustment of village landholdings occurred in 1965 as Jinghai became part of Tianjin.[13] After the mid-1960s, the minor fluctuations in land per capita have been caused by either population shifts or by the use of arable land for non-agricultural purposes (e.g. schools, factories, housing).

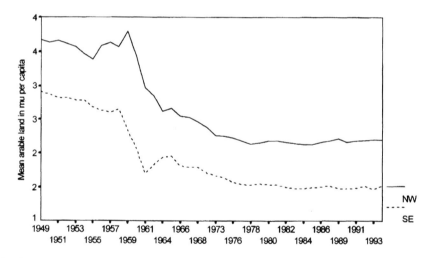

Fig. 3: Mean per capita landholdings in the northwest and southeast villages, 1949–1994.

From 1960 to 1961, Ganglong's southeast villages lost an average of over 500 mu of land each (about 82 acres) as the larger commune was broken up into smaller, more manageable communes (see Figure 3 above).[14] Particularly interesting is which specific villages lost and gained land during the first decade of Communist rule. Of the southeast villages, those that took the brunt of this land giveaway had the most land to begin with: Xiaobaotun, Fuguantun, Huoxing, Yonghe and Jinqiu lost almost 1000 mu of land each. This land was re-assigned to neighboring villages in Ganglong or villages from neighboring townships. Three of these, Huoxing, Yonghe and Xiaobaotun had been self-sufficient in grain production in pre-collectivization times by the standards introduced above. The opposite was true of the north-west villages: those which possessed the smallest landholdings initially, *lost* land in this transfer: Quanjiakou and Sanxiaotun lost over 200 mu each to neighboring villages which already had much more land, per capita. Considering that they only had 520 mu and 430 mu, respectively, to begin with in 1960, this is no small loss of land.

Thus it is that the village land adjustment policies carried out by county and/or commune leadership reinforced the more commercial tendencies of the southeastern villages. These policies forced the only three southeastern villages which formerly had been self-sufficient in staple crops to become grain-deficit villages. Consequently, they were impelled to diversify their economies in order to ensure the subsistence needs of their villagers. Similarly, two of the three northwest villages which did not have enough land to be grain self-sufficient in pre-collectivization times would now become even more dependent on non-agricultural activities. One of these villages, Quanjiakou, today has the strongest rural industries on the northwest side of the river.

In 1965 Jinghai County was placed under municipal Tianjin jurisdiction—and thus was no longer part of Hebei Province. The four brigades of Shimiao (prior to that, part of a larger commune together with the twenty-three Ganglong villages) were then promoted to the level of "town" (*zhen*). As a "town" those four brigades, at least in administrative terms, did not require all the land they had held and therefore their land was divided up among the twenty-three villages of the new Ganglong Commune, which regained an average of 200 mu each.[15] However, none of the villages which lost so much in 1961 were big land winners in the 1965 village land giveaway.

Aside from market proximity and land reallocations, another possible reason for the importance of the northwest-southeast differences among villages is that land quality differs on either side of the river. A few Ganglong residents indicated to me that they believed the land southeast of the Grand Canal to be intrinsically of better quality than that on the northwest side. All else being equal, grain yields over the forty-odd years, which might be considered an indication of land quality, can be found in Figure 4 below.[16]

In fact, up until 1955 it was actually the northwest villages that produced slightly higher grain yields than the southeast villages. This would seem to indicate that, initially at least, land quality on both sides of the river was about the same or, more conservatively speaking, that the southeast land was not significantly better than northwest land.[17] Nor did the northwest villages grow substantially more coarse grains in those days, which might mislead us into thinking that the higher yields were due to the type of crop grown.[18]

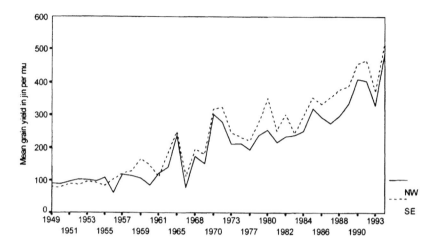

Fig. 4: Grain yields in jin per mu, 1949–1994.

The higher yields of the southeast villages beginning in the mid-1950s correspond with the increasing collectivization of village land: as collectivization, the stress on grain production, and suppression of non-farming sidelines progressed, the southeast villages began to have higher grain yields. Several interwoven reasons account for this. One is that prior to collectivization farmers in southeast villages did not always manage their land with the same care as the northwest farmers did, mainly because they had other, more important, sources of income. A work team investigating why southeast village Daren still lagged behind, even in 1965, provides one example:

> The pre-1949 [Daren] agricultural base was not very good. At that time 80% of households made brooms, baskets, sold their children and junk for their living. Although they had a few mu of land, some households hired or invited people to cultivate it. Now there are very few people over the age of 40 who know how to do all agricultural activities...people now still don't take agriculture seriously...they believe that you can't get anywhere with agriculture (*nongye mei chuxi*).[19]

Although Daren represents an extreme, most of the southeastern villages did have other more market-oriented ways to make a living before collectivization and subsequent policies stressing agricultural production. They did not stress staple crop agriculture, and generally did not have enough land to rely on agriculture, the way the northwest villages did. Once collectivization was in full swing and there was no longer a lively market system in which to sell their goods and services, the politics of the times stressed grain production. It was then that the southeast villages began to throw their energy into improving their land and agricultural skills: by the mid-1960s, there was a big push to fill in depressions in the land and use fertilizer. Because southeast villages had less land and were trying to become self-sufficient in grain—a policy advocated ardently by Mao—they were better able to fertilize and improve their relatively closer and smaller amounts of village land than the northwest villages—which by comparison had very high land-labor ratios. The northwest village land was generally much farther from the residential part of the village, and this made intensive and frequent land management difficult. With more laborers working on smaller amounts of land, southeast villagers were able to farm more intensively, irrigate better and in general manage fields more efficiently. This is an important reason for the higher grain yields on the southeast side of the Grand Canal in the commune years.[20]

Therefore, the categories "northwest" and "southeast" with respect to Ganglong village socioeconomic performance, can be best understood as proximity to market and population-to-land ratios. The most important features defining the differences between the northwest and southeast villages are the remnants the barrier the Grand Canal posed in accessing the Shimiao market and the land policy decisions which locked-in initial village agricultural or commercial orientations.

HUMAN CAPITAL AND SOCIAL CAPITAL

In the paragraphs above, I discussed geography and landholdings as determinants of village socioeconomic performance. Another widely accepted determinant of development status, human capital (e.g. education and skills), will be discussed in this section. In addition, I address the more controversial idea of social capital. Social capital and social trust (social cohesiveness or social solidarity) have been shown to be the key factors in communities and societies successful both socially and economically. In Italy, Putnam found that "the creation and destruction of social capital [is] marked by virtuous and vicious cycles." [21]

These virtuous and vicious cycles are all too conspicuous in the context of Ganglong economic development, and they have been noted—but not explained—in the rural Chinese development context in general.[22] The villages which have been able to build (or build upon existing) ways of working together for the public good generally continue to progress and improve their collective lot. Those villages which have not built, or have actually even destroyed, the ability for social cooperation can expect increasing social and economic stagnation or degeneration. Political leadership plays an important role because good village leadership is well-positioned to help build (or break) the ties of social capital and social cohesiveness.[23]

A poignant example of how village leaders can facilitate the creation and expansion of social capital is found in Cuitai and Yonghe. The Party

Secretaries of these villages sponsor annual parties at Lunar New Year in which all village natives living and working outside the village are invited to come and talk about their experiences working in industries or businesses elsewhere with those villagers still living and working in Ganglong Township. This way, new information about business and industrial practices and policies, as well as market information from outside the village and township can be exchanged and hopefully utilized right there at home. According to Cuitai's Party Secretary Wang, these information-exchange parties have been very useful. This is just one way in which an innovative and interested Party Secretary can foster village cohesiveness and enterprise by taking advantage of villager social capital.

One preliminary measure of social capital, or social cohesiveness, is whether or not there is a large proportion of any one surname in a village. Presumably the traditional ties of lineage make it more likely that same-surname people work better together because they have the greater interests of the lineage in mind.[24] Indeed, of the several joint-shareholding businesses in Ganglong, the vast majority were run by brothers, cousins, and/or nephews and their paternal uncles.[25] As has been the case for generations in Ganglong, brothers still often exchange and share agricultural tools and livestock, farming land together.

I use the word "preliminary" to describe surnames as a proxy for social cohesiveness for two important reasons. The first is that not all families with the same surname and living in the same village are guaranteed to get along with each other—or even belong to the same lineage. For example, there were two Li lineages in Baihu village, totally unrelated as far as village informants knew. Similar cases can be found in other villages. The second reason is that families with different surnames may still work quite well together, either because they are related maternally, or simply because they just get along well, as was the case of the Chen's and Wang's in Cuitai. Almost all of the villages contain maternal relatives who, though they do not share the same surname, tend to be loyal to their mother's lineage. Thus, the surname count may not accurately reflect social cohesiveness.

On the other hand, the fact that a large proportion of one surname does make a difference in a village was mentioned again and again in my stay in the township. A village leader from the majority surname is better able to mobilize more people—to pay their electric bills or dig irrigation canals— sometimes for no other reason than that he is related to a majority of the residents and can call upon personal relationships to get things done. Young Party Secretary Tan from Yonghe, for example, felt that if he had a large lineage behind him the way Party Secretary Wang from Cuitai did, he would not face such tremendous obstacles in mobilizing villagers. I repeatedly ran into examples of this in Ganglong; similar examples can be found in the archival documents. A work report from 1965 mentions some of the "problems" related to having a high proportion of one single surname in Daren:

> Ninety percent of the households are surnamed Ren . . . so the ability to criticize oneself and others is weak . . . in some matters struggle cannot even be initiated [because] they always maintain a good-natured demeanor in interpersonal relations, and thus there is no discipline among village cadres and people.[26]

So it was that the large proportion of one surname this village was a source of headaches for Ganglong Commune communist party officials, but was good for village solidarity.

The high proportion of Hao's in Niudian and their lineage solidarity was likewise credited with an especially peaceful Cultural Revolution. A former Party Secretary in Niudian who was actually denounced during the later part of the Cultural Revolution noted that

> Niudian did not get as crazy as Cuitai did during the Cultural Revolution. Because everyone was related, people even helped the landlords and rich peasants by giving them food, clothes or helping them build houses. During the Cultural Revolution people still made offerings of mantou to the ancestors (*shang gong*), though they did it secretly. I knew they did [when I was Party Secretary then], but didn't yell at or beat anyone over it [as happened in other villages].[27]

These examples further strengthen the case for the importance of a strong lineage in creating village cohesiveness, trust and collective social capital, which can potentially be used in the pursuit of village economic endeavors.[28]

Likewise, both human and social capital were embedded in the skills which accompanied market-oriented activities in the precollectivization era. Table 6.2 above identified the villages and the non-subsistence activities which were major contributors to household livelihood in the villages in pre-Liberation times. The human capital skills associated with the art of mat and basket weaving, for example, were (are) passed down from generation to generation in the same household. Along with the skills involved in basket-weaving itself, a series of other types of skills and/or knowledge geared to marketing was also taught: knowing the best season and location to market baskets, judging what prices could be obtained in each season and location, and being able to conduct market transactions using basic math skills. Marketing goods inevitably meant that a basket-peddler would meet other people selling both baskets and other goods. Sometimes a basket-weaver might decide to sell to a middleman because a sale farther away might fetch a better price. Providing information on markets and other subjects, as well as access to low cost services such as transport and short-term loans, exemplify some types of human and social capital a basket seller might have. The roles of weaver and seller might be divided up within the family, so that people who were good weavers wove while good marketers marketed. In any case, a family of weavers/marketers would have a set of experiences, market connections and skills that could be reproduced within the family with each new generation.

The human capital skills, at least, did not die with collectivization. In some cases, village-wide economic activities like basket-weaving were organized into special production units within the commune system in the early years of communism.[29] During the recovery period after the Great Leap Forward (1961–1963) the private household economy was allowed to revive for a short time, giving a new generation some experience with family-based production and marketing. Policies encouraging sidelines in the mid-1960s and then again after the death of Lin Biao in the early 1970s gave villages (and residents) with experience in commodity production opportunities to refresh and utilize their market-oriented skills, even though household production for sale was periodically forbidden.

Thus, when markets reopened on a large scale in 1978, households were allowed to decide whether to engage in private non-farm businesses and what types of business to engage in. Those villages with large segments of the population having human capital skills in commodity production and marketing were in the best position to take advantage of the emerging markets. Similarly, one legacy of the commune period is that, in some of the previously more commercial villages, these skills were coordinated into the creation and operation of brigade and/or village enterprises. These village-level collective enterprises provided the fixed assets and foundations upon which to enter the new market environment in more large-scale endeavors. While the villages which had strong precollective crop agriculture bases were in a favorable position during the commune years (in that they were always ensured ample amounts of grain, vegetables, and oil for cooking, lighting and fuel, they were at a disadvantage when preparing to engage in more market-intensive activities after Mao's death.

The few factories that existed in the northwest villages were set up by mandate from the commune or county authorities during the commune years and, in most cases, shrivelled up soon after their raw materials—originally supplied by state plan—were diverted to other enterprises. Similarly, buyers of their products were able to choose cheaper and better quality goods from closer factories. Thus we find that in the reform era, the villages which had strong experiences with commodity market production and sales before collectivization are the ones which have been able to take advantage of human and social capital—either in collective rural industry or in private business. The new institutional environment of market socialism favors these types of economic activities.

The early Communist *hukou* (residence) policies undoubtedly reinforced the original configuration of social capital. Instituted over ten years beginning in the 1950s (Cheng and Selden 1994), the *hukou* policies limited personal mobility so that people could not migrate to other areas with better opportunities, either agricultural or non-agricultural. In this way, most male villagers—along with the fabric of social and human capital into which they were tightly woven—stayed in their home villages, further perpetuating their village's vicious or virtuous cycles.[30] If "stocks of social capital, such as trust, norms, and networks, tend to be self-reinforcing and cumulative," then pegging down humans—the sources of social capital—necessarily reinforces existing social patterns, be they advantageous or harmful to socioeconomic development.[31] Initial village cohesiveness as well as specialized skills can be expected to continue and even multiply. Conversely, in those villages where initial conditions were not as harmonious, where there was little interest in education, where skills which might lift them out of poverty were lacking, there tends to be ever more "defection, distrust, shirking, exploitation, isolation, disorder, and stagnation."[32]

FACTORY ENTERPRISE ESTABLISHMENT

In Chapters Four and Five, I showed that the two villages with the strongest and most numerous village-run industries in the six-village sample tended to have the highest levels of individual and social (i.e. village) well-being).[33] If we are interested in differential development, the question of how rural industrial enterprises were and are established in the first place must be addressed.[34] Thus the following discussion takes place in two parts, corresponding to the chronological processes by which factory enterprises have been established in Ganglong. The first part hinges on factors in the precollectivization era influencing reform-period factory establishment, and the second part considers a micro-study of the how individual factories have been set up in Ganglong. Taken together, both show the interconnectedness of broader historical, social, and political processes with the specific characteristics of some villages, their residents, and leaders.

There are two basic paths for establishing a factory in Ganglong, both during the commune period and beyond: imitating an existing, nearby factory or using village social connections to build a factory of a type not found locally. Both paths hinge on social capital—for better or worse. That village leaders would not attempt to build a factory producing something novel to the area if there were no strong connections to be utilized indicates a weakness in village and leadership social capital.[35] The other explanation, however understandable, is that the village leadership would refuse to use the connections they did have out of fear of failure and the consequent problems failure would bring. This may also be seen as a leadership weakness.[36]

An old cadre from Cuitai said that the policy initiated by Liu Shaoqi in the mid-1960s to promote rural industry is what prompted that village to begin its first industrial enterprise.[37] Thus, in 1965 the first village factory in Cuitai—and indeed the first factory in the whole of what was then Ganglong Commune—was set up. Cuitai chose a metal polishing factory because there was a fairly successful one in the Shimiao market town. At the time, machinery and equipment was very scarce, so Cuitai representatives went to a scrap metal store in Tianjin to buy the parts they needed for the factory.[38]

In essence, Cuitai officials' only experience with a successful local factory at the time was the metal polishing one in the nearby Shimiao market town. The Cuitai response was to copy what seemed like a good thing. As it turns out, this copycat impulse drove much of the early industry in Ganglong Commune and continues to be an impetus for the continued pickled vegetable factory fetish today.[39] Needless to say, the result is that later copycat factories seem to falter because all nearby villages have copied the one or two success stories and the market subsequently becomes saturated.[40]

Later, however, Cuitai realized the problems caused by merely copying others and began to use its far-reaching connections to set up a metal link watch-band factory in 1972. This factory was built at the suggestion of a Cuitai native who was then working as an engineer in a factory that produced the same thing in Tianjin. Through this social connection a branch of that factory was set up in Cuitai. The large private factory in Yonghe in the early 1990s was also developed this way: the owner-manager's father-in-law used to be a marketing representative for the Yonghe village factories, and had met lots of people in that position. It was through these connections that he arranged for his son-in-law to learn and apply the skills needed to produce a specialized part for railroad operation which, reportedly, no other company in all of the Northeast makes.[41]

The two collective industries in Cuitai were set up with villager and/or village leadership initiative. While having a factory early on would seem to be a positive development upon which management and production skills could be built and expanded into other factories, this is not necessarily the case. This is particularly so if the initiative to set up factories comes from above rather than from within the village where the factory is located. Many of the factories set up in the Ganglong villages were created only because county or commune leaders felt they should have been; these same upper levels of government found inputs and marketing outlets for them. One example is the rubber-processing factory built in Lizhuang during the commune years. It went out of business because its supply of molds and rubber was centrally allocated from a factory in Southern China; as soon as the commune system fell apart, the southern factory found another customer located closer by in the South.[42]

Another example is a metal wire factory in Yonghe which went out of business because, when it was first built in 1986, the government still controlled raw material allocation of the metal this factory needed. By 1988, most raw materials had to be purchased on the free market, which meant that the leaders of this enterprise had to look for the materials they needed themselves, and could not find enough to keep themselves in operation. Social capital—including initiative, resourcefulness, far-sightedness and village cohesion—is indeed important for the creation and maintenance of a successful rural industry.

There is more evidence that social solidarity (or in this case lack of it) has consequences for economic performance. The two villages with the strongest non-agricultural "sideline" (*fuye*) enterprises in the pre-Cultural Revolution era, Panzhuangzi and Wanjun, reportedly had especially brutal experiences during the Cultural Revolution. These enterprises, a woodworking shop and iron-processing factory, were seen as "capitalist tails" and subsequently ransacked, machines and other equipment destroyed, and their leaders and managers viciously attacked (Xia 1996). This resulted in a leadership divided, fearful, and incapable of making important decisions. As one informant sees it, this is why these two villages have less than good economic performance today.[43]

One more type of social capital, or connection, which can lead to a successful factory is that which ultimately connects a village leadership with the Tianjin municipal and Jinghai County "welfare industry." "Welfare factories" are those which, because they employ at least 60% disabled workers, benefit from special privileges such as access to cheaper-than-market inputs and exemption from taxes, among other helpful policies. Only one welfare factory is allowed per village, and one township-run factory per township.[44] The two Ganglong villages with welfare industries are the two villages with the highest industrial outputs on either side of the river—Dingxiang on the southeast side, and Quanjiakou on the northwest side. My guess is that there are only so many disabled people in the area and this limits the number of newer welfare factories. Those that got there first—Dingxiang and Quanjiakou, due to either connections or far-sighted leaders—have a distinct advantage.[45]

From these cases about the origins of viable village industry, I argue that the relative success of industrial enterprises is due, in large part, to the culmination of those same virtuous and vicious cycles of human and social capital (including access to information), as well as the persistence of market orientation put into play in part by pre-bridge proximity to market, all described above. Financing for village industry in China is equally reliant on good relations with county, township, other villages, banks, and credit cooperative officials.[46] But if a factory was built with money saved up by the village, such as the new pickled vegetable factory opened in Niudian (built with 600,000 yuan from village savings), then this too shows a tremendous amount of robustness and resourcefulness on the part of existing village industry and village leadership. I believe this is most convincingly explained in terms of cumulative social and human resources.[47]

Rural collective factories provide advantages to a village socioeconomy in many ways. As discussed in Chapter Four, a thriving factory may bring in revenue to build roads and schools, to purchase agricultural machinery to service village lands, and so on. These are public goods benefiting all village residents. Rural industries in one's own village also provides the convenience of having jobs close to home and the ability to appeal to the consciences of their own officials about poor pay and working conditions at "collective" factories.[48] An additional benefit of factory work is that often workers will be sent to other locations for specialized training in machine skills or other skills needed by the factory. This has value for the factory (which gets an upgrade in human resources), the employee (who learns more, meets new people and potentially makes new and useful connections), and the village (which may also eventually benefit from the employee's new contacts).

Clearly, not all of the rural industrial enterprises in all the villages are thriving, which is why there have been so many ups and downs in the number of factories per village, particularly after 1989.[49] The villages without healthy industries have few, if any, other sources of revenue, and are therefore unable to provide public services and infrastructure. Certainly, the more profits there are, the more can be done for residents. Of course, this does not always work in practice, as the example of Dingxiang, the most profitable village in Ganglong, shows. Dingxiang could easily provide the best in agricultural services to reduce the second shift of fieldwork for villagers who have worked all day in other non-farm jobs, but it does not (or did not as of 1995). This is one reason that measures of village collective industrial income and/or productivity are not highly correlated with villager well-being.

These first three sections warrant a short summary. The initial agricultural or commercial orientation of villagers depended on the proximity to market. Subsequent strengthening and locking-in of these patterns came from Communist policies in 1950s and 1960s. Collectivization and the commune system could not easily erase human and social capital which were accumulated in the pre-collectivist era. Villages with higher concentrations of strong market skills and other human capital endowments gained from market participation in the precollectivist period and reproduced down through the institution of the family. These will be the villages with higher levels of well-being in the post-Mao reform period, whether their success comes from private business enterprise or collective economic endeavors. The advantage of collective rural industry is that, given a village leadership with a sense of responsibility toward village residents, profits from industry can be used for public works benefiting the whole village. This is not possible in villages where there is only private business.

EXPLAINING THE NORTHWEST/SOUTHEAST VILLAGE ANOMALIES

In Table 5.6 at the end of Chapter Five, I showed that although there was a distinct tendency for southeast villages to be better off and northwest villages to be worse off, a few anomalies appeared. The villages of Gaoduizi and Huoxing in the southeast were doing relatively poorly in 1994 while Quanjiakou, Sanxiaotun (and Sunjiazhuang) in the northwest were doing quite well in socioeconomic terms. In this chapter I have argued that the distance from market and pre-collectivization predilection toward either staple-crop agriculture or a diversified village economy are the main predictors of whether villages had higher levels of well-being in 1994. The fact that the northwest villages of Quanjiakou, Sanxiaotun (and Sunjiazhuang, which was on the cusp in ranking) are doing better than the other northwest villages is evidence of this fact. These villages were all right across the river (less than a kilometer away as the bird flies) from the Shimiao market town, had boats operating from there to market, and all had diversified economies prior to collectivization.

Huoxing falls just behind Quanjiakou, Sanxiaotun and Sunjiazhuang, so it is not terribly far behind. However, its poor performance in relation to the other southeast villages does warrant an explanation. The reasons are just the opposite of those helping to explain the anomalous performance of Quanjiakou, Sanxiaotun and Sunjiazhuang. In precollectivization times, Huoxing had one of the highest land/population ratios (4.83 mu per person) and one of the highest grain outputs per capita (252 jin per capita) on the southeast side of the river, both statistics which indicate a more staple-crop-based economy. It was also the second farthest from the Shimiao market. Together, all of these characteristics would predict a poorer socioeconomic status in 1994 given the discussion above.[50]

There may be another reason why Huoxing has not done so well: Huoxing was notorious for being a base for the Yiguandao Sect—a local religious sect with Daoist/Buddhist roots deemed by the Chinese Communist Party to be counter-revolutionary, mainly because the sect was sympathetic to the KMT.[51] Even in 1968, there were still 20 households in Huoxing labelled as "enemies, corrupt officials and rightists," more than in any other Ganglong village. It is altogether possible that some people (and even entire families) either were killed, run out of town, or died off—along with their skills and connections which might have made a difference in the reform period.

The story behind Gaoduizi is slightly more complicated but also hinges on the loss of initial human capital skills and natural resources. Looking at the grain output per capita figures for the 1949–1953 period, Gaoduizi had the lowest of the twenty-three villages—half as much as the next lowest village—with only 39 jin of grain per person per year. This is obviously ridiculously low and, as I suggested before, indicates that the residents in this village had other economic pursuits with which to support themselves. Additionally, Gaoduizi also had the second smallest landholdings per capita and the highest proportion of poor and lower middle peasants (89%) on the southeast side of the river. Local informants said that in fact most people in Gaoduizi used to fish, at least part time, in the Machang aquaduct which runs behind the village.[52] Reportedly, about 20% had fishing boats. In 1965, at the same time waters stopped flowing to the Grand Canal, there were no more fish to be caught. As one local historian put it,

> From 1965 to 1976 was the high time for the Maoist policy "grain is the key link" [*yi liang wei gang*, which stressed grain production over other economic activities], so even if the river had actually had water, I am afraid that no one would have dared to go fishing. In the reform period it is okay to engage in fishing for a living again, but no one had any boats anymore, and there was nowhere to fish.[53]

That Gaoduizi's residents had a difficult time reorienting themselves toward crop agriculture is reflected in Ganglong Commune work reports in the early 1960s. By the late 1960s Gaoduizi had one of the strongest grain harvests in the commune. In the other villages, handicrafts and artisanship were funnelled into cooperatives while small-scale commerce and peddling were revived periodically in the more liberal periods throughout the commune years. But fishing was gone forever for Gaoduizi villagers and there was no opportunity to rediscover their past fishing-and-marketing skills. Although they might have redirected their existing skills to other, more commercial activities, the skills associated with fishing were not as conducive to transfer as, for example, peddling a wide range of products. With no relevant skills to build upon and a twenty-some year history of concentrating on crop agriculture, Gaoduizi today has the lowest levels of well-being on the southeast side. It was in the same situation in 1949–1953, but for different reasons.

STATISTICAL EXPLORATION OF THE DETERMINANTS OF VILLAGE WELL-BEING IN 1994

The previous few sections laid out in narrative terms some propositions about some of the determinants—many historical—of well-being in the Ganglong villages. In this section I articulate these propositions in concrete terms and then test them with the available data using statistical methods.[54] Results of the regressions, descriptions of the variables used, and their correlations with each other follow. Based upon the analysis in Chapter Five, I use the aggregate number of durables per village (DURAB94) as reported in the village accountant records as my dependent variable and proxy for village and villager well-being.

Proposition One: The proximity to market in pre-bridge times (MKT-PROX65) will have a positive and significant effect on well-being in 1994 (DURAB94), and will be stronger than the distance to market in 1994 after bridges were built. As I argued above, the proximity to the Shimiao market in the time before bridges were built set up the initial institutional environment which encouraged residents of the closest villages to engage in the market).

Proposition Two: Commercial activities in the precollective era (COMMERC53) will have a positive and significant effect on well-being in 1994 (DURAB94). Substantial commercial activities in the precollectivization era indicates a store of human and social capital that has persisted over time due to 1) the reproduction of the relevant skills and networks via the family and, 2) several opportunities to revive and refresh these skills and networks during the more liberal periods throughout the commune years.

> **Corollary**: Proximity to market in the time before bridges were built (MKPROX65) will be less important for well-being (DURAB94) than presence of commercialization (COMMERC53) in precollectivization Ganglong because market proximity is a precursor to commercialization.

Proposition Three: A large proportion of one surname group (CLAN94) in a village in 1994 will have a positive and significant effect on well-being in 1994. Generally speaking, a large proportion of one surname indicates a strong sense of community and more desire to work together for the public good than a village with several unrelated lineages. In villages with a large proportion of one single surname, it will be easier to mobilize residents for public works and other tasks.

Proposition Four: High levels of grain consumption per person in the 1949–1953 precollectivization period (GRNCONSM53) will have a significant negative effect on well-being in 1994 (DURAB94). Villages with higher levels of grain consumption in the 1949–1953 period, all else being equal, are the more agriculturally-based villages, both then and in 1994. According to the explanation given above, the traditionally more agricultural villages should be losing out in the reform period.

Proposition Five: Land quality (GNYD4994) should not have a strong effect on well-being (DURAB94). If it does have an effect, however, it can be

Table 6.3. Determinants of well-being in the Ganglong villages, 1994.+

Dependent Variables>> Independent variables \/	Estimated Coefficients (T-statistic)		
	I DURAB94	II DURAB83	III DURAB94
MKTPROX65	11.18 1.75+	.55 .20	—
MKTPROX94	—	—	9.41 1.57
COMMERC53	94.72 4.45**	7.95 .91	97.02 4.48**
LAND94	.04 1.43	—	.03 1.28
LAND83	—	-.01 -.72	—
GRNCONSM53	-.82 -3.01**	.05 .39	-.85 -3.12**
POPUL94	-.01 -.11	—	-47419.30 -.01
POPUL83	—	.01 .38	—
GNYD4994	-.25 -.72	—	-.29 -.79
GNYD4983	—	-.08 -.43	—
CLAN94	69.41 3.16**	2.38 .26	74.71 3.44**
Constant	501.60	12.93	507.95
Adj. R^2	.687	-.146	.676

*signif. to the .05 level   * signif. to the .01 level

expected to be positive. Controlled for land and population, average grain yields in jin per mu (1949–1994) can be used as a measure of land quality.[55]

Table 6.3 gives the results of three regressions. Since the per household number of the five durables is the best measure of Ganglong village and villager well-being in 1994 (see Chapter Five), I built my models using the number durables as a proxy for average villager well-being. As a comparison, there are observations at two different time points, 1994 (DURAB94) and 1983 (DURAB83). I use 1983 because it was the first year durables information was available. Since my argument about well-being in Ganglong is one about change over time, the two time-point comparison is necessary to evaluate differences in well-being between the last year of the commune system and 1994.[56]

Looking first at Model I as predicted in Propositions One through Four, the effects of the large lineage (CLAN94) and all the precollectivization variables—relationship to pre-bridge proximity to market (MKTPROX65), the dummy variable representing villages with widespread year-round market-oriented activities (COMMERC53—see Table 6.2) and grain consumption per capita (GRNCONSM53)—are all quite strong.

The precollective commercial orientation had the strongest (positive) effect on well-being: villages with substantial commercial activity prior to collectivization are more likely to be better off in 1994. Similarly, the effect of precollectivization per capita grain consumption on contemporary well-being was strong and negative. This indicates that the more traditionally agricultural villages—those that produced the most grain for consumption—are less well-off today than their more commercial counterparts. Pre-bridge market proximity also had a relatively strong positive effect on well-being although, as expected, it was a bit weaker than the effect of precollective commercialization. Because the commercial orientation to market would be the result of varying distances of the villages to market, it should logically be one step back in process; these findings support such a conclusion. Lineage strength, as measured by having one large surname group representing at least 50% of village households, also had a strong, positive effect on well-being as measured in the five durables, but not washing machines.

Although the effect of average grain yield in jin per mu, 1949–1994 (GNYD4994), on well-being is very weak as I predicted, it is unexpectedly negative, going against my prediction that it should be positive. The correlation between the two variables is positive to begin with, but becomes negative when the commercialization variable is added to the regression equation. This would indicate that for the more traditionally commercialized villages, higher grain yields have a negative effect on well-being. Perhaps this points to an effeciency loss: traditionally commercial villages would do better spending their time on their comparative advantage—commerce and transport—rather than on grain production.

None of the variables tested in Model II had an effect on well-being in 1983. Contrary to the reasonable assumption that the further one moves forward in history, the weaker the historical variables, this finding is strong evidence for my overall argument that the institutions operating in the era of market reform have revitalized some important historical factors that lay dormant during the commune years. One specific conclusion these results indicate is that a formerly commercialized village does not have any advantage with respect to well-being than the other, more agricultural villages in the last year of the commune system (1983), but by 1994 they did. This is points to the idea that precollective commercialization is being rewarded in the era of market reform.[57] Similarly, villages closer to the market in pre-bridge times, villages with low grain consumption per capita in precollective times, and villages with lineages accounting for the majority of households are gaining under market reforms.

Model III, the regression which substituted market proximity in 1994 (with bridges) for pre-bridge market proximity finds that the effect of contemporary market proximity is slightly weaker, although still positive and significant. This supports the idea that the pre-bridge market proximity is the more salient factor: historical transport barriers and market access from over 30 years ago are still influencing Ganglong villages.

Results of the correlations between household-level and village-level variables in Chapter Five found that gross village income was strongly and positively correlated with household per capita food expenditures but not durables—durables were the best overall measure of village and villager well-being. Gross village income is all income from both agricultural and collective non-agricultural activities but does not take into account debt, taxes or expenses. Per capita income was not significantly correlated with any of the measures of household well-being, but I ran a regression using it because of its widespread use in gaging socioeconomic levels within and outside of China. As could be expected from the poorly (or outright incorrectly) measured and reported income variables, regressions were not very informative, and I have not included them here.

CONCLUSION

In this chapter I have laid out a story, based upon archival, ethnographic and statistical evidence, of how the twenty-three villages of Ganglong Township began, at some distant time, experienced a differentiation in primary economic activities—subsistence agricultural versus production and exchange for commodity and service markets. This division of labor was set in motion by a simple proximity to market and was quite developed by the years just prior to Communist-led collectivization. The skills, experiences and mindsets corresponding to the agriculture versus commercial lifestyles were passed down, generation to generation, and went dormant (or simply under cover) in the years when commercial activities were suppressed by Communist ideologies and institutions. Once commercial activities were officially sanctioned and encouraged in the post-Mao years, those villages and villagers with stores of human and social capital geared toward commercial activities have been the ones which have made the largest gains in well-being.

The statistical analyses conducted with available data support the conclusions from archival evidence. Comparing 1983 and 1994 levels of well-being finds that the influence of market proximity, traditions of commerce or agriculture, and a single surname group majority were highly significant determinants of well-being in 1994 but *not* in 1983. This is further evidence that the new institutions of market socialism are having a differential effect on Ganglong villages: the historical variables of market proximity and commercial tradition have become decisive after the fall of the commune, as has single surname density.

At the same time, good leadership is also a key element in village prosperity. Especially successful in Ganglong are those villages with strong lineages-cum-leadership which were and are able to foster village solidarity, a sense of the collective good and pride in one's home village. More importantly, good leaders provide public services such as plowing, good schools, paved roads and social welfare for all villagers—not just wealthy individual entrepreneurs.

Having rural industry is an incentive to be a local leader; primarily agricultural villages have little to attract good leaders and subsequently there has been a downward spiral in leadership in those agricultural villages. Similarly, talented people in villages lacking solidarity and pride have little incentive to work to improve things. So it is that vicious and virtuous cycles of development involving human capital (leadership and skills) and physical resources, sometimes set into motion decades ago, are vividly observable in today's Ganglong villages.

The importance of human and social capital to socioeconomic development is not a new idea. What is new is just how the interplay of multiple forces, many with strong historical roots, contributes to the building up of certain types of human and social capital in some villages and not others— despite distances of *as little as less than one mile*. In particular, it is ironic that communist land and residency policies—and the unintended consequences of these policies—enforced the agricultural-commercial split which would prove damaging to the very villages and villagers which were the strongest supporters of the revolution in the first place.

NOTES

[1] Particularly important is the extent and quality of village leadership educational levels and connections with the outside world of government, finance and business in both prior years and contemporary times. These are not very easy to measure—or access.

[2] By virtue of the transport links available in Shimiao and its large KMT presence (residences and administration), I believe that Shimiao qualifies as an "intermediate market town," though I did not do the in-depth research necessary to assert this with complete confidence. A local historian wrote me that "Shimiao was/is the most important market in all of Jinghai County" (Xia, 1998). The Changxi market bought and sold (and buys and sells today) more local agricultural produce and supplies; trade in industrial and/or non-local goods in Changxi had to come through Shimiao or an even more distant, larger market.

[3] Sun and Zhou (1990:161).

[4] *Jinghai juan* 1993:7.

[5] While writing this book I have reflected on the differences between my own concept of "commercialization" and Philip Huang's. Huang (1985) believes that Skinner's view of the standard market as a meeting place to exchange information was not accurate, at least for the North China Plain villages Huang studied. His main evidence came from a 70–year old informant, Li Guangzhi, from Shajing (a moderately commercialized village in Huang's categorization). Li supposedly went to market whenever he could, but did not chat with acquaintances—or anyone else and, Huang reports, neither did other Shajing residents (Huang

1985:221). Huang interviewed elder residents of another "moderately commercialized" village, Dabeiguan, and found the same thing. My interpretation of this, in light of findings in Ganglong, is that both Shajing and Dabeiguan were subsistence crop oriented villages, much like many of the northwest villages in Ganglong. Looking at the types of crops Shajing and Dabeiguan produced (Table A2 in Huang's book), it is almost certain that Li and other informants were full-time subsistence-oriented farmers. Without any "real" business—buying and selling produce, handicrafts or other commodities—*on a regular basis*, it is not surprising that Li did not stop to chat with people. The people who really benefited from the social and economic ties to the market town are those who spent much time there engaging in market-oriented activities. In comparison to them, Li was a "country bumpkin." Skinner's model was not "wrong" for North China, perhaps just wrong for some types of villages and villagers.

[6] Skinner's main task in Part I is explaining the rise of rural markets which he shows to be largely a function of population density (among other factors). While his causal chain runs from people to markets, my causal hypothesis runs in the opposite direction from markets to people: the presence of Shimiao market actually structured (and structures) local people's economic activities in that market. These are complementary theories in that they describe processes which are temporally distinct: the rise of markets is followed by a process of market-orientation towards the already-established market.

[7] As will be seen in the next section, Land Reform virtually (if not totally) limited farming to that in one's own village of residence, whereas previously a farmer could conceivable rent land anywhere he or she wanted. Thus, the grain produced in a village after Land Reform would be the only self-produced grain available—any grain beyond that would have to be bought or traded.

[8] Throughout the book, I refer to "market activities" or "market orientation," by which I mean orientation to a commodity market—i.e. producing, buying and selling consumer and/or industrial goods and cash crops rather than staple foods, land or labor (though to some extent the latter seem to accompany commodity market activity).

[9] The link between landholdings and socioeconomic performance in pre-Communist times was not necessarily the same as it is today. Relying on local informants' memories, Ganglong residents reported that, in contrast to my contemporary findings, it was the smallest Ganglong area villages in landholding terms (Quanjiakou, Sunjiazhuang, Sanxiaotun, Xiayuan) that were the poorest in pre- and early Communist times. On the other hand, some of the richest people—landlords and merchants—lived within the villages with much more land (e.g. Fuguantun, Lujiatun, Wanjun), although this does not tell us about the village as a whole. The opposite situation can be found as well: Langwo, which traditionally had a very small population but large-landholdings was quite poor, while Baihu village, which was short on landholdings, nevertheless was very wealthy.

[10] I have yet to find any source, including village elders, who are able to tell me how this worked in practical terms. For example, a peasant living in village A tilled land belonging to a landlord in village B. Did this land eventually become village A's or village B's? From what I have been told, it seems that initially, the land was

considered part of village A, but if it was not adjacent to the residential and other farming areas belonging to village A, then it would have been traded for a similar amount of land in village A.

[11] Certainly there is more to land reform than I discuss here. Land reform redistributed land from landlords and rich peasants to land-poor and landless households. The collectivization process in the 1950s then took the land out of private hands again. What is important for my purposes here, is that the *village*-level landholding adjustments in the years up to 1965 would determine how much land each *household* would get after decollectivization.

[12] But it was not until five months later that Changxi Commune was returned to Qing County (*Jinghaixian zuzhi shiliao* 1992:88).

[13] *Jinghaixian zuzhi shiliao*: 78–79.

[14] The missing years in Figure 3 for per capita landholdings are: 1963, 1969–70, 1972–75, 1988. For all of the figures in this chapter, there are years in which data are missing. Available years will either be shown on the x-axis or the missing years will be noted in an endnote such as this.

[15] In fact, twenty-two of the twenty-three Ganglong villages gained land in 1965, in amounts between 3 mu and 500 mu. Only Langwo lost any land—about 20 mu.

[16] In Figure 4, grain yields from 1949 to 1961 are calculated on the basis of sown area while those from 1964 to 1994 are calculated from harvested areas. Data missing for 1962–63, 1965, 1967, 1972, 1976, 1979, 1992.

[17] The flood in 1956 disproportionately affected the northwest harvest, accounting for the dip in northwest grain yields that year.

[18] More accurately, the northwest villages did, and still continue to, grow *slightly* higher proportions of coarse grains than southeast villages. Therefore, all else being equal, if cropping differences were important in the precollectivization period, the same type of yields should be observable throughout the 1949–1994 period. Coarse grains included any of the grains other than wheat and rice. Official figures for grain production and consumption in the Ganglong area prior to the mid-1970s include soya beans, lima beans, red (azuki) beans, mung beans, *jidou* (another kind of bean), potatoes and sweet potatoes, and all fall into the category of "coarse grains." Annual accountant records show that only 10% to 40% of grain grown before between 1961 and 1984 was fine grains.

[19] Ganglong Doc#23L, 1965.

[20] Also noteworthy is the fact that grain yields in all villages rose sharply toward the end of the 1960s through the early 1970s, after which they stagnated for almost twenty years until the late 1980s. One conclusion which might be drawn from this is that the market reforms, at least initially, had little effect upon farmer incentive. Other conclusions might be that the fertilizers and mechanization beginning in the late 1960s gave crop agriculture a growth spurt but that these technologies soon reached their limits. At commune dissolution, most of the machinery was sold and most farmers were not prepared to spend their money on good seed and chemical fertilizer (which perhaps were not widely available), so any gains from land being returned to private management were cancelled by inverted economies of scale and lack of proper inputs. For a fairly thorough discussion of the efficiency gains of the Household Responsibility System (HRS) after

commune dissolution, see Chapter Seven and the Appendix to Chapter Seven in Putterman (1993). Lin (1992) contains more positive evidence of the efficiency gains of the HRS.

[21] Putnam (1993:170).

[22] Knight and Song (1992:3). So too have others found these cycles in other non-China contexts of development and economic change (e.g. North 1990; Rona-Tas 1998:121–122).

[23] Even during the commune period, Parish and Whyte (1978:59) found that commitment and leadership problems were very much related to older, precollectivization social relations—further evidence of the longevity of vicious cycles, and by extension, virtuous cycles.

[24] Even during the mid-1970s when we might expect lineage/surname allegiances to be particularly low, Parish and Whyte (1978:58) and Wilson (1994) find a positive relationship between lineage strength and economic strength. Wilson (1994) also finds that Party Secretary lineage has a positive effect for same-lineage village households.

[25] Huang (1998) gives a thorough list of how kin and lineage ties are infused into rural industry, mostly private and shareholding enterprises. She also discusses how village leaderships, often drawn from the strongest village lineage(s) can influence the running of collective rural industry. But she but stops short of making the connection I hope to: that strong lineages were/are in a better position to set up and manage collective industries by virtue of being able to draw on kinship sentiments to work for the collective good.

[26] Ganglong Document #23L, 1965.

[27] Niudian notes, May 24, 1995.

[28] I will not pretend to ignore the seeming anomaly in the statement that Niudian showed more solidarity during the Cultural Revolution while Cuitai was divided and the findings of the previous chapters that Cuitai seems to be doing much better than Niudian in village and villager well-being.

Again, I do not claim that higher proportions of one surname in a village will lead to higher levels of well-being across the board, but I would argue that it (and/or intra-village cohesiveness of other types) is a necessary, but not sufficient condition. Moreover, at least two intervening factors are at play in these two particular cases. First, there is evidence in the archival records that most of the serious fighting in Cuitai was caused by several "sent-down youth" living in Cuitai during the Cultural Revolution (Ganglong Document #18-1 1968:5). Second, further discussion of the Cultural Revolution in Cuitai uncovered the most heated fighting was against the majority Wangs by a small—but originally very powerful—Han lineage.

[29] Ganglong Doc#1 and 1L-B.

[30] The one hope for change came in the form of brides from other villages, counties and provinces. Often the arrival of one bride would be followed by yet another from this woman's natal village, followed by another, and so on. In this way very close ties to another village could, in theory, cause significant changes in the husband's village.

[31] Putnam (1993:177).

[32] Putnam (1993:177).

33 Of course, this holds only for areas with conditions conducive to the development of rural industries, especially coastal and/or suburban areas where transport and communications links are well-developed. Rural industry is not a universal solution to the problems of inequality in other areas.

34 The issue of rural collective industrial enterprise development *after* they have been set up, particularly their performance in comparison with state-sector industry, is a much-studied topic. Sjoberg and Zhang (1998) give a review of existing literature and new evidence that Chinese rural township governments negotiate with both township and village collective enterprises on taxation and credit which allows them "soft budget constraints." Though they do not say so explicitly, these soft budget constraints are differential, presumably depending on the characteristics each enterprise—size, scope, product, importance to township revenue coffers, individual enterprise leadership, and social and political capital.

35 Actually, it may be attributed to a lack of social cohesion and pride in one's village. In Chapter Three I recounted a conversation with the Wanjun village accountant, who lamented that Wanjun was poor and had no industry. Later I found out that Wanjun was a bedroom community for Tianjin railroad workers, but that the village could not or would not take advantage of these connections. Another village official said that there are plenty of talented people but they have all left the village and are doing business elsewhere. Wanjun had a very tumultuous Land Reform: there were a few rich landlord families and reportedly more than a few very poor families in the same lineages. In Wanjun's case, Land Reform splintered the traditional ties of lineage, and created many hard feelings. Niudian on the other hand, despite the existence of very rich and very poor of the same lineage in that one village, had a very peaceful Land Reform and Cultural Revolution. (The village was in fact criticized for lacking the proper political consciousness).

36 Obviously, I am using "social connections" here in a positive sense. The type of connections I see as constructive to a village's socioeconomy could also be used for individual gain and corruption, which I am sure they sometimes are—even in the villages which seem to do much for collective well-being. This is connected to the character of the leadership and its relationship with its constituency. A totally corrupt leadership by definition does not worry about the public welfare of its citizens and does not see any obligation to them. Under these circumstances any social connections will be used for private gain. Where leaders feel that they have some obligations to their constituents (say, when the leadership is of the same lineage as a large segment of the population), social connections will, at least sometimes, be used for public gain. Baihu is a good example of the first type, while Cuitai and Niudian are good examples of the second.

37 Liu Shaoqi, a member of the Chinese Communist Party Central Committee and close colleague of Mao Zedong for years, was vilified, put under house arrest; he later died in confinement during the Cultural Revolution, ostensibly for his promotion of liberal reforms such as household contracting.

38 There is yet another theory by Skinner which complements the idea of human and social capital, particularly in the realm of imitation or diffusion. In a more recent and almost startling work, Skinner (1994) gives evidence that in contemporary China, there is a geographic diffusion of new economic, political, social

and technical activities and knowledge which operates at successive points in the market hierarchy. Adapted for use in Ganglong Township, this theory would predict that the new skills and knowledge needed for economic success in post-Mao China, will spread from nearby cities to the Shimiao market, to the nearby villages and, lastly, to those which are farther away from market centers.

[39] Chinese development since the Communists came to power has in many ways been a history of experimenting in one locality and then encouraging other areas, communes, and work units to "study" (copy) the experimental model.

[40] Watson (1992:187) also finds that rural industries which are *not* copycats tend to do better.

[41] This is one example of how commune-era social networks were used profitably in the reform-period. My example of the basket weaver/seller's social networks would seem to leave little room for use in the reform period, which is why lineage and village ties become so important as mines of social capital in the commune period and its immediate aftermath. By the 1990s, new social capital based on market interaction, factory co-workers from other villages, etc. has been built, though lineage and village ties still exist.

[42] This is also true of Panzhuangzi, which had an extremely successful factory in the late 1960s, and was seen as model for other villages to follow at the time. According to the current Party Secretary there, the reason for the factory's deterioration is that there were no more skilled leaders to manage it. If set up under the commune system, this factory could have been a training ground for other potential leaders but instead it folded. In a village like Cuitai, Daren, Dingxiang or Fuguangtun, a lack of experienced leaders is almost unimaginable: handed-down skills and experience abound.

[43] It is noteworthy that several ironsmiths still reside in Wanjun today, evidence that the commune system also fostered human capital. However, there were one or two ironsmiths in the pre-Liberation period to begin with. It would have been interesting to see whether the skills stayed in certain households or lineages, or whether the brigade-run shop was able to propagate the skills more widely.

[44] There is also a township-run "welfare" oil refining business. It is a shareholding (*gufenzhi*) enterprise with shares held by the village it is located in (Cuitai), the township and a state-run oil company. It is apparently doing very well. The manager is the younger brother of the Cuitai village Party Secretary. In a conversation with the manager, he finally openly remarked to me that it was doing well in large part because it was a "welfare" (*fuli*) enterprise.

[45] I got a little insider information about how the Dingxiang welfare factory is run. One household I surveyed in Langwo has four children, two of whom are handicapped. The son suffered an accident in the 1963 flood and as a result has limited use of his hands and feet. The oldest daughter seems to be mildly mentally handicapped, although she speaks fairly well and is able to do most of the cooking. Dingxiang representatives apparently went to all nearby villages to find handicapped people for their "welfare" factory, and hired this family's son. They also said they would give 40 yuan per month to the mentally-handicapped daughter, though she does not work there at all. They had to get special identification cards for the two kids proving that they were disabled. These identification cards are now kept at the Dingxiang factory; the parents say factory officials

bring them out whenever county or other officials visit the factory to investigate. These cards "prove" that Dingxiang has "hired" the appropriate number of disabled people. But most of the work is done by "normal" people who work there (I was also told this by a man from Baihu who works at the same factory).

The son is supposed to make 260 per month, but his mom says he is lucky if he brings home 170. Some months he does not bring home any wages because the factory supposedly has no money. The son is unable to ride a bike, so he has to walk to work and back. If the water in the river is high, which it is for half the year, he has a very long walk. For all these reasons and more, the Dingxiang factory is detested by officials and villagers of other villages. I never encountered similar malevolence toward the Quanjiakou welfare factory.

46 I was quite surprised at the amount of short and long-term loans given and received among the villages in Ganglong.

47 In the case of social capital needed to set up and run factories, former officials are in a good position because they have connections to the Communist Party. A further source of social capital not tied to lineage and native place is the army—and many village leaders were former soldiers. If they chose to use these connections (as Party Secretary Tan from Yonghe did in his ramen noodle selling to the Russians), they can be quite powerful.

48 This way village factory leaders can continue to benefit personally from rural industry while they exercise duty toward their constituents (who will not complain as much about true or imagined abuses of the system).

49 In the aftermath of the Tiananmen Incident, a retrenchment was implemented on the national level, and many rural industrial enterprises suffered greatly or collapsed altogether. On the other hand, considering the importance of the government in input procurement and marketing, perhaps Tiananmen just hastened already weakened industries to their death.

50 Jinqiu is/was farther away from Shimiao than Huoxing, but just 2 Chinese *li* from Changxi market. Jinqiu had less land and much lower figures for grain output per capita, making it less agricultural.

51 The KMT (GMD) or Nationalist Party, which ruled China from 1911 to 1949 carried out a civil war with the Communists for years and was ultimately forced to retreat to Taiwan.

52 Xia (1996); Li (1996).

53 Xia (1996).

54 It is unfortunate that I have no reliable statistical data with which I can explore the relationship between collective rural industry and clan strength. I computed two regressions with potential measures of collective industry strength, but in neither case was surname density significant.

55 I use an average for all years, 1949–1994, under the assumption that quality in earlier years and later years is different and that early land quality may be just as important to present-day well-being.

56 The arable land per village (LAND94 and LAND83) and population per village (POPUL94 and POPUL83) are the actual arable land and population figures in 1994 and 1983, respectively.

57 Here I assume that consumer durables was an equally important determinant of well-being in 1983 as it was in 1994. No doubt, as D. Gale Johnson pointed

out in a review of a draft of this section, the lack of a relationship also reflects the fact that there were simply fewer durables in 1983 (and therefore little variability in the dependent variable). Personal communication August, 2001.

CHAPTER 7.

CONCLUSION

THE WINNERS AND LOSERS IN MARKET REFORM

I N THE DEBATE ABOUT WHO IS "WINNING" UNDER RURAL MARKET REFORM, THIS STUDY provides a novel perspective in two ways. My analytic focus is on the village-as-community, whereas most studies of market transition are solely concerned with which types of individuals and households are benefiting from the new institutions of post-socialism.[1] Because of the distinct impact that village-level factors have upon village residents, I argue that as units of analysis, villages (communities) make up an extremely critical, though rarely discussed, dimension of this debate. The other, more important, point is that this question can be pushed further back in time. Transition studies are concerned with comparing who was doing well under the command economy and who is doing well in the aftermath.

And so, despite the Great Leap Forward, despite the Cultural Revolution, despite all the Communist policies aimed at leveling out differences among households and villages, almost two decades of market reforms have reversed the pro-agriculture trends of the Communist period villages by the mechanisms and processes described in Chapter Six. At the same time, it is a sad irony that the earliest villages to embrace communism are now the poorest ones, while those which had been staunchest supporters of the "Nationalist bandits" in the civil war today are able to offer more in the way of social welfare and generally higher living standards to their citizens. But how long will this tendency continue? Will villages still continue to look more they way they did on the eve of collectivization in twenty years? In fifty?

In the short run, predictions about the future of differential development in Ganglong are rather dim. The strength of this township study is that it con-

151

trols for macro-level political, social and economic variables, thereby clarifying specific processes leading to differential development. If transportation obstacles and human and social capital from fifty years ago are still influencing village development in the 1990s, there is little hope that this trend will end in the next decade or two without strong human or natural intervention.

For the long term, the institutional lag responsible for some of the village differences is likely to diminish, and this will mitigate somewhat the path dependent nature of Ganglong's development. Younger generations may find that they can learn market-rewarded skills from peers, education and other non-family sources. As people continue to look beyond village, township and provincial boundaries for information and opportunities, formerly family-centered knowledge and skills and village ways of doing things will certainly spread to other families and villages which traditionally did not have them. A full marketization of land would also speed up the process of change, though this is unlikely to occur soon. But the lessons from Ganglong also indicate that any predictions must be tempered by the possibility that emerging new institutions, policies and events (e.g. WTO entry) will trigger a new set of processes that may alter the developmental balance of the Ganglong's villages. After all, collectivization arrested commercial development for almost thirty years.

More important than the future of Ganglong is the underlying question that this study poses for larger coastal/inland differences in China. Just as there are path-dependent factors at work keeping some of the Ganglong villages from reaping the benefits of reform, many similar factors are at work in the inland regions. These include the legacy of land endowments, market orientation and subsequent human skills, transport links, commune-era policies such as the *hukou* system, and cultural differences among the peoples of different areas. If institutional lag effects have had such a profound effect on twenty-three contiguous villages in one 14–square mile township in suburban China, then it will be a very long time indeed before inland areas can catch up to the Chinese coast, even under the best of conditions. Furthermore, the findings from Ganglong Township—that local-level processes and institutions are a crucial part of the development picture—suggest that uniform national or even provincial policies are ill-equipped to offer much relief to poverty-stricken households and villages.

There are also implications beyond China's borders, especially for other post-socialist states and developing countries experimenting with market reform. Skills, experiences, and memories of the market—or lack of them—is, along with particular policies and other institutional environments, perhaps a place to begin an effort to explain the varying success of market reforms in different regions of the former Soviet Union, Eastern Europe, Vietnam and Cuba.

KINSHIP AND VILLAGE WELL-BEING

More than two decades ago, agricultural and other forms of economic deci-sion-making were returned to the household. Yet surprisingly, the village as a distinct social, economic, political and geographic entity still greatly influ-ences the individual and household well-being of its residents today. This is true mainly because of the unique village micro-geographies, specific village histories and social forces which have given rise to virtuous and vicious cycles of growth and stagnation in each village. Particularly important are village endowments of human and social capital, as well as the institutional arrange-ments, which made these types of capital fairly stable over time. At the vil-lage level, these factors are crucial to understanding village socioeconomic differences in the mid-1990s.

The role of kinship in socioeconomic development in contemporary China is one form of social capital in desperate need of further research. I draw this conclusion from my ethnographic evidence and the similar, but nonetheless striking, results of the multivariate analysis in Chapter Six: there is a strong relationship between villages having a majority of households with a single surname and current levels of village well-being. For the year prior to decollectivization, however, there is no evidence of this positive relationship between surname density and well-being. This implies that household economic independence in the era of market reforms has been matched by kinship dominance of collective industry—at least in those villages possessing both strong lineages and healthy collective industry. With respect to egalitarian distribution and social welfare within a village, kinship accounta-bility in political, social and economic affairs certainly seems to work quite effectively.

Under what circumstances will this trend strengthen or diminish with time? To what extent may these findings be generalized? Under what condi-tions does kinship tyranny rather than kinship harmony occur? Would we find similar results in areas of China where single- (or near-single) surname villages are much more common? If so, what types of mitigating factors are respon-sible for higher levels of well-being in such areas? Future research in this area will no doubt develop more sophisticated ways to assess kinship strength and determine the degree of village solidarity.

THE METHODOLOGICAL LESSONS FOR DEVELOPMENT RESEARCH

In Chapter Five I linked the household economy to village socioeconomic sta-tus. Those studying Chinese rural development and the Chinese government itself have, out of convenience and lack of a better alternative, used village per capita income to assess socioeconomic status. This book outlines some problems with linking village and personal well-being too closely, and sug-gests a new method for assessing socioeconomic well-being: conducting strategic household surveys in a few township villages and then comparing them with the village accountant records in the same township.

This method, correlating survey and village data, uncovers problems with certain types of village-level data. For example, village-level grain harvest and yield data in the post-commune years are extremely suspect when compared to household information because, without detailed household production information, village accountants can only guess. Undoubtedly, there will be other types of inconsistencies in survey and village-level data in different areas of China. Although a knowledgeable researcher can speculate about problems in village-level data, conducting household surveys to gain a fuller understanding of local conditions will take much of the guesswork out of the equation. Gathering information about the accuracy of accountant records and relevant local issues from in-depth household survey and ethnographic data is a powerful and efficient use of resources.

Researchers interested in rural Chinese living standards will benefit by employing this method of combining household-level survey data with village-level data collected by village accountants. For example, by correlating the most important household and village measures of well-being, I discovered that the village-level number consumer durables per household was an excellent and robust measure of current well-being in the Ganglong villages. Given the dubious quality of other available measures of socioeconomic status (e.g. per capita village income, per capita gross value of agricultural and industrial output, etc.), I would urge rural development researchers in China to use consumer durables as a measure of well-being instead. Better yet, those with access to household surveys should similarly test all the variables they have access to, including consumer durables, in order to determine which village-level measures in the areas they study are the most reliable.[2]

This method also provides statistical support for the ethnographic observation that per capita village income, as a measure of well-being, is very misleading. Unfortunately, these per capita income figures are often used (usually aggregated into county and provincial per capita income figures) by the Chinese government for policy making and analysis. In addition to the fact that per capita income turned out *not* to be strongly related to any measure of household well-being in this study, there is at least one other reason why village per capita income data should be used with great caution: these figures contain information upon which taxation and/or subsidies will be levied or given. Therefore these figures have a political nature and are often altered by village officials, as the Dingxiang and Cuitai Party Secretaries actually told me they themselves had done. In this sense, too, using consumer durables as a general measure of village and villager well-being is all the more attractive.

That the village accountant records have some problems is well-known. This study's contribution is to provide a method for deciding which village-level quantitative data are most reliable. These quantitative measures can then be used as yet another way to test and reformulate theories based upon ethnographic and/or archival information.

PATHS UNPURSUED

There are undoubtedly other lines of inquiry which would shed light upon the story of Ganglong's differential development laid out in Chapter Six. Since differential levels of household and village well-being are almost universally attributed to the presence—or lack—of rural industries, understanding the origins of rural industry is unquestionably one of the most underrated pieces of the differential development puzzle. In tracing some of the reasons for successful industry in Ganglong, it became clear that a more thorough investigation of the origins of a large cross-section of enterprises is necessary to make more definitive statements about the establishment of rural industries. The preliminary findings from Ganglong are a starting point for future studies of rural industry. The first place to look for rural industry origins should be precollective handicrafts, processing and commercial activities, as well as the actual individuals and families who engaged in them. Did these activities get organized by production teams or brigades during the collective period and subsequently become the infamous village-run enterprises of the post-Mao reform period? How important were kinship relations and village solidarity in the establishment and operation of collective and post-commune industries? To better understand the processes involved, in addition to studying areas where kinship/lineage ties are relatively weak, it would be very instructive to conduct studies of the link between kinship/lineage relations and village solidarity in areas where lineage relationships are traditionally much denser.

A closer investigation of village stratification during the commune period itself is another important area for future research. Such research might lead to a more generous evaluation of the commune system, the legacy of which some readers may feel I have underestimated. In fact, I do believe the legacies are far-reaching, but perhaps in different ways than expected. It was during the commune era that village landholdings were rearranged, thereby adjusting land-labor ratios in ways that profoundly impacted village economies. It was during the commune era that new agricultural techniques were popularized and differentially benefited the land-poor but labor-rich southeastern, more commercial villages. It was during the commune era that rural industries were encouraged and villagers' prior skills and experiences were developed in new ways that would serve them well in the reform period later. The village conflicts and divisions due to the Great Leap, Four-Cleanups, and Cultural Revolution also affected the ability of villages to work together for collective benefit. Closely related to the specifics of commune-era events and legacies is the question of whether, and to what extent, village leadership influenced differential government subsidies, privileges, and taxation which might have contributed to or detracted from overall villager well-being.[3]

I continue to be intrigued by the ethnographic evidence that each Ganglong village has a distinct collective identity recognized by other villages (e.g. Cuitai's reported stress on education and the claim that, historically, it possessed more scholars than surrounding villages). Cuitai residents themselves speak proudly of being a *"wenhua cun,"* a "cultural" (here, meaning "educated") village. Today, there are several Cuitai children in universities in China, Germany and Russia; no other village reported students studying abroad. Lower-middle school officials that I interviewed also commented upon Cuitai's distinctive stress on education. Other villages are known for their collective amicability (Niudian), arrogance (Dingxiang), daring private business ventures (Jinqiu), or total disregard for what others think of them (Daren).

Are these simply handed-down stereotypes with no basis in reality? Or do they represent some core aspect of each village's unique (and very collective way) of viewing and dealing with the outside world? Obviously, if substantiated, some of these village "personalities" would have more of an impact upon socioeconomic development than others. Finding ways to get at these differences and systematically document and assess them would contribute both to studies of rural culture and development research.

A FINAL NOTE FOR STUDENTS OF CHINA

The presence of these distinctive village personalities and evidence of very different socioeconomic development trajectories among the villages of a small and otherwise ordinary township brings me to a simple but profound fact discovered in this study: villages in close proximity can be quite different. It is very tempting to conclude, upon finding a certain phenomena in a North China village but not in a South China village, that these are differences between North and South (or coast vs. inland, mountain vs. plain). In fact they may be truly local differences based upon complex but subtle micro-level geographic, social, political and historical factors.

One example of this over-simplification is Freedman's (1958) influential classification of lineage types, whereby strong single-lineage villages are more prevalent in the South and several-surname villages are more common in the North. Subsequent scholars took this broad categorization and reified it. While proportionally there are more single-lineage villages in the South and they were/are economically better off than Northern counterparts, this does not mean that lineages were/are less important in all areas of the North or that single or near-single-lineage villages do not exist in the north. As the case of Ganglong demonstrates, northern lineages greatly influence villager well being. They may be important simply in different or unforeseen ways.[4]

Local and micro-level differences are often downplayed to the detriment of scholarship on rural China. If nothing else, I hope that readers of this book will begin, if they have not already, to look beyond the larger dichotomies of north-south, inland-coastal and urban-rural to explore the fascinating, complex, and important issues of inter- and intra-village dynamics.

NOTES

[1] See especially Nee (1989, 1992, 1996), Rona-Tas (1994 and 1998) and Yan 1992.

[2] In addition to household surveys, or as an alternate approach if household surveys are not feasible, I recommend a second method to combat resorting to per capita income figures. This requires asking village officials to give a brief run-down of all the private enterprises in each village in a township in order to estimate private enterprise income. The private enterprise data, merely number and type within a village, could also easily be added to the official accountant records to track ups and downs over time and be used as a gage of private commercial activity. This way, researchers would have some supplementary data with which to weigh per capita income figures.

[3] For example, Parish and Whyte (1978:59) found regressive taxation in the Guangdong villages they studied, indicating that villages with poor harvests would be penalized through taxation.

[4] See Fang (1992) for a new lineage classification and a more in-depth challenge to the notion that single-surname villages in the North are both weaker and less common than in the South.

NOTE ON METHODS AND SOURCES

THE INITIAL ARRANGEMENTS WITH MY HOST INSTITUTION, THE TIANJIN ACADEMY of Social Sciences (TASS), were that I was to be accompanied at all times in Ganglong Township by a colleague from TASS. After the first two weeks, and a day or two more five or six times throughout the year to help negotiate with the villages or County Archive, my TASS host did not accompany me at all. Within the first three months, local and TASS officials apparently decided that I was all right on my own. This left me a wonderful (and rare for a foreigner in the rural Chinese context in the 1990s) opportunity to get to know people and do household surveys unaided. In addition to utilizing household and village surveys, I collected local data from township and Jinghai County Archives, and obtained other background information from the TASS, Tianjin Municipal and Nankai University libraries. Again, the names of the villages, townships, market towns and people in this book (and the relevant document names in the References) have been changed.

Comparable township/commune records allow a detailed examination of each village's socioeconomic situation, down to the last pig, chicken, tractor, and jin of fertilizer and grain, not to mention the plethora other kinds of information for most years, 1949 to 1994. I have tried to use and present the data creatively and clearly so that it is accessible to both quantitatively- and qualitatively-oriented readers. In addition to the numeric data, the archival materials also contain some wonderful narrative information, mainly work reports, memos to superiors and proceedings of Commune Party meetings which give colorful clues to conditions in the Ganglong villages in the 1960's and 1970's.

Additional material comes from my own semi-formal interviews with village leaders in all but two of the twenty-three villages, from the 150 household questionnaires I conducted in 1995, from observations while living in one of the villages, from participation in agricultural work with villagers in several of the other villages, and from informal conversations with village and township officials, as well as the villagers themselves. I cannot stress enough how much the ethnographic element in my work has informed my use of the quantitative data. Using the almost intuitive knowledge and hunches of a field worker often allowed me to formulate hypotheses for ostensible anomalies in the numbers, which then could be explored and tested statistically. Likewise, the numbers sometimes hinted at trends and relationships I had not thought of on my own.

THE VILLAGE-LEVEL SURVEYS

During 1995, I conducted interviews with village officials from all but two of the villages (most of these were done in the weeks my TASS colleague was with me), most of them in the first month I was in Ganglong Township. These surveys, designed to give an overall view of each village, covered the basic demographics, land, agricultural and industrial situation in each village, but also included a lengthy section on village history and culture. The questions pertaining to finances or agriculture were based on the 1994 fiscal year and the 1994 harvests. While I waited all year for the opportunity to interview officials in Lujiatun and Wuguantun, there was a leadership vacuum in both villages all year, despite the efforts of the Township Party Committee to set up a village governance team of leaders. Therefore, an official visit was impossible, although I did visit both unofficially.

THE ONE HUNDRED AND FIFTY HOUSEHOLD SURVEYS

The household surveys were based on the World Bank Living Standard Measurement Survey (LSMS) developed by the World Bank and adapted for use by a team of North American social scientists and their Chinese counterparts in the State Planning Commission in 1992.[1] I later adapted the survey for my own purposes in Ganglong Township. It took between ninety minutes and five hours per household to implement, depending on how complex the household, farm and off-farm activities were, and whether the people answering the questions had a mind for the kind of details the survey elicited. I conducted the surveys in Wanjun, Niudian, and Baihu between April and June, 1995; the Langwo, Yonghe and Cuitai surveys took place between October and December, 1995. In each village, I asked about the previous year—starting from the month and day I did the interview. This avoided a sometimes-bewildering range of opinions on what "last year" was.[2]

    To set up the household surveys, I had the help of my colleague from TASS. We first cleared it with township officials, who called the villages to let them know we were coming. Proceeding one village at a time, we arranged the logistics together. I then implemented the survey on my own over a period of two or three weeks, only to start the process again in the next village afterwards. At the village, setting up the systematic random sampling of households went like this: the village accountant (usually) brought out the residency (*hukou*) booklets. Since we wanted twenty-five households in each village, we would divide the total number of households by twenty-five and count by that number to get the random sample. For instance, in Baihu there were 154 households, so we divided 154/25 = 6.2. Starting on the third household in the list, we counted every six households and wrote down the name of the household head of twenty-five households. These would be the families I would interview. Occasionally, we would have to find replacements: a family had moved, the interviewee was mute, and in one case (and one case only) there was a man who refused to be interviewed. Reportedly he was a Party Secretary who had been struggled against in the Cultural Revolution and was still very wary of speaking to foreigners.

In each village, an older villager, usually a former cadre, was assigned to arrange a time for the interview and guide me to the survey household home. Most often this "guide" would stay for the first interview to get a sense for the kinds of questions I was asking. In subsequent households, he or she would get quite bored and leave after the first few questions—which consisted rather tediously of the names, ages and other basic demographic information for each household member. Because there was at least one person in almost every household working in a non-farm job, I reimbursed the households 20 yuan per household for completing the interview with me. This helped ensure that people were home when I arrived for the interview (though there were more than a few times when no one was home and my guide had to scramble to find another household on the list). While I asked that husband, wife and adult children be at home to answer questions that applied to them, in many cases there was only the head of household or spouse there to answer for everyone.[3] In other cases, the whole extended family was there, as were neighbors, because it was a unique chance to see and talk with a foreigner in person.

I usually conducted one household survey in the morning and one in the afternoon, with the exception of market days when most people who would otherwise be home were off to market. I often stayed for lunch, if invited, particularly if the village was far from my "home" village (as was the case with Langwo, Niudian, Wanjun and Yonghe). This was another opportunity to get to chat in a non-official way. At the conclusion of the surveys in one village, I would give the village leaders 500 yuan, requesting that at least part of it go to my guide for all her or his hard work on my behalf.

ARCHIVAL WORK

The vast majority of historical evidence on Ganglong villages presented is from the Jinghai County Archives, which store an impressive set of official records for each of the townships. Township records, in turn, contain information right on down to the village, and occasionally production team level. The 1980–1994 records were still housed at the Ganglong Township government offices when I was there (they normally keep the past ten years' worth of records on hand for their own use). I copied the figures for these years by hand from township records. As a data source, these records have both advantages and drawbacks.[4] From a sociologist's point of view, the main drawback is that an analysis based on these data is constrained to the information that officials deemed worth collecting at the time. Mostly, these data reflect Communist Party preoccupations with basic demographic variables, land, labor, means of production, grain, grain consumption, etc. If a researcher were to use these records exclusively to try reflect life in Ganglong during the early fifties for example, s/he would come away with the inaccurate impression that everyone in Ganglong's villages at this time made their livings from raising grain and oil crops. In fact there was more non-grain-based private business than any researcher might ever have suspected. Therefore, I have necessarily supplemented these records with interviews and other information collected in the course of my fieldwork.

In subsequent years, village accountants collected more and more types of information for these annual records; data for the late 1970s is extraordinarily extensive. The 1980s and 1990s records reveal counts of fans, refrigerators, TVs, motorcycles, etc. in each village, which, as readers will see, makes a researcher interested in village and villager well-being quite happy. Unfortunately, for the years before the mid-1960s, not very many types of information are available. The advantage is that the same basic information for each village was systematically recorded for each year, making possible in-depth comparisons of available information.

The archival materials do have other drawbacks; information for some years is incomplete or missing. The year 1975, for example, is missing most data for several of the villages while the agricultural produce figures for a few other years is limited to either spring or fall harvests, but not both. Some of the numbers or categories on the original record sheets are not clear, inconsistencies in reporting can be found, and categories appear to change from year to year without any explanation. One example of the last problem is in the reported agricultural income. In some (but not all) years, this included forestry, animal husbandry and fishery income in addition to crop income. Often it is not clear which definition of agricultural income the accountants were using. Despite the drawbacks, however, a researcher can discover much of interest and import in local-level Chinese archives.

NOTES

1 I was part of that particular project, which was later aborted. Two of the original organizers, Paul Glewwe, formerly of the World Bank, and Loren Brandt of the University of Toronto, went on to complete the project in 1995, with a new American participant and a new Chinese counterpart—the Research Centre for the Rural Economy in the Ministry of Agriculture.

2 For surveys conducted after the fall harvest in November and December, 1995, people often spoke of that harvest (still this year to me) as "last year" (*tounian*). I imagine they were referring to the agricultural year. November, 1994, was even referred to as "the year before last" (*qiannian*) in surveys done in April, 1995.

3 While the "head of household" (*huzhu*) was in most cases male, there were at least two or three female heads of household in each village. These were households in which the eldest male had died, leaving his wife as household head, households in which the eldest male had "non-agricultural residence" (*feinongye hukou*), meaning that he belonged to a non-agricultural work unit and was therefore not considered part of the village-as-work-unit, nor was he allocated any land. For village purposes, then, his spouse is called upon to pay agricultural taxes, engage in any corvee labor, etc.

4 See Putterman (1993) for a detailed economist's assessment of such data.

CORRELATION COEFFICIENTS FOR INDICATORS OF WELL-BEING FROM HOUSEHOLD SURVEY DATA

Accountant records >>	Con-sumer dur-ables	Wash-ing mach-ines	TVs	House-hold income	House-hold expend-itures	Nonfarm income	Land value	Land per capita	House-hold wealth
Household survey ∨									
Consumer durables	1.0000								
Washing machines	.7091**	1.0000							
TVs	.6170**	.3864**	1.0000						
Household income	.3968**	.2822**	.3451**	1.0000					
Household expend-itures	.4709**	.3982**	.3491**	.4396**	1.0000				
Nonfarm income	.4597**	.3319**	.3307**	.7130**	.4491	1.0000			
Land value	.0931	.0914	-.0249	-.0179	-.0531	-.0909	1.0000		
Land per capita in mu	-.1478	-.1446	.0034	.0169	-.0006	-.1008	-.3200**	1.0000	
Household wealth	.4428**	.2470**	.1787**	.5102**	.5717**	.5142**	-.0271	-.0158	1.0000
Value of food consumed	.4499**	.3894**	.3192**	.3173**	.6051**	.3592**	.0075	.0277	.4577**

* Significant to the .05 level (2-tailed test).
** Significant to the .01 level (2-tailed test).

LIST OF VARIABLES USED IN THE REGRESSIONS

CLAN94 is a dummy variable whereby villages in which the proportion of the largest surname group is greater than 50%=1, while those with a percentage smaller than 50%=0.

COMMERC53 is a dummy variable for major commercial activities within villages in the precollectivization period. Villages where most households derived their livelihood from anything other than substitence crop agriculture=1, others=0.

MKTPROX65 is the pre-bridge distance to market for getting to the closest market—either Shimiao or Changxi—on foot or bicycle (and boat if one lived on the northwest side of the river), multiplied by negative one.

MKTPROX94 is the distance to the closest market *with* bridges today—either Shimiao or Changxi, multiplied by negative one.

DURAB94 is the average number of the five consumer durables per household—fans, TVs, washing machines, refrigerators, and motorcycles—in each village in 1994.

DURAB83 is the average number of the five consumer durables per household—fans, TVs, washing machines, refrigerators, and motorcycles—in each village in 1983.

GNYD4994 is average grain output per mu of land sown, 1949-1985 and 1986-1994 average grain output per mu of harvested land.

GRNCONSM53 is average amount of grain consumed per person in each village in the years 1949-1953.

LAND94 is the amount of village arable land in 1994.

LAND83 is the amount of village arable land in 1983. This variable is only used in the DURAB83 regression equation.

POPUL94 is village population in 1994.

POPUL83 is village population in 1983. This variable is only used in the DURAB83 regression equation.

Table C.1: Correlation coefficients for the variables used in the regressions (including the regressions in Table C.4 below).

	CLAN94	COMMERC53	DURAB83	DURAB94	GNYD4994	GNYD4983
CLAN94	1.0000	.0382	.1279	.3108	.2363	.1761
COMMERC53	.0382	1.0000	.3945	.6520**	.6279**	.5256*
DURAB83	.1279	.3945	1.0000	.2389	.3496	.2287
DURAB94	.3108	.6520**	.2389	1.0000	.4359*	.3508
GNYD4994	.2363	.6279**	.3496	.4359*	1.0000	.8931**
GNYD4983	.1761	.5256*	.2287	.3508	.8931**	1.0000
GRNCONSM53	.4932*	-.2614	-.0563	-.3203	-.2966	-.3716
LAND83	.0338	-.5490**	-.3534	-.2350	-.6914**	-.5996**
LAND94	.0400	-.5517**	-.3579	-.2259	-.6997**	-.6070**
MKTPROX65	.1476	.4652*	.2757	.5542**	.6422**	.6709**
MKTPROX94	.0904	.4165*	.2916	.4935*	.6237**	.6632**
POPUL83	.0122	-.2996	-.2290	.0256	-.3822	-.3022
POPUL94	-.0257	-.2808	-.2125	.0111	-.3825	-.3184

	GRNCONSM53	GRSINC94	LAND83	LAND94
CLAN94	.4932*	.2848	.0338	.0400
COMMERC53	-.2614	.3741	-.5490**	.5517**
DURAB83	-.0563	.1051	-.3534	-.3579
DURAB94	-.3203	.2229	-.2350	-.2259
GNYD4994	-.2966	.5806**	-.6914**	-.6997**
GNYD4983	-.3716	.3794	-.5996**	-.6070**
GRNCONSM53	1.0000	.0944	.4774*	.4689*
LAND83	.4774*	-.3086	1.0000	.9988**
LAND94	.4689*	-.3110	.9988**	1.0000
MKTPROX65	-.4172*	.2589	-.5911**	-.5942**
MKTPROX94	-.4104	.2548	-.5470**	-.5533**
POPUL83	.1985	-.2024	.8183**	.8082**
POPUL94	.2061	-.1988	.8030**	.7909**

	MKTPROX65	MKTPROX94	POPUL83	POPUL94
CLAN94	.1476	.0904	.0122	-.0257
COMMERC53	.4652*	.4165*	-.2996	-.2808
DURAB83	.2757	.2916	-.2290	-.2125
DURAB94	.5542**	.4935*	.0256	.0111
GNYD4994	.6422**	.6237**	-.3822	-.3825
GNYD4983	.6709**	.6632**	-.3022	-.3184
GRNCONSM53	-.4172*	-.4104	.1985	.2061
LAND83	-.5911**	-.5470**	.8183**	.8030**
LAND94	-.5942**	-.5533**	-.3504	.7909**
MKTPROX65	1.0000	.9787**	-.2859	-.2844
MKTPROX94	.9787**	1.0000	-.2597	-.2550
POPUL83	-.2859	-.2597	1.0000	.9947**
POPUL94	-.2844	-.2550	.9947**	1.000

REFERENCES

Abramovitz, Moses. 1995. "The Elements of Social Capability." In *Social Capability and Long-Term Economic Growth*, edited by B. H. Koo and Dwight Perkins. New York: St. Martin's Press, Inc.

Arthur, W. Brian. 1988. "Self-Reinforcing Mechanisms in Economics." In *The Economy as an Evolving Complex System*, edited by P. W. Anderson, Kenneth J. Arrow, and David Pines. Reading, MA: Addison-Wesley Publishing Co.

Arthur, W. Brian. 1989. "Competing Technologies, Increasing Returns, and Lock-in by Historical Events." *The Economic Journal* 99:116–131.

Arthur, W. Brian. 1994. *Increasing Returns and Path Dependence in the Economy*. Ann Arbor: The University of Michigan Press.

Ash, Robert F. and Y.Y. Kueh, eds. 1996. *The Chinese Economy under Deng Xiaoping*. Oxford: Oxford University Press.

Azizur, Rahman Khan and Carl Riskin. 1998. "Income and Inequality in China: Composition, Distribution and Growth of Household Income, 1988 to 1995." *The China Quarterly* 154:221–253.

Benjamin, Dwayne and Loren Brandt. 1999. "Markets and Inequality in Rural China: Parallels with the Past." *American Economic Review* 89:292–295.

Bian, Zenghui. 1986. "Tianjinshi dili yange yizhi chugao (Draft of knowledge about Tianjin's geographical changes)." In *Tianjin shi di zhishi*, vol. 1, *Tianjin diming congkan*, edited by Bian Zenghui. Tianjin: Tianjinshi diming weiyuanhui bangongshi.

Bian, Zenghui. 1987. "Tianjin shi di zhishi (Knowledge about Tianjin's history and geography)." Pp. 252 in *Tianjin diming congkan*, vol. 1, edited by C. Chen. Tianjin: Tianjinshi diming weiyuanhui bangongshi.

169

Brinton, Mary C. and Victor Nee. 1998. The New Institutionalism in Sociology. New York: The Russell Sage Foundation.

Byrd, William A. and Lin Qingsong (Ed.). 1990. *China's Rural Industry: Structure, Development and Reform.* Oxford: Oxford University Press for The World Bank.

Chai, Joseph C. H. 1996. "Consumption and Living Standards in China." In *The Chinese Economy under Deng Xiaoping,* edited by Robert F. Ash and Y. Y. Kueh. Oxford: Oxford University Press.

Chan, Anita, Richard Madsen and JonathonUnger. 1992. *Chen Village under Mao and Deng.* Berkeley: University of California Press.]

Chen, Fan. 1996. "China's Rural Property Rights System Under Reform." In *The Third Revolution in the Chinese Countryside,* edited by R. Garnaut, Shutian Guo and Guonan Ma. Cambridge: Cambridge University Press.

Chen Tong. 1995. "Zhongguo nongcun shequ gongyehua jiqi zhengce xuanze." *Nongye jingji wenti.* March:29–32.

Cheng, J.Y.S. and M.J. Zhang. 1998. "An analysis of regional differences in China and the delayed development of the Central and Western regions." *Issues & Studies* 34:35–68.

Cheng, Tiejun and Mark Selden. 1994. "The Origins and Social Consequences of China's *Hukou* System." *The China Quarterly* 1994: 644–668.

Cheng, Yuk-shing. 1996. "A Decomposition of Income Inequality of Chinese Rural Households." *China Economic Review* 7:155–167.

Christiansen, Flemming. 1992. "'Market Transition' in China: The Case of the Jiangsu Labor Market, 1978–1990." *Modern China* 18:72–93.

Christiansen, Flemming and Zhang Junzuo, eds. 1998. *Village, Inc.: Chinese Rural Society in the 1990s.* Honolulu: University of Hawai'i Press.

Coase, Ronald. 1960. "The Problem of the Social Cost." *Journal of Law and Economics,* October 1960 (3):1–44.

Cook, Sarah. 1998. "Work, Wealth, and Power in Agriculture: Do Political Connections Affect the Returns to Household Labor?" in *Zouping in Transition: The Process of Reform in Rural North China,* edited by A. G. Walder. Cambridge, MA: Harvard University Press.

Coughlin, Richard M. 1991. *Morality, Rationality, and Efficiency: New Perspectives on Socio-economics.* Armonk, N.Y.: M.E. Sharpe.

Croll, Elisabeth. 1994. *From Heaven to Earth: Images and Experiences of Development in China.* New York and London: Routledge.

Crook, Isabel and David. 1979. *Ten Mile Inn: Mass Movement in a Chinese Village.* New York: Pantheon (Random House).

Dasgupta, Partha. 1993. *An Inquiry into Well-Being and Destitution.* Oxford: Clarendon Press.

David, Paul A. 1985. "Clio and the Economics of QWERTY." *American Economic Review* 75:332–337.

Du, Runsheng with Thomas, R. Gottschang, ed. 1995. *Reform and Development in Rural China*. Translated by Winrock International, Beijing. New York: St. Martin's Press.

Eastman, Lloyd E. 1988. *Family, Fields and Ancestors: Constancy and Change in China's Social and Economic History, 1550–1949*. New York and Oxford: Oxford University Press.

Epstein, Amy. 1997. "Village Elections in China: Experimenting with Democracy." In *China's Economic Future: Challenges to U.S. Policy*, edited by The Joint Economic Committee of the Congress of the United States. Armonk, NY and London: M.E. Sharpe.

Etzioni, Amitai and Paul R. Lawrence. 1991. *Socio-Economics: Toward a New Synthesis*. Armonk, N.Y: M.E. Sharpe.

Fan, Cindy C. 1997. "Uneven Development and Beyond: Regional Development Theory in Post-Mao China." *International Journal of Urban and Rural Research* 21(4):620–639.

Fang, Qian. 1992. *A Re-interpretation of China's Rural Socialist Transformation: Lineages, Power Transfer, Village Leadership Patterns in North China*. Ph.D. Thesis, University of Pennsylvania.

Fei, Xiao Tung. *Chinese Village Close-Up*. Beijing: New World Press.

Fligstein, Neil. 1991. "The Structural Transformation of American Industry: An Institutional Account of the Causes of Diversification in the Largest Firms, 1919–1979." Pp. 311–336 in *The New Institutionalism in Organizational Analysis*, edited by W. W. Powell and P.J. DiMaggio. Chicago: University of Chicago Press.

Friedland, Roger and A.F. Robertson. 1990. *Beyond the Marketplace: Rethinking Economy and Society*. New York: Aldine de Gruyter.

Friedman, Edward, Paul G. Pickowicz, Mark Selden with Kay Ann Johnson. 1991. *Chinese Village, Socialist State*. New Haven: Yale University Press.

Ganglong gongshe bangongshi dangwei. 1949–1960. (#1) *1949–1960 nian jiben shuzi tongji pian.*

Ganglong gongshe bangongshi dangwei, Jinghaixian. 1961. (#2) *1961 nian fenpei juesuan, liangshichan [sic], gouxiao, nongyeshui tongji biao.*

Ganglong gongshe bangongshi guanwei. 1963 [sic—should be 1962]. (#3) *nian fenpei juesuan, zijin pingheng, nongzuowu chanliang, bozhong mianji, renkou tongji.*

Ganglong gongshe bangongshi guanwei. 1962. (#4) *Nongyeshui zhengshou fenpei biao jichu shuzi.*

Ganglong gongshe bangongshi guanwei. 1963. (#3L) *Teda hongshui shouzai tongji biao.*

Ganglong gongshe bangongshi dangwei, 1963. (#5) *Siqing zhengfeng, zhengshe baogao jielun.*

Ganglong gongshe bangongshi guanwei. 1963. (#6) *Jiben qingkuang, liangshi chanliang, shouyi fenpei biao.*

Ganglong gongshe bangongshi guanwei. 1963. (#7) *Nongye shuishou tongji biao.*

Ganglong gongshe bangongshi dangwei. 1964. (#8) *Shenghuo jiuji gongzuo baogao.*

Ganglong gongshe bangongshi guanwei. 1964. (#9) *Jiben qingkuang, nongzuowu chanliang xiaji fenpei, shouyi fenpei biao.*

Ganglong gongshe bangongshi dangwei. 1964. (#4L) *Siqing yundongzhong zhangmu qingli, jingji tuipei, zichan qingli, jingji bu qing tongji biao.*

Ganglong gongshe bangongshi guanwei. 1964. (#9L) *Baihu, Sanxiaotun dadui dierci renkou pucha dengjibiao.*

Ganglong gongshe bangongshi guanwei. 1964. (#12L) *Niudian, Quanjiakou dadui dierci renkou pucha dengjibiao.*

Ganglong gongshe bangongshi guanwei. 1964. (#17L) *Wanjun dadui dierci renkou pucha dengjibiao.*

Ganglong gongshe bangongshi guanwei. 1965. (#12) *Jiben qingkuang, xiaji fenpei, shouyi fenpei biao.*

Ganglong gongshe bangongshi gewei. 1965. (#23L) *Shejiao, siqing tuipei, dundian, gongzuo zongjie, baogao.*

Ganglong gongshe bangongshi guanwei. 1966. (#14) *Nongye jiben qingkuang tongji nianbao: shiji chanliang, shouyi fenpei tongji biao.*

Ganglong gongshe bangongshi guanwei. 1966. (#15) *Nongyeshui xiaji zhengshou fenpei qingce.*

Ganglong gongshe bangongshi gewei. 1967. (#16) *Nongye shengchan tongji nianbao xiaqiu bozhong mianji shichan tongji biao.*

Ganglong gongshe bangongshi gewei. 1967. (#34L) *Ge dadui nongzuowu bozhong mianji, shengxu bannian biao.*

Ganglong gongshe bangongshi dangwei. 1968. (#18) *Zhaokai geweishu dahui, pindaihui chengli, zhengdang zhengfeng, qingli zhuanan gongzuo, jianghua, yijian, zongjie.*

Ganglong gongshe bangongshi gewei. 1968. (#19) *Nongzuowu shiji chanliang, fenpei, nongyeshui tongji biao.*

Ganglong gongshe bangongshi gewei. 1968. (#38–39L) *Gedadui nongye shengchan tongji biao.*

Ganglong gongshe bangongshi gewei. 1969. (#20) *Nongye shengchan jihua, chanliang fenpei, nongyeshui tongji biao.*

Ganglong gongshe bangongshi gewei. 1969. (#42L) *Kaimen waifeng, nongye shengchan, duidi douzheng, yao shou baowei, da pipan, xin?anjian, bao-gaoyijian*

Ganglong gongshe bangongshi gewei. 1970. (#21) *Nongzuowu shichan, shouyi fenpei tongjibiao.*

Ganglong gongshe bangongshi gewei/dangwei. 1971. (#23) *Jianli gongshe dangwei, nongye shengchan, jihua shengyu, youfu xinfang qingshi, tongzhi, baogao, gui(??)*

Ganglong gongshe bangongshi gewei. 1971. (#24) *Nianbao, bozhong mian-ji, shichan, shouyi fenpei, nongyeshui jishu tiaozheng, tongji biao.*

Ganglong gongshe bangongshi gewei. 1972. (#26) *Shouyi fenpei huizong biao.*

Ganglong gongshe bangongshi gewei. 1972. (#27) *Nongyeshui biao.*

Ganglong gongshe bangongshi dangwei, gewei. 1972. (#50L) *Nongye, shuili, gongzuo baogao, zongjie, tiaozi tongzhi.*

Ganglong gongshe ge dadui. 1972. (#52L) *Fuye, tifang, qingcha, quanmin da zongjie.*

Ganglong gongshe bangongshi gewei/dangwei. 1973. (#28) *Zhaokai shuang quan hui, guanche xian pin dai hui, pixiu zhengfeng baogao yijian.*

Ganglong gongshe bangongshi gewei. 1973. (#29) *Bozhong mianji, chan-liang, shouyi fenpei tongji biao.*

Ganglong gongshe bangongshi dangwei. 1973. (#54L) *Nongye, caiwu, weisheng, jihua shengyu, zhiqing gongzuo, zongjie, baogao, tongji.*

Ganglong gongshe bangongshi gewei. 1973. (#55L) *Ganbu zhengce luoshi qingkuang tongjibiao.*

Ganglong gongshe bangongshi gewei. 1973. (#57L) *Ge dadui bozhong mian-ji, shouzai mianji, da shengxu tongjibiao.*

Ganglong gongshe bangongshi gewei/dangwei. 1974. (#31) *Kaizhan quan-min da zongjie, pilin pikong, nongye shengchan guihua, kuaiji xuexiban baogao.*

Ganglong gongshe bangongshi gewei. 1974. (#32) *Nongye shengchan nian-bao, chanliang.*

Ganglong gongshe bangongshi gewei. 1975. (#35) *Shouyi fenpei, zijin pingheng tongji biao.*

Ganglong gongshe bangongshi gewei. 1975. (#62L) *Nongye shengchan, caiwu guanli, hezuo yiliao, jihua shengyu, tongzhi, zongjie, banfa, xianjin jiti, xianjin geren, huaming biao.*

Ganglong gongshe bangongshi gewei. 1975. (#63–64L) *Gedadui nongye shengchan tongji nianbaobiao.*

Ganglong gongshe bangongshi gewei. 1975. (#65–66L) *Gedadui nongzuowu shichan biao.*

Ganglong gongshe bangongshi gewei. 1975. (#67L) *Nongcun jingji dianxing diaocha, qiudong bozhong mianji biao.*

Ganglong gongshe bangongshi gewei. 1976. (#36) *Nongyeshui biao.*

Ganglong gongshe bangongshi gewei. 1976. (#37) *Nongye shengchan tongji nianbao biao.*

Ganglong gongshe bangongshi gewei. 1976. (#70L) *Zhenzai jiben qingkuang diaochabiao.*

Ganglong gongshe bangongshi gewei. 1976. (#71L) *Gedadui shouyi fenpei tongji nianbaobiao.*

Ganglong gongshe bangongshi gewei. 1977. (#40) *Nongye shengchan tongji nianbao, guding caichan tongji biao.*

Ganglong gongshe bangongshi gewei. 1977. (#41) *Xianjin shouyi fenpei. Zijin pingheng tongji biao.*

Ganglong gongshe bangongshi dangwei. 1978. (#43) *Zhaokai disijie dangdaihui tongzhi, minge fenpei, yicheng, kaimuci, baogao, houxuanren mingdan, jueyi, fayan, bimuci, daibiao mingdan.*

Ganglong gongshe bangongshi gewei. 1977. (#76L) *Ge dadui, fuyechang shezhi danwei, xianjin shouyi fenpei, zijin pingheng tongjibiao.*

Ganglong gongshe bangongshi gewei. 1978. (#45) *Nongye shengchan tongji nianbao biao, quannian shichan tongji biao.*

Ganglong gongshe bangongshi gewei. 1978. (#46) *Shouyi fenpei, zijin pingheng huizong biao.*

Ganglong gongshe bangongshi gewei. 1978. (#80L) *Shehui ziying bufen quannian nongzuowu shichanbiao.*

Ganglong gongshe bangongshi dangwei. 1978. (#44) *Zhaokai xue dazhai huiyi chengxu, kaimuci, baogao, fayan, juexinshu, bimuci, biaozhang mindan.*

Ganglong gongshe bangongshi gewei. 1979. (#48) *Nongye shengchan tongji nianbao, quannian nongzuowu shichan tongji biao.*

Ganglong gongshe bangongshi dangwei, gewei. 1979. (#84L) *Zhaokai qing fengshou biaomo dahui, kaimu ci, jianghua, fayan, laomo mingdan, bimuci.*

Ganglong gongshe bangongshi gewei. 1979. (#50) *Xianjin shouyi fenpei, zijin pingheng, huizongbiao.*

Ganglong gongshe bangongshi gewei. 1979. (#51) *Nongyeshui biao, queliangdui diaocha biao.*

Ganglong gongshe bangongshi gewei. 1979. (#91L) *Ge dadui xianjin shouyi fenpei, zijin pingheng huizong biao.*

Ganglong gongshe bangongshi dangwei. 1980. (#52) *Zhaokai ganbu hui, jingying guanli gongzuo bao.*

Ganglong gongshe bangongshi gewei. 1980. (#54) *Zhaokai sanjie yici rendaihui pi fu, yubeihui chengxu, yicheng, kaimuci, baogao, ti'an jueyi, bimuci.*

Ganglong gongshe bangongshi guanwei. 1980. (#56) *Nongye jiben qingkuang tongji nianbao biao, xiaqiu shichan tongji biao.*

Ganglong gongshe bangongshi guanwei. 1980. (#57) *Xianjin shouyi fenpei shenpi biao.*

Ganglong gongshe bangongshi guanwei. 1980. (#58) *Nongyeshui biao, nongyeshui jichu shuzi bianhua shebao biao.*

Gao, Yutong, ed. 1929. *Jinghai xianzhi.*

Gilley, Bruce. 2001. *Model Rebels: The Rise and Fall of China's Richest Village.* Berkeley: UC Press.

Gore, Lance L. P. 1999. "The Communist Legacy in Post-Mao Economic Growth." *The China Journal* January 1999:25–54.

Granovetter, Mark. 1990. "The Old and the New Economic Sociology: A History and Agenda." Pp. 89–112 in *Beyond the Marketplace: Rethinking Economy and Society,* edited by Roger Friedland and A.F. Robertson. New York: Aldine de Gruyter.

Granovetter, Mark and Richard Swedburg. 1992. *The Sociology of Economic Life.* Boulder: Westview Press.

Griffin, Keith and Zhao Renwei. 1993. *The Distribution of Income in China.* Houndmills and London: St. Martin's Press, Inc.

Guo, Rongxing. 1999. "The Spatial Division of the Chinese Economy." In *How the Chinese Economy Works.* New York: St. Martin's Press, Inc.

Guo, Wenjing. 1989. *Tianjin gudai chengshi fazhan shi.* Tianjin: Tianjin guji chubanshe.

Guojia tongjiju nongcun shehui jingji diaocha zongdui. 1996. *Zhongguo nongcun tongji nian jian.* Beijing: Zhongguo tongji chubanshe.

Guojia tongjiju nongcun shehui jingji diaocha zongdui. 1995. *Zhongguo nongcun tongji nian jian.* Beijing: Zhongguo tongji chubanshe.

Hartford, Kathleen. 1985. "Socialist Agriculture is Dead; Long Live Socialist Agriculture! Organizational Transformations in Rural China." Pp. 31–61 in *The Political Economy of Reform in Post-Mao China,* edited by E. J. Perry and C. Wong. Cambridge, MA: The Council on East Asian Studies at Harvard University.

Hebeisheng dizhengting. 1934. *Hebeisheng gexian gaikuang yilan.*

Hebeisheng zhengfu shiyeting shichachu. 1931. *Hebeisheng gongshang tongji.*

Hebeisheng jiansheting. 1928. *Hebeisheng zhengfu jiansheting diaocha baogao, Volumes 1, 3, 4.*

176

References

Hebeisheng renmin zhengfu. 1995. *Hebei jingji tongji nianjian.* Beijing: Zhongguo tongji chubanshe.

Hebeisheng renmin zhengfu, ed. 1996. *Hebei jingji nianjian.* Beijing: Zhongguo tongji chubanshe.

Hebeisheng zhengxie wenshi ziliao yanjiu weiyuan hui, Hebeisheng difangzhi bianzuan weiyuanhui. 1986. *Hebei jindai dashiji.* Shijiazhuang: Hebei renmin chubanshe.

Hedstrom, Peter and Richard Swedberg, eds. 1998. *Social Mechanisms: An Analytical Approach to Social Theory.* Cambridge: Cambridge University Press.

Hinton, William. 1966. *Fanshen: A Documentary of Revolution in a Chinese Village.* New York: Alfred A. Knopf, Inc.

Ho, Samuel P.S. 1994. *Rural China in Transition: Non-agricultural Development in Rural Jiangsu, 1978–1990.* Oxford: Oxford University Press.

Hsiao, Kung-ch'uan. 1960. *Rural China: Imperial Control in the Nineteenth Century.* Seattle: University of Washington Press.

Hu Biliang and Hu Shunyan. 1996. *Zhongguo xiangcun de qiye zuzhi yu shequ fazhan: Hubeisheng Hanchuanxian Duanxiacun diaocha* (Enterprise Organization and Community Development in Rural China: Survey Report of Duanjia Village, Hubei Province). Edited by Chen Jiyuan and C. Herrmann-Pillath. Taiyuan: Shanxi jingji chubanshe.

Huang, Philip C.C. 1985. *The Peasant Economy and Social Change in North China.* Stanford, California: Stanford University Press.

Huang, Xiyi. 1998. "Two-way Changes—Kinship in Contemporary Rural China" in Christiansen, Flemming and Zhang Junzuo, eds. *Village, Inc.: Chinese Rural Society in the 1990s.* Honolulu: University of Hawai'i Press.

Jang, Soo Hyun. 1998. *Chinese Peasants on the Wheels of Change: Rural Reform and Its Impact in a Tianjin Village.* Doctoral dissertation Thesis, Anthropology, University of Illinois at Champaign-Urbana, Urbana, Illinois.

Jian, T.L., J.D. Sachs and A.M. Warner. 1996. "Trends in Regional Inequality in China." China Economic Review, V7 N1:1–21.

Jiang, Jing. 1987. "Tianjin dongcai shihua." *Jinghai wenshi ziliao* 1:69–71.

Jing, Jun. 1996. *The Temple of Memories: History, Power, and Morality in a Chinese Village.* Stanford: Stanford University Press.

Jicha zhengwu weiyuanhui 1936–1937. "Hebei gexian jinsan niandu geye zuofang tongji." *Jicha diaocha tongji congkan,* pp. 41–51.

Jinghai, xianzhengfu and Tianjin shekeyuan "Jinghai shihua" bianxie zu. 1989. *Jinghai shi hua.* Tianjin: Tianjin guji chubanshe.

Jinghai juan bianji weiyuanhui, eds. 1993. *Jinghai juan. Zhongguo guoqing congshu: baixianshi jingji shehui diaocha.* Beijing: Zhongguo dabaike quanshu chubanshe.

Jinghaixian nongye hezuohuashi bianxie bangongshi. 1988. *Jinghaixian nongye hezuohua shiliao.* Jinghai: Jinghaixian nongye hezuohua shiliao.

Johnston, M. Francis. 1999. "Beyond Regional Analysis: Manufacturing Zones, Urban Employment and Spatial Inequality in China." *The China Quarterly* 157:1–21.

Ke, Bingsheng. 1996. "Regional Inequality in Rural Development." Pp. 245–264 in *The Third Revolution in the Chinese Countryside*, edited by R. Garnaut, Guo Shutian and Ma Guonan. Cambridge: Cambridge University Press.

Kelliher, Daniel. 1992. *Peasant Power in China: The Era of Rural Reform, 1979–1989.* New Haven and London: Yale University Press.

Khan, Azizur Rahman. 1993. "The Determinants of Household Income in Rural China." Pp. 95–115 in *The Distribution of Income in China*, edited by K.Griffin and Zhao Renwei. Houndmills and London: St. Martin's Press, Inc.

Khan, Azizur Rahman and Carl Riskin.1998. "Income and Inequality in China: Composition, Distribution and Growth of Household Income, 1988–1995." *The China Quarterly* 154:221–253.

———. 2001. *Inequality and Poverty in China in the Age of Globalization.* Cambridge: Oxford University Press.

Khan, Azizur Rahman, Keith Griffin, Carl Riskin and Zhao Renwei. 1993. "Sources of income inequality in post-reform China." *China Economic Review* 4:19–35.

Knight, John. 1992. "Price Scissors and Intersectoral Resource Transfers: Who Paid for Industrialization in China?" Oxford University Institute of Economics and Statistics Applied Economics Discussion Paper Series.

Knight, John and Lina Song. 1992. "Income Inequality in Rural China: Communities, Households and Resource Mobility." Working paper for Institute of Applied Economics, University of Oxford.

Knight, John and Lina Song. 1993. "Workers in China's rural industries." Pp. 174–215 in *The Distribution of Income in China*, edited by Keith Griffin and Zhao Renwei. Houndmills and London: St. Martin's Press, Inc.

Koo, Bon Ho and Dwight H. Perkins, eds. 1995. *Social Capability and Long-Term Economic Growth.* New York: St. Martin's Press, Inc.

Kueh, Y. Y. 1995. *Agricultural Instability in China, 1931–1991: Weather, Technology and Institutions.* Oxford: Oxford University Press.

Lardy, Nicholas. 1985. "State Intervention and Peasant Opportunities." In *Chinese Rural Development: The Great Transformation.* William Parish, ed. Armonk, NY, M.E. Sharpe: 33–56.

Lavely, William. 1991. "Marriage and Mobility under Rural Collectivism" in *Marriage and Inequality in Chinese Society*. Rubie S. Watson and Patricia Buckley Ebrey, eds. Berkeley: University of California Press.

Li, Enyin. 1987a. "Jinghaixian cunzhen mingcheng suyuan." *Jinghai wenshi ziliao* 2:132–144.

Li, Enyin. 1987b. "Jinghai diyu yange jianshu." *Jinghai wenshi ziliao* 1:1–4.

Li, Xiujun. 1996. Personal Letter.

Lin, Justin Yifu. 1992. "Rural Reforms and Agricultural Growth in China." *American Economic Review* 82: 34–51.

———. 1990. "Collectivization and China's Agricultural Crisis in 1959–1961." *Journal of Political Economy* 98:1228–52.

Linge, Godfrey, ed. 1997. *China's New Spacial Economy*. Hongkong and Oxford: Oxford University Press.

Linge, Godfrey and D. K. Forbes, eds. 1990. *China's Spacial Economy: Recent Developments and Reforms."* Hongkong and Oxford: Oxford University Press.

Lu, Hanlong. 2000. "To Be Relatively Comfortale in an Egalitarian Society." *In The Consumer Revolution in Urban China*, edited by Deborah S. Davis. Berkeley: University of California Press.

Lu, Xueyi and Huang Ping. 1995. "Cujin nongcun jingji shehui xietiao fazhan." *Nongye jingji wenti,* January, 1995:25–32.

Luong, Hy Van. and Jonathon Unger. 1998. "Wealth, Power, and Poverty in the Transition to Market Economies: The Process of Socio-Economic Differentiation in Rural China and Northern Vietnam." *The China Journal* 40 (July): 61–93.

Lyons, Thomas P. and Victor Nee. 1994. *The Economic Transformation of South China: Reform and Development in the Post-Mao Era*. Ithaca: Cornell East Asia Program.

Ma, Guonan. 1994. "Income Distribution in the 1980s." In *China's Quiet Revolution: New Interactions Between State and Society*, edited by David S. G. Goodman and Beverley Hooper. New York: St. Martin's Press, Inc.

Ma, Rong. 1994. "Xizang jumin shouru, xiaofeizhong de chengxiang chayi." In *Zhongguo bianyuan diqu kaifa yanjiu*, edited by Pan Naigu and Ma Rong. Hongkong: Oxford University Press.

Marglin, F.A and S.A. Marglin. 1990. *Dominating Knowledge: Development, Culture and Resistance.* Oxford: Clarendon Press.

Mckinley Terry. 1996. *The Distribution of Wealth in Rural China*, Edited by M. Selden. New York and London: M.E. Sharpe.

Nee, Victor. 1989. A Theory of Market Transition: From Redistribution to Markets in State Socialism." *American Sociological Review* 54(1989):663–681.

———. 1991. "Social Inequalities in Reforming State Socialism: Between Redistribution and Markets in China." *American Sociological Review* 56:267–282.

———. 1996. "The Emergence of a Market Society: Changing Mechanisms of Stratification in China." *American Journal of Sociology* 101:908–49.

———. 1998. "Sources of the New Institutionalism." Pp. 1–16 in *The New Institutionalism in Sociology*, edited by M. C. Brinton and Victor Nee. New York: The Russell Sage Foundation.

Nee, Victor and Paul Ingram. 1998. "Embeddedness and Beyond: Institutions, Exchange, and Social Structure." Pp. 19–45 in *The New Institutionalism in Sociology*, edited by M. Brinton and V. Nee. New York: The Russell Sage Foundation.

Nee, Victor and Su Sijin. 1990. "Institutional Change and Economic Growth in China: The View from the Villages." *Journal of Asian Studies* 49:3–25.

Nelson, Richard R. and Sidney Winter. 1982. *An Evolutionary Theory of Economic Change.* Cambridge, MA and London, UK: The Belknap Press of Harvard University Press.

Nongyebu nongye zhengce yanjiuhui (Ed.). 1992. *Zhongguo nongye wenti yanjiu.* Beijing: Nongye chubanshe.

North, Douglass C. 1990. *Institutions, Institutional Change and Economic Performance.* Cambridge: Press Syndicate of the University of Cambridge.

———. 1998. "Economic Performance Through Time." Pp. 247–257 in *The New Institutionalism in Sociology*, edited by M. Brinton and V. Nee. New York: The Russell Sage Foundation.

Oberschall, Anthony. 1996. "The Great Transition: China, Hungary and Sociology Exit Socialism into the Market." *American Journal of Sociology* 101:1028–1041.

Oi, Jean. 1989. *State and Peasant in Contemporary China: The Political Economy of Village Government.* Berkeley: University of California Press.

———. 1992. "Fiscal Reform and the Economic Foundations of Local State Corporatism." *World Politics* 45:99–126.

———. 1999. *Rural China takes off : institutional foundations of economic reform.* Berkeley: University of California Press.

Paine, S. 1981. "Spacial aspects of Chinese development: issues, outcomes and policies, 1949–1979." *Journal of Development Studies* 17:133–195.

Pan, Naigu and Ma, Rong. 1994. *Zhongguo bianyuan diqu kaifa yanjiu.* Hongkong: Oxford University Press.

Parish, William. 1985. *Chinese Rural Development: The Great Transformation. .* Armonk, NY: M.E. Sharpe, Inc.

———. 1994. "Rural Industrialization in Fujian and Taiwan" in *The Economic*

Transformation of South China: Reform and Development in the Post-Mao Era, edited by T. Lyons and V. Nee. Ithaca: Cornell East Asia Program.

Parish, William L. and Ethan Michelson. 1996. "Politics and Markets: Dual Transformations." *American Journal of Sociology* 101:1042–1059.

Parish, William L. and Martin King Whyte. 1978. *Village and Family Life in Contemporary China*. Chicago and London: The University of Chicago Press.

Parish, William L., Xiaoye Zhe and Fang Li. 1995. "Nonfarm Work and the Marketization of the Chinese Countryside." *The China Quarterly* 1995:697–730.

Pei, Xiaolin. 1998. "Townshi-Village Enterprises, Local Governments, and Rural Communities: The Chinese Village as Firm during Economic Transition." In *Cooperative and Collective in China's Rural Development*, edited by E. B. Vermeer, Frank N, Pieke and Woei Lien Chong. Armonk, NY: M.E. Sharpe.

Perkins, Tamara. 1999. PhD dissertation, University of California, San Diego. Back to the Future: Well-Being in a Rural Tianjin Township.

———. 1997. "Early Communist Policy, Path Dependence and Village Development." Unpublished paper presented on March 16, 1997, at the Association of Asian Studies Annual Conference in Chicago, Illinois.

Pennarz, Johanna. 1998. "Adaptive Land-Use Strategies of Sichuan Smallholders—Subsistence Production and Agricultural Intensification in a Land-Scarce Poverty Area of China." In Christiansen, Flemming and Zhang Junzuo, eds. *Village, Inc.: Chinese Rural Society in the 1990s*. Honolulu: University of Hawai'i Press.

Potter, Sulamith Heins and Jack M. Potter. 1990. *China's Peasants : The Anthropology of a Revolution*. Cambridge [England] and New York : Cambridge University Press.

Powell, Walther W. and Paul J. DiMaggio. 1991. *The New Institutionalism in Organizational Analysis*. Chicago: University of Chicago Press.

Prosterman, Roy, Tim Hanstad and Li Ping. 1998. "Large-scale Farming in China: An Appropriate Policy?" *Journal of Contemporary Asia* 28:74–102.

Putnam, Robert D. 1993. *Making Democracy Work: Civic traditions in Modern Italy*. Princeton: Princeton University Press.

Putterman, Louis. 1993. *Continuity and Change in China's Rural Development*. New York, Oxford: Oxford University Press.

Quarnstrom, Glenda Liu. 1994. *The Political Economy of Rural Reform in Post-Mao China*. Doctoral Dissertation: University of Hawaii.

Ravallion, Martin and Chen Shaohua. 1999. "When Economic Reform is Faster then [sic] Statistical Reform: Measuring and Explaining Income

Inequality in Rural China." *Oxford Bulletin of Economics and Statistics* 61:33–56.

Riskin, Carl. 1991 (1987). *China's Political Economy: The Quest for Development Since 1949.* Oxford: Oxford University Press.

———. 1993. "Income distribution and poverty in China." Pp. 135–170 in *The Distribution of Income in China,* edited by K.Griffin and Zhao Renwei. Houndmills and London: St. Martin's Press.

———. 1996a. "Rural Poverty in Post-Reform China" in *The Third Revolution in the Chinese Countryside,* edited by R. Garnaut, Guo Shutian and Ma Guonan. Cambridge: Cambridge University Press.

———. 1996b. "Social Development, Quality of Life and the Environment" in *Crisis and Reform in China,* edited by E. Bliney. Commack, NY: Nova Science Publishers, Inc.

Rizzello, Salvatore. 1997. "The Microfoundations of Path Dependency." Pp. 98–118 in *Evolutionary Economics and Path Dependence,* edited by L. Magnusson. Cheltenham, UK: Edward Elgar.

Rodwin, Lloyd. 1994. "Rethinking the Development Experience: Aims, Themes and Theses" in *Rethinking the Development Experience: Essays Provoked by the Work of Albert O. Hirschman,* edited by L. Rodwin. Washington, D.C. and Cambridge: The Brookings Institution and The Lincoln Institute of Land Policy.

Rona-Tas, Akos. 1998. "Path Dependence and Capital Theory: Sociology of the Post-Communist Economic Transformation." *East European Politics and Societies* 12:107–131.

———. 1994. "The First Shall Be Last? Entrepreneurship and Communist Cadres in the Transition from Socialism." *American Journal of Sociology* 100:40–69.

Rozelle, Scott. 1996. "Stagnation without Equity: Patterns of Growth and Inequality in China's Rural Economy." *China Journal* 35:63–96.

———. 1994. "Decision-Making in China's Rural Economy: The Linkages Between Village Leaders and Farm Households." *China Quarterly* 1994:362–391.

———. 1994a. "Rural Industrialization and Increasing Inequality: Emerging Patterns in China's Reforming Economy." *Journal of Comparative Economics* 19:362–391.

Rozelle, Scott and Richard N. Boisvert. 1994. "Quantifying Chinese Village Leaders' Multiple Objectives." *Journal of Comparative Economics* 18:25–45.

Rozelle, Scott, Lily Tsai, Minggao Shen and Hongbin Li. 1997. "Market Emergence and Leader-Manager Contracts in China's Village Enterprises." Paper presented at the 1997 Annual Meetings of the Association of Asian Studies. Chicago, IL, March 13–16.

Ruf, Gregory Anthony. 1994. *Pillars of the State: Laboring Families, Authority and Community in Rural sichuan, 1937–1991.* Ph.D. Thesis, Columbia University.

Schelling, Thomas C. 1998. "Social Mechanisms and Social Dynamics." In *Social Mechanisms: An Analytical Approach to Social Theory,* edited by Peter Hedstrom and Richard Swedberg. Cambridge: Cambridge University Press.

Schoppa, R. Keith. 1992. "Contours of Revolutionary Change in a Chinese County, 1900–1950." *The Journal of Asian Studies* 51:770–795.

Selden, Mark. 1985. "Income Inequality and the State" in *Chinese Rural Development: The Great Transformation,* edited by W. Parish. Armonk, NY: M.E. Sharpe.

———. 1993. *The Political Economy of Chinese Development.* Armonk and London: M.E. Sharpe.

Shiyebu zhongguo jingji nianjian bianji weiyuanhui. 1936(?). *Zhongguo jingji nianjian, liuce, nongyepian.* Shangwu yinshuguan chubanshe.

Shuili shuidian kexue yanjiuyuan. 1981. *Qingdai haihe luanhe honglao daongan shiliao.* Beijing: Zhonghua Shudian.

Sjoberg, Orjan and Zhang Gang. 1998. "Soft Budget Constraints in Chinese Rural Enterprises" in Christiansen, Flemming and Zhang Junzuo, eds. *Village, Inc.: Chinese Rural Society in the 1990s.* Honolulu: University of Hawai'i Press.

Skinner, G. William. 1964. "Marketing and Social Structure in Rural China, Part I." *The Journal of Asian Studies, (*JAS reprint from 1965*)* 24.

———. 1965. "Marketing and Social Structure in Rural China, Part II." *Journal of Asian Studies (*Reprint by Association for Asian Studies*)* 24.

———. 1994. "Differential Development in Lingnan." In *The Economic Transformation of South China: Reform and Development in the Post-Mao Era,* edited by T. Lyons and V. Nee. Ithaca: Cornell East Asia Program.

Smelser, Neil and Richard Swedberg, eds. 1994. *The Handbook of Economic Sociology.* Princeton: Princeton University Press.

Spence, Jonathan . 1990. *The Search for Modern China.* New York and London: W.W. Norton and Company.

Sun, Dechang and Zhou Zuchang. 1990. *Tianjin jindai jingjishi.* Tianjin: Tianjin shehuikexue yuan chubanshe.

Svejnar, Jan and Josephine Woo. 1990. "Development Patterns in Four Counties" in *China's Rural Industry: Structure, Development and Reform,* edited by W. Byrd and Q. Lin. Oxford: Oxford University Press for The World Bank.

Swedberg, Richard. 1993. *Explorations in economic sociology.* New York: Russell Sage Foundation.

Swedburg, Richard. 1991. "Major Traditions of Economic Sociology." *Annual Review of Sociology* 17:251–276.

Swedburg, Richard, Ulf Himmelstrand, and Goran Brulin. 1987. "The Paradigm of Economic Sociology." *Theory and Society* 16:169–213.

Szelenyi, Ivan. 1988. *Socialist Entrepreneurs : Embourgeoisement in Rural Hungary*. Madison, WI: University of Wisconsin Press.

Szelenyi, Ivan and Eric Kostello. 1996. "The Market Transition Debate: Toward a Synthesis?" *American Journal of Sociology* 101:1082–1096.

Shimiao gongshe bangongshi dangwei. 1962. A(#1L) *Guanyu Lujiatun deng dadui cun naoshi guocheng he zhengfeng gongzuo qingkuang de baogao.*

Tianjin shehui kexue yuan jingji yanjiu suo, Tianjinshi nongye shipin weiyuan-hui jingji yanjiushi, Tianjin nongcun jinrong yanjiusuo. 1985. *Tianjin nongye jingji gaikuang.*

Tianjin shekeyuan lishisuo "Tianjin jianshi" bianxie zu, ed. 1987. *Tianjin jianshi*. Tianjin: Tianjin renmin chubanshe.

Tianjin zhuanqu qixiangju, Tianjin zhuanqu qixiangju. 1961? *Tianjin qixiang ziliao, 1890–1960*, vol. 1. Tianjin: Tianjin zhuanqu qixiangju.

Tianjinshi fangxun zhihuibu. 1963. *Tianjinshi fangxun jishu ziliao. Tianjinshi fangxun jishu ziliao fulu*. Tianjin: Tianjinshi fangxun zhihuibu.

Tianjinshi Jinghaixian tongjiju. 1993. *Jinghaixian guomin jingji he shehui tongji ziliao*. Tianjin: Tianjinshi Jinghaixian tongjiju.

Tianjinshi minzhengju jianzhengchu. 1984. *Tianjinshi geji xingzheng quhua yange*. Tianjin: Tianjinshi minzhengju jianzhengchu.

Tianjinshi qixiangju. 1972 August. *Tianjinshi qixiang ziliao, 1961–1970*, vol. 2. Tianjin: Tianjinshi qixiangju.

Tianjinshi tongjiju, ed. 1995. *Tianjin tongji nianjian*. Beijing: Zhongguo tongji chubanshe.

Tianjinshi tongjiju, ed. 1996. *Tianjin tongji nianjian*. Beijing: Zhongguo tongji chubanshe.

Tianjinshi turang pucha bangongshi, Tianjinshi turang feiliao yanjiusuo, Tianjinshi nongye quhua bangongshi. 1990. *Tianjin tuzhongzhi*. Tianjin: Tianjin kexue jishu chubanshe.

Tianjinshi wenshi yanjiuguan sanshi zhounian jinian zhuanji. 1983. *Tianjin wenshi congkan*. vol. 1. Tianjin: Tianjinshi wenshi yanjiuguan.

Tsui, Kai-yuen. 1998. "Trends and Inequalities of Rural Welfare in China: Evidence from Rural Households in Guangdong and Sichuan." *Journal of Comparative Economics* 26:783–804.

Tsui, Kai Yuen. 1991. "China's Regional Inequality, 1952–1985." *Journal of Comparative Economics* 15:1–21.

UNDP (United Nations Development Program) 1993. *Human Development Report 1993*. New York and Oxford: Oxford University Press.

Unger, Jonathan. 1994. "'Rich Man, Poor Man': The Making of New Classes in the Countryside." In *China's Quiet Revolution: New Interactions Between State and Society*, edited by David Goodman and Beverley Hooper. New York: St. Martin's Press, Inc.

Vermeer, Eduard B., Frank N, Pieke and Chong, Woei Lien, eds. 1998. *Cooperative and Collective in China's Rural Development*. Armonk, NY: M.E. Sharpe.

Walder, Andrew G, ed. 1998. *Zouping in Transition: The Process of Reform in Rural North China*. Cambridge, MA: Harvard University Press.

Walder, Andrew. 1996. "Markets and Inequality in Transitional Economies: Toward Testable Theories." *American Journal of Sociology* 101:1060–1073.

Wang, Fei-ling. 1998. *Institutions and Institutional Change in China: Premodernity and Modernization*. New York: St. Martin's Press, Inc.

Wang, Jingmo. 1987. "Machang jianhe." *Jinghai wenshi ziliao* 2:153–158.

Wang, Shaoguang and Hu Angang. 1999. *The political economy of uneven development : the case of China*. Armonk, NY: M.E. Sharpe.

Wang, Xiaoyi and Zhu Chengbao. 1996. *Zhongguo xiangcun de minying qiye yu jiazu jingji: Zhejiangsheng Xiangnanxian Xiangdongcun diaocha* (Nonstate enterprises and family economy in rural China: Survey report of Xiangdong Village, Zhejiang Province). Edited by Chen Jiyuan and C. Herrmann-Pillath. Taiyuan: Shanxi jingji chubanshe.

Watson, Andrew. 1992. "The Management of the Rural Economy." Pp. 171–199 in *Economic Reforma and Social Change in China*, edited by A. Watson. London: Routledge.

Watson, Andrew, Christopher Findlay and Chen Chunlai. 1996. "The Growth of Rural Industry: The Impact of Fiscal Contracting." Pp. 277–292 in *The Third Revolution in the Chinese Countryside*, edited by R. Garnaut, Shutian Guo and Guonan Ma. Cambridge: Cambridge University Press.

Watson, Andrew, Harry X. Wu, and Christopher Findlay. 1997. "Regional Disparities in Rural Development." In *China's New Spacial Economy*, edited by Godfrey Linge. Hongkong and Oxford: Oxford University Press.

Watson, James A. 1986. "Anthropological Overview: The Development of Chinese Descent Groups." Pp.274–292 in *Kinship Organization in Late Imperial China, 1000–1940*, edited by Patricia B. Ebrey and James L. Watson. Berkeley: University of California Press.

Whiting, Susan. 2001. *Power and Wealth in Rural China: The Political Economy of Institutional Change*. Cambridge: Cambridge University Press.

Whyte, Martin King. 1995. "The Social Roots of China's Economic Development." *The China Quarterly* 1995:999–1019.

———. 1992. "Introduction: Rural Economic Reforms and Chinese Family Patterns." *The China Quarterly* 1992:317–322.

Wiens, Thomas B. 1985. "Poverty and Progress in the Huang and Huai River Basins" in *Chinese Rural Development: The Great Transformation*, edited by W. Parish. Armonk, NY: M.E. Sharpe.

Wilson, Scott. 1994. *About Face: Social Networks and Prestige Politics in Contemporary Shanghai Villages.* Ph.D Thesis, Cornell University.

Wu, Ou. 1931. Tianjinshi nongye diaocha baogao. Shehuiju.

Wu, Dasheng, Ju Futian, Zou Nongjian. 1993. *Jiangnan nongcun shinian da bianqian.* Nanjing: Jiangsu renmin chubanshe.

Xia, Qing'an. 1998. Personal letter.

Xia, Qing'an. 1996. Personal letter.

Xia, Qing'an. 1995. *Xiayuan cunzhi.* Xiayuan, Ganglongxiang, Jinghaixian, Tianjin: unpublished manuscript.

Yan Lin. 1981. *Nongye tongji.* Beijing: Nongye chubanshe.

Yan, Yunxiang. 1992. "The Impact of Rural Reform on Economic and Social Stratification in a Chinese Village." *The Australian Journal of Chinese Affairs* 0 :1–23.

Yang, Dali. 1996. *Calamity and Reform in China: State, Rural Society and Institutional Change Since the Great Leap Famine.* Stanford: Stanford University Press.

Yang, Minchuan. 1994. "Reshaping Peasant Culture and Community: Rural Industrialization in a Chinese Village." *Modern China* 20:157–179.

Yin Jing, Zhang Chaozhong, Yao Tongfa. 1988. *Jinghai zai jueqi.* Tianjin: Tianjin shehui kexue zazhishe.

Yu Henian. 1986. "Tianjinwei kao chugao" in *Tianjin shi di zhishi, Tianjin diming congkan*, edited by B. Zenghui. Tianjin: Tianjinshi diming weiyuanhui bangongshi.

Yu Xie, and Emily Hannum. 1996. "Regional Variation in Earnings Inequality in Reform-Era Urban China." *American Journal of Sociology* 101:950–992.

Zhang, Jianhua. 1995. "Zhidu chuangxin yu nongye fazhan: guanyu chuantong nongye gaizao de zhidu fenxi." *Nongye jingji wenti.* April:46–50.

Zhang, Kejun and Cha Luzhong , 1988. "Fazhan hengxiang jingji lianhe." *Nongcun gongzuo tongxu.* August, 1988, pp. 44–48.

Zhang, Xinyi. 1933. *Hebeisheng nongye gaikuang guji baogao.* Lifayuan tongjichu.

Zhang, Yinong. 1989. *Zhongguo shangye jianshi.* Beijing: Zhongguo caizheng jingji chubanshe.

Zhang, Zhonggen, Huang Zuhui. 1995. "Jihui chengben, jiaoyi chengben yu nongye de shidu jingying guimo." *Nongye jingji wenti.* May:19–22.

Zhao, Guoliang. 1988. *Zhongguo nongcun jingji tizhi gaige dashiji.* Beijing: Qiushi chubanshe.

Zhao, Renwei. 1993. "Three Features of the Distribution of Income during the Transition to Reform." In *The Distribution of Income in China,* edited by K. Griffin and Zhao Renwei. New York: St. Martin's Press.

Zhonggong Tianjinshi Jinghaixianwei zuzhibu and Zhonggong Tianjinshi Jinghaixianwei dangshi ziliao zhengji weiyuanhui. 1992. *Zhongguo gongchandong Tianjinshi Jinghaixian zuzhishi ziliao, 1944–1987.* Tianjin: Tianjin renmin chubanshe.

Zhongguo nongye kexueyuan nongye jingji yanjiusuo. 1995. "Muqian woguo jingji fazhan suochu de jieduan yu tiaozheng gongnong guanxi de silu." *Nongye jingji wenti.* March:2–7.

Zhongguo tongji nianjian bianweihui. 1995. *Zhongguo tongji nianjian.* Beijing: Zhongguo tongji chubanshe.

Zhongguo tongji nianjian bianweihui. 1996. *Zhongguo tongji nianjian.* Beijing: Zhongguo tongji chubanshe.

Zhongyang shujichu nongcun zhengce yanjiushi he guowuyuan nongcun fazhan yanjiu zhongxin noncun diaocha lingdao xiaozu. 1986. "Quanguo nongcun shehui jingji dianxing diaocha qingkuang zonghe baogao (jielu)." *Nongcun jingji wenti* 1986:4–13.

Zhou, Qiren. 1994. *Nongcun biange yu zhongguo fazhan, 1978–1989*, vol. 1–2. Hong Kong: Oxford University Press.

Zhou, Kate Xiao and Lynn T. White III. 1995. "Quiet Politics and Rural Enterprise in Reform China." *Journal of Developing Areas* 29:461–490.

Zhu, Ling. 1991. *Rural Reform and Peasant Income in China: the impact of China's post-Mao rural reforms in selected areas.* New York : St. Martin's Press.

Zukin, Sharon and Paul DiMaggio. 1990. *Structures of Capital : The Social Organization of the Economy.* Cambridge [England]; New York: Cambridge University Press.

Zweig, David. 1997. *Freeing China's Farmers: Rural Restructuring in the Reform Era.* Armonk: M.E. Sharpe.

REFERENCES CITED BY TITLE

(cross-referenced above by author/editor)

Hebeisheng gexian gaikuang yilan. Hebeisheng dizhengting. 1934.

Hebeisheng gongshang tongji. Hebeisheng zhengfu shiyeting shichachu. 1931.

Hebei jingji tongji nianjian. Hebeisheng renmin zhengfu, (Hebei people's government). 1995. Beijing: Zhongguo tongji chubanshe.

Hebeisheng nongye gaikuang guji baogao. Zhang Xinyi. 1933. Lifayuan tongjichu.

Hebeisheng zhengfu jiansheting diaocha baogao, Volumes 1, 3, 4. Hebeisheng jiansheting. 1928.

Jicha diaocha tongji congkan, pp. 41–51. Jicha zhengwu weiyuanhui, eds. 1936–1937. Hebei gexian jinsan niandu geye zuofang tongji.

Jinghai juan. Zhongguo guoqing congshu: baixianshi jingji shehui diaocha. Jinghai juan bianji weiyuanhui, eds. 1993. Beijing: Zhongguo dabaike quanshu chubanshe.

Jinghai xianzhi. Gao Yutong, ed. 1929.

Qingxian xianzhi. 1931. [located in the Tianjin Academy of Social Sciences library].

Tianjin tongji nianjian. Tianjinshi tongjiju, ed. 1996. Beijing: Zhongguo tongji chubanshe

Tianjin tongji nianjian. Tianjinshi tongjiju, ed. 1995. Beijing: Zhongguo tongji chubanshe.

Xiayuan cunzhi. Xia Qing'an. 1995. Xiayuan, Ganglong xiang, Jinghaixian, Tianjin: unpublished manuscript.

Zhongguo gongchandong Tianjinshi Jinghaixian zuzhishi ziliao, 1944–1987. Zhonggong Tianjinshi Jinghaixianwei zuzhibu and Zhonggong Tianjinshi Jinghaixianwei dangshi ziliao zhengji weiyuanhui. 1992. Tianjin: Tianjin renmin chubanshe.

Zhongguo jingji nianjian, liuce, nongyepian. Shiyebu zhongguo jingji nianjian bianji weiyuanhui. 1936(?). Shangwu yinshuguan chubanshe.

Zhongguo nongcun tongji nianjian. Zhongguo nongcun tongji nianjian bianweihui. 1996. Beijing: Zhongguo tongji chubanshe.

Nongyebu nongye zhengce yanjiuhui (Ed.). 1992. *Zhongguo nongye wenti yanjiu.* Beijing: Nongye chubanshe.

Zhongguo tongji nianjian. Zhongguo tongji nianjian bianweihui. 1996. Beijing: Zhongguo tongji chubanshe.

Zhongguo tongji nianjian. Zhongguo tongji nianjian bianweihui. 1995. Beijing: Zhongguo tongji chubanshe.

INDEX